I0638898

THE NEW COMPLETE SAMOYED

Czar Alexander III and family in 1887 with the princes' family pet, Kamtscnatka.

The NEW Complete

SAMOYED

by

ROBERT H. and DOLLY WARD

SECOND EDITION

HOWELL
BOOK HOUSE
New York

Copyright © 1985 by Howell Book House Inc.

All rights reserved. No part of this book may be reproduced or
transmitted in any form or by any means, electronic or mechanical,
including photocopying, recording or by any information storage
and retrieval system, without permission in writing from the Publisher.

Howell Book House
Macmillan Publishing Company
866 Third Avenue, New York, NY 10022
Collier Macmillan Canada, Inc.

Library of Congress Cataloging in Publication Data

Ward, Robert H.
   The new complete Samoyed.

   Rev. ed. of: The complete Samoyed. 1971.
   1. Samoyeds (Dogs) I. Ward, Dolly. II. Ward,
Robert H. The complete Samoyed. III. Title.
SF429.S35W36   1985   636.7′3   83-49207
ISBN 0-87605-298-7

Macmillan books are available at special discounts for bulk purchases
for sales promotions, premiums, fund-raising, or educational use.
For details, contact:

                Special Sales Director
                Macmillan Publishing Company
                866 Third Avenue
                New York, NY 10022

10 9 8 7

Printed in the United States of America

Lindi and future Ch. Starchak's Witangemote.

*W*e dedicate this revised edition to our daughters, Lindi Leigh and Marion Dee, and to our grandchildren— Lance, Megyn, and Molly.

Mardee has become the third dog judge in our family, and established the Hoof n' Paw prefix.

All of us still have Samoyeds,

. . . and Corgis,

. . . and Hounds,

. . . and Morgans,

and . . .

The Authors

Few authors of dog books can match the expertise, experience and active participation with the breed that Bob and Dolly Ward bring here.

Until retirement Bob was a high school administrator and Dolly a teacher. But for more than four decades, dogs have been the major interest. They have owned and shown Corgis, Poodles, Dobermans and Boxers, and Bob even served as an all-breed handler from 1947 to 1954, but the No. 1 breed has been Samoyeds.

Although Bob had a pet Sammy as a boy, the Wards' serious devotion began with the acquisition of the puppy that became one of the great studs of the breed, Ch. Starchak, C.D., 1943-1957. Since 1944, they have been prominent in virtually every area of Samoyed sport. In obedience, they finished 7 Sammys and 2 Corgis to C.D.X. For over 15 years, they competed in Samoyed sled-dog racing. They supported local and national clubs. Both Bob and Dolly are past presidents of the Samoyed Club of America, and Dolly is currently president of the Samoyed Club of Los Angeles.

Bob became an AKC-approved judge in 1954, and Dolly in 1960, and they are among the select number of Samoyed specialists also approved to judge other breeds and Groups. Currently Bob judges Hounds, Working, Non-Sporting, Herding and BIS. Dolly judges Working, Non-Sporting, Herding, half the Toy Group and BIS. They have judged at Specialty and all-breed shows throughout the United States, and in Canada, Mexico, England, Ireland, Sweden, Australia, New Zealand, Japan, Hong Kong and Taiwan.

As authors in a lighter vein, to reach the kindergarten set with colorful education on dogs and their care, Bob and Dolly wrote a series of coloring books— *Color Me Puppy* and *Color Me Obedient*, illustrated by Mel Fishback-Riley.

For the Wards, dogs and horses have been a family affair, and this is continuing in new generations with the Kelley Livingston Moore family on Sam Hill, Paso Robles, and with Mardee Ward's success with her Hoof 'n Paw Samoyeds.

Contents

Television talk show host Merv Griffin with his Samoyed bitch, Samantha.

The Name:

The correct pronunciation of Samoyed is
SAMMY—YED
(Accent on the last syllable.)

The name was chosen by E. Kilburn-Scott, English pioneer of the breed, and honors the Samoyed tribes of Siberia from whom the founding stock was obtained.

In both England and America, the breed was originally written as *Samoyede*. The final "e" was dropped by the English in 1923, and by the American Kennel Club in 1947, and the simplified spelling is now used in reference to either the people or the breed.

The word *samoyed* is literally translated as "living off themselves." Some reporters have interpreted this as implying cannibalism, but we believe the truer implication is one of self-sufficiency—a nomadic people who managed to live off the land by their moving about.

The Russians sometimes called the dogs *Voinaika*, which can be translated to mean either carriage, lead or direction dogs, or guard, hunting and war dogs. But the natives themselves called the dogs *Bjelkiers*, "white dogs that breed white."

In 1984, Mrs. Ivy Kilburn Morris, daughter of E. Kilburn-Scott, stated: "I am sorry to see that the name of the breed is being incorrectly pronounced, e.g. SAM-OY-ED instead of SAM-YED (the "O" being slurred, not joined to the "Y"). The breed is named after the race of people of the same name, and the pronunciation was agreed upon by Mr. Kilburn-Scott and the Arctic explorers. It was pronounced correctly for at least 50 years, and it is difficult to understand why it has been changed in this ugly Anglicized way, as there is no such sound as "OY" in any language other than English."

Ch. Quicksilver's Razz Ma Tazz, wh. 8/5/81, the top winning Samoyed of all time. At end of 1984, Tazz's record included: 54 all-breed Bests in Show; 232 Bests of Breed; 202 Group placements, of which 141 were Firsts. Tazz was Best of Breed at the Samoyed Club of America Specialties, 1983 and 1984, and the winner of the Quaker Oats Award for the Working Group in both years. Co-owned by Danny and Chris Middleton (his breeders) and Eugene Curtis, and handled by Roy Murray.

Crizta Knight Break at 8 weeks old.

Foreword

by Herman L. Fellton

(Mr. Fellton is one of America's most respected dog authorities, and was chairman of the AKC's special committee studying the alignment of breeds into Groups. He is approved to judge all breeds of the Hound, Working, Non-Sporting and Herding Groups, plus many of the Terrier breeds.)

ALTHOUGH not a Samoyed breeder, I have known, liked and admired the breed for a long time and have judged it many, many times at all-breed shows and at specialty shows—both in the United States and abroad. So I am delighted to have been invited to write this Foreword for Bob and Dolly Ward's excellent book about this breed.

A breed of physical vigor and splendid character, the Samoyed is perhaps the most beautiful breed in the Working Group. It is an eye-catching dog with its glistening silver-sheened white coat standing straight out from the body, over an undercoat of soft, short, thick, close white wool. This, together with its dark pigmentation, its dark almond-shaped eyes and, especially, its rather unique expression, including the slight upward curve at the corners of the mouth creating the characteristic "Samoyed smile," forms an irresistible, spectacular, aesthetically pleasing picture. A good specimen of the breed is truly a dog breeder's work of art.

But the "Sammy" is not only beautiful; it is a true working dog, having served as a herder of reindeer, as a sledge dog and as a household companion, watchdog and helper. Its strong, sturdy, medium-sized, muscular body and its speed and endurance attest to its ability to perform all of these functions. The breed standard requires that it present a picture of beauty, alertness and strength, with agility, dignity and grace.

One of the oldest domesticated breeds of dogs, the Samoyed was bred and developed by the nomadic Samoyed tribes in Siberia and has made the transition from reindeer-skin tents in the Arctic to modern dwellings in the temperate zones with grace and aplomb. It is a well-mannered dog with a disposition that is friendly (albeit somewhat reserved) and devoid of viciousness.

13

The Samoyed is probably best known to the public for its work as a sledge dog in both Arctic and Antarctic explorations. Borchgrevink, Amundsen and Shackleton—among others—in the Antarctic, and Nansen and Abruzzi in the Arctic, utilized "Sammys" for their expeditions—with an unexcelled record of achievement. In these days of airplane and mechanical snow-sled transportation, it is difficult for us to comprehend the hardships, hazards and difficulties both dogs and humans had to overcome in those early expeditions, but overcome them they did, adding even more luster to the breed. More often than one likes to think about, some of these sled-pullers were slaughtered to furnish food for the remaining dogs in the expedition. Many of today's Samoyed strains are descendants of the sled dogs who survived the expeditions.

The Wards have done a remarkably fine job in writing this definitive book about this great breed. It is comprehensive, well-written, objective and authoritative. It should be read and studied by all novice and veteran Samoyed owners, exhibitors, handlers, breeders and judges. I am delighted to recommend this book to all those interested in the breed.

BIS winner Am. & Can. Ch. Moonlighter's Ima Bark Star shares a gallery seat with owner Wayne Nonhof and friends.

Acknowledgments

IT HAS BEEN 15 years since we worked on the first edition. Because so much has happened, this second edition has become more of a new book than a revision.

However, the beginning of the breed remains the same. That was easy!

Important for us in writing the history was our contact with some who had seen the early English and United States imports. Prime among these was Mrs. Ivy Kilburn Morris, the most prominent authority on the Samoyed, and the longest identified with its breeding, care, training and judging. Mrs. Morris (nee Ivy Kilburn Scott) is a daughter of the Kilburn Scotts, the original importers of the breed to England. (Professor Scott originated the breed standard.) Mrs. Morris was the breeder of Ch. Tobolsk, the very influential dog imported by Percy Roberts to the United States in 1919.

We are indebted to Richard Beauchamp, editor-publisher of *Kennel Review* magazine, for an update. Recently, while on a judging trip to Capetown, South Africa, Dick met Mrs. Morris. They were having tea when the subject of *The Complete Samoyed* came up. Mrs. Morris rose, went directly to a cabinet and got from it a letter which the authors had written thanking her for prior help with breed information in 1970. What a small world the dog fraternity is!

Mrs. Morris sent us more material via Mr. Beauchamp in October 1984, and we quote: "I played a very active part in my mother's famous Samoyed kennel near London. I wish to state emphatically that the Samoyed is NOT just a sledge-dog; any breed can pull a sledge. Capt. Robert Scott, a family friend of my father, never intended to use any breed of dog on his expedition to the Antarctic. . . . Though a working dog, the breed is the most beautiful of all breeds."

Much of the new information in this edition came to us in response to an open plea made to readers of the *Samoyed Quarterly*, edited by Don Hoflin. We thank the breeders and exhibitors who cooperated so wonderfully in sending us histories, records and splendid pictures.

15

We are pleased and honored to have the new Foreword written by Mr. Herman Fellton. All Samoyed enthusiasts will appreciate his tribute to the breed.

Included with particular pride are the new Samoyed drawings skillfully created by Liisa Laguire. Her grasp of the breed characteristics shows brilliantly in her work, and it's obvious that she owns Samoyeds together with Pembroke Welsh Corgis, her paramount breed. Liisa also handles several other Working/Herding breeds exceptionally well, including German Shepherd Dogs.

Our judging assignments in other countries, as well as in the United States and Canada, have put us in contact with many people deeply and sincerely involved with the breed. These contacts have provided many pleasures and have considerably added to our knowledge and appreciation of dogs. Although too many to list by name, we thank you in Sweden, Norway, Finland, Denmark, Holland, England, Scotland, Ireland, Mexico, Brazil, Australia, New Zealand, Japan, and Taiwan, ROC—all who helped with pictures, your precious time and contributions for the text.

Our thanks to Mrs. Carol Chittum for the new ideas on Spinning, to Don and Del Wells for the new chapter on Obedience, and to Peggy Borcherding (editor of the *Samoyed Club of America Bulletin*), Constance Meylan, Lindi Ward Moore, Mike and Bobby Smith, Ruth Tausend, Ted Awaya, and John Ronald (past president of the SCA) for their visible support. Thanks, too, to our Junior Showmanship winner of 25 years ago—Mardee Ward—for bringing us up-to-date on Grooming, Show Handling and Training. And to our grandchildren—Lance, Megyn and Molly—who have their Sams as companions now, and will one day read about them here.

Our special thanks to editor Ab Sidewater, who has stuck by us through both editions. His good humor was morale-building for us, and his expertise rewards you, the readers.

Sam-a-ly yours,
BOB and DOLLY WARD

Ice Way's Ice Crystal at 7 months. Owners, Joel Carlin and Jane Montgomery, North Carolina.

"Great Dogs Are Like White Water"

The history and progress of a breed can be seen as a river.
Then its great dogs are like white water:
They rise, momentarily and brilliant in the sun—
To hang there suspended in the mind's eye,
Long after darkness has fallen
And they have rejoined the river on its way to the sea.
Though they make up but a tiny portion of the breed,
They nevertheless contribute significantly
To our total experience of that breed.
They are the dogs who not only win often and/or produce well,
But they are the dogs who capture the imagination
Of judges and fanciers alike,
Who become fixed in our minds when we think of the river . . .
                    —(Reprinted from the *Siberian Quarterly*, with special permission.)

With the concept of White Water before us, let us look through these pages and meet some of those who have risen momentarily, and those who did leave progeny to white cap the waters again and again.

17

Samoyed across the South Pole with the Roald Amundsen Expedition.

ETAH, lead dog of the Amundsen expedition, pictured at 11 years of age. In his later years, ETAH was a pet of the Princess de Montyglon.

18

Introduction

IN the comparatively short span of ninety years, the Samoyed has risen from an almost extinct breed to one of the more popular—currently 29th in AKC registrations.

The tribes of the Samoyed people, from whom the dogs were obtained by the early explorers, have been dispersed by the Russians, and their mode of living altered by industrialization. It is fortunate for us that the handful of dogs released in the period of 1890 to 1912 were handled so skillfully that the breed was preserved. With wars and political upheaval, not more than a half dozen were obtained from Russia in the 1920s, and since then the door has been closed.

Because the Samoyed is one of the breeds most nearly akin to the prehistoric or natural canine, it has been one of the easier breeds to duplicate. The erect ears, the smiling face, the buff to white coat, the plumed tail—all come naturally. The disputes that there have been over proper size for a Samoyed are a problem created by humans, and not by nature. We would indeed be more successful as breeders if we would trust nature more. As it is, we have been quite fortunate, for Samoyeds have no coat color problem, no docking, no cropping, and no trimming. In man's desire to "improve" the breed, he did concentrate upon the black points—the eye rims, the nose, and the lips. While this contrast of black against the white face is very pleasing, records show that the pink or Dudley (pink with black) noses were natural.

Research reveals that the black, black and white, and even brown and white dogs which existed in the sled packs along with the white Bjelkiers were Laika and Ostiak dogs from around Archangel, and were of a different ancestry. The Bjelkiers were from a thousand miles east of Archangel, in the area east of the Yenisei River stretching to the Olenek River, where the Samoyed tribes of the Tungunese and Yakuts lived. If this difference in the dogs was not so, we Samoyed breeders have found a way to refute the Mendelian theory, for there have been no mixed colors in England or America plaguing the registrations for the past 75 years.

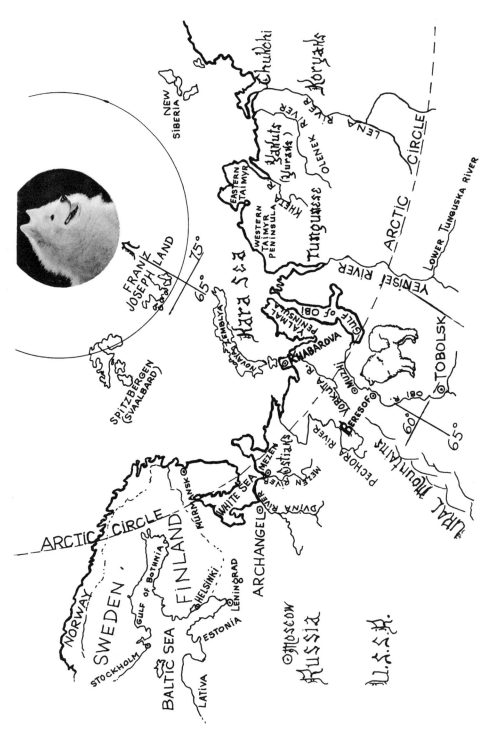

NEW SIBERIA

Chukchi

Koryaks

LENA RIVER

Yakuts (Yuraks)

OLENEK RIVER

EASTERN TAIMYR

KHETA R.

Tunguese

ARCTIC CIRCLE

LOWER TUNGUSKA RIVER

FRANZ JOSEPH LAND

75°

65°

WESTERN TAIMYR PENINSULA

YENISEI RIVER

TOBOLSK

SPITZBERGEN (SVAALBARD)

Kara Sea

NOVAYA ZEMBLYA

YAMAL PENINSULA

GULF of OBI

OBI R.

KHABAROVA

MUZH

YORKUTA R.

BERESOF

OB R.

60°

180

65°

URAL MOUNTAINS

PECHORA RIVER

MEZEN R.

Ostiaks

MEZEN RIVER

ARCTIC CIRCLE

KURMANSK

WHITE SEA

DVINA RIVER

ARCHANGEL

NORWAY

SWEDEN

GULF OF BOTHNIA

FINLAND

HELSINKI

LENINGRAD

ESTONIA

MOSCOW

Russia

U.S.S.R.

STOCKHOLM

BALTIC SEA

LATIVA

1

Discovery of the Samoyed

THE white dog with the smiling face, the dog we know as the Samoyed, was brought to the attention of Western civilization through Dr. Fridtjof Nansen, the noted Norwegian explorer.

Dr. Nansen firmly believed that sledging with dogs was the answer to conquering the Arctic wastes. He recommended the dogs, and the services of his dog broker, Alexander I. Trontheim of Tobolsk, Siberia, to many explorers. This proved most fortunate. The majority of the dogs used in their expeditions thus came from the same area and, because the natives' dogs had not been interbred with outsiders for thousands of years, were of a strongly-developed strain. As we shall see later in detail, it was dogs from these expeditions—brought to England largely through the efforts of Mr. and Mrs. Ernest Kilburn-Scott—that became the nucleus for the breed as we know it today.

Tribes of the Siberian Tundras and the Eskimos of North America had early discovered that the safest method for traveling the frozen regions was the sledge, usually drawn by dogs. (Dr. Nansen, in his book *Northern Mists*, quotes the explorer Ibn Batuta (1302-1377): "Four dogs to sledges going to the 'Land of Darkness'—dogs or guides, a leader who has been there before is worth 1,000 dinars.") But it was in Siberia that this method of locomotion was first applied to polar exploration.

In the 17th and 18th centuries the Russians made extensive sledge journeys and charted the Siberian coast from the borders of Europe to the Bering Strait. Baron Wrangell wrote of traveling the barren wastes of Siberia with sledge teams, and of their use by the "Yassak" men (tax collectors for the Czar).

(*Samojedinkoiria* 1800-*iuvulta.*) Samoyed dogs in upper Lapland in the early 1800s. From an early tintype.

The Russians usually traveled with many dogs and few men. The early English explorers, in contrast, used many men and few dogs. Dr. Nansen's research, and the experience of a trip across Greenland on skis in 1888, convinced him of the wisdom of using dogs in overwhelming ratio to men.

In preparing his expedition toward the North Pole in 1894, Nansen asked his friend, Russian explorer Baron Edward von Toll, to procure good sledge dogs from Siberia. The Baron had used these on his trip to the Arctic.

Sled team and polar bear.

Baron von Toll engaged Alexander Trontheim to purchase thirty dogs. When he heard that Trontheim was preparing to purchase Ostiak dogs, he asked that the dogs be purchased instead in eastern Siberia from the Tungunese branch of the Samoyed people, whose draught dogs were better than the Ostiaks.

Trontheim headed toward the Petchora district to obtain the dogs. Hearing of a disease raging in that area among the dogs, he turned instead to Berezof, which is located n. 64° latitude and e. 64.5° longitude, and here purchased 40 sledge dogs. Trontheim hired a native named Terentieff, who used a herd of 450 reindeer and sledges to convey him, the 40 dogs, and 9600 pounds of food for the dogs to the coast at Khabarova. This, a distance of 400 miles, was the arranged meeting place where Fridtjof Nansen was to pick up the dogs. The trip took three months.

Dr. Nansen's account of his first meeting with the dogs reads: "Many of them appeared to be well-bred animals, longhaired, snow-white, with upstanding ears and pointed muzzles. With their gentle, good-natured-looking faces, they at once ingratiated themselves into the affections. Some of them resembled a fox, and had shorter coats, while others were black or spotted. Evidently they were of different races, and some of them betrayed by their drooping ears, a strong admixture of European blood."

What Nansen saw as a difference in the dogs stemmed from a difference in the people that owned them. There were two types of Samoyed tribes— one nomadic, the other pastoral—and each had their own kind of dog.

The nomadic Samoyed tribes had the all-white *Bjelkier* dogs, who served as hunting and draught dogs for their owners. *Bjelkier* means "white dog that breeds white." In native usage, the term was also applied to the ermine, the white fox, and the white bear.

The pastoral tribes had dogs of the Renvall-Hund or Elkhound type. Some were white, some black and white, and some brown and white.

The books *Dogs of All Nations* by Count Henry de Blyandt, *The Voyage of the Vega* by Dr. Otto Nordenskiolds, and *In Northern Mists* by Fridtjof Nansen, all repeat this classification of the nomads with white hunting dogs and the reindeer-pastoral tribes with their smaller Renvall-Hund type, which were white, black and white, and brown and white, weighing thirty to fifty pounds.

In reports by explorers and expeditions sent out by the Smithsonian Institute, the Peabody Fund, and the British Zoological Society, accounts have been given of the various dogs in the Siberian area. One account told of white sled dogs hitched four abreast being used to pull barges on the Yenisei River. The Yenisei River is 200 miles east of the town of Berezof where Trontheim procured Nansen's dogs. The Smithsonian Institute Report of 1898 quotes from *Die Tungusen* by Dr. B. Langkavel, who in 1872 said:

"The tent-living Samoyeds use only reindeer as draught animals and have the dogs for herding, but the remainder of the Samoyeds and Yakuts use dogs and indeed each one can pull two to three and one-half *pud* [a pud is 32 pounds]."

Another German explorer, in 1892, told of the people in the area of the Sameanda. He declared there were two types of tribes: the dog people who had no reindeer and the reindeer people who had no dogs. The two classes of natives were continually battling because the dogs would kill the reindeer and the reindeer people would then kill the dogs. These dogs were described as pure white, quite gentle, but terrific hunters. Their speed deeply impressed the expedition.

Thus we had tribes of similar peoples with fairly similar dogs, yet there were distinct differences. The question arises, "Did these tribesmen have a breeding program?" When we read accounts of the devious means used by the Europeans to obtain the dogs which the natives refused to sell, we know that the natives prized their dogs highly. Small wonder, for the natives' total existence depended upon their possessing good dogs. They must have felt the same intense personal pride in their strains that breeders exhibit today.

Explorers and Expeditions Influencing the Breed

The great age of polar exploration, from 1870 to 1912, brought all Arctic dogs to notice. However, we shall confine ourselves here to the explorers of note who used the Bjelkier, now known as the Samoyed.

Fridtjof Nansen. Dr. Nansen, a professor in seven chairs or departments at the University of Norway, designed his own ship for his expedition. *The Fram* was so well-built and excellent in its design that it was used for five expeditions over a period of 35 years.

Nansen did considerable research in making his selection of the dogs for the sledging phase of his expedition. The cataloging of the weights of the 28 dogs selected for the final journey toward the North Pole, recorded after nearly a year and a half of living and working in the Arctic regions, shows that the 19 males averaged 58.7 pounds, and the 9 bitches averaged 50.5 pounds.

The weights of Nansen's dogs (in pounds):

Males:

Storraeven, 70	Isbjon, 61.5	Russen, 58
Kaifas, 69	Haren, 61.5	Potifar, 57
Sultan, 68	Baro, 60.5	Narrifas, 46
Pan, 65	Barrabas, 59.5	Barnet, 39
Perpetuum, 63	Kapperslangen, 59.5	Livjaegeren, 38.5
Gulen, 60.5	Lilleraeven, 59	
Flint, 61.5	Blok, 59	

Fridtjof Nansen's drawing of himself and Frederic Johansen en route to Franz Joseph Land in kayaks, lashed together by their dog sleds.

Bitches:

Kvik (Nansen's own from Greenland), 78

Ulenka, 57	Katta, 45.5
Freia, 50	Sjoliget, 40
Suggen, 61.5	Bjelki, 38
Barbara, 49.5	Kvindfolket, 37

Nansen's theory for sledging was a disastrous one for the dogs. He and partner Frederic Johansen set out with many dogs, but planned that as they ran out of food, the weaker dogs would be fed to the stronger ones. The trip over the ice packs eliminated all the dogs but two, their lead dogs Kaifas and Suggen. And even these two had to be sacrificed when they arrived at open water, for the men were cautious about taking them in their kayaks.

After selecting the draught dogs of the Samoyed people for his attempt at the Pole, Dr. Nansen recommended them to other explorers. He sent an all-white Samoyed bitch, named Grasso, to the Duc d'Abruzzi as a good example of a sled dog.

Jackson-Harmsworth Expedition. Major Frederick G. Jackson led this English expedition to Franz Josef Land, above the Arctic Circle. Here they met Nansen and Johansen, returning from their 18-month journey by sledge and kayak, and brought them home. Major Jackson was also very interested in the Samoyed, and returned some to England. He presented his best dog, Jacko, to Queen Alexandra. Jacko was all-white, and the get of Nimrod out of Jenny. Dr. Kotelitz, a physician with the expedition, brought the bitch Kvik back with him, and she is found in early pedigrees. Eight other dogs brought back by Major Jackson went to Mr. Kilburn-Scott's kennels in 1899.

The Duc d'Abruzzi, or Luigi Amadeo, the distinguished Italian adventurer, aimed for the North Pole, and sought the counsel of Fridtjof Nansen. Upon advice, he ordered 120 dogs from Alexander Trontheim in July, 1898. Not many explorers have given detailed comment on their use of dogs, but the Duc left the following: "Although born in an intensely cold country, they were not insensible to temperatures below a –30° centigrade. When it was very cold they were often seen to raise their paws out of the snow from time to time, and to go about looking for straw or wood to lie upon . . ."

The Duc's account of the harnessing of the dogs is very interesting to sled drivers because he was the first to use the double tandem hitch. He wrote:

> While Trontheim showed us how Nansen had harnessed the dogs abreast by separate traces attached to the sledge [fan hitch], as was done by the Samoyeds and Esquimaux to allow them more liberty in their movements and to utilize all their strength, it had great disadvantages. The traces became all mixed up and required much continual, tiresome labor. To avoid this inconvenience I decided when at Christiana to follow this method used by the Yakuts of the Lower Lena River who make use of a single long trace, to each side of which the dogs are harnessed by shorter traces attached to the central trace. The dogs showed strength and endurance and I felt more confidence in them after a four-day trip of 70 miles. Rings were fixed on the central trace on a level with the dogs' heads when they were pulling, and to which they were hooked by short chain, which also served to tie them up during the night. Our dog harness, like that made by other explorers, consisted of three or four layers of canvas, two lines of which passed between the animals' forelegs and two along its back, where they were all united to the trace.

Most interesting is the Duc's description of his best lead dog, an all-white Bjelkier named Messicano.

> We are decidedly rivaling not only Nansen, but also Wrangell, who was celebrated for the rapidity of his marches. We are able to accomplish these remarkable stages now, partly because we have only four sledges, and partly on account of the tracks which Messicano, the leading dog, was able to follow again today, even where they had been almost entirely effaced by the wind. It is a small white dog, with thick hair, and very intelligent eyes. It is so called Messicano on account of the abundance of hair which fringes its legs, resembling trousers which widen at the feet. Ever since our departure from Templitz Bay, it has held the first place of the first sledge, because it followed the man at the head of the convoy better than the others. Has followed obediently from the outset, being the most obedient to the word of command. Although not as big as some of his companions he always pulls, and falls upon the dogs of the other sledges which try to pass it. One would say that it feels all the importance of its position, and is proud of it. Messicano gallops like a dwosky horse with its nose always down in the snow. Sometimes it loses the track and then goes more slowly. Messicano shows its anxiety, it whines and runs up and down with its tongue out until it finds the track again. Then he darts off in the right direction, often for long stretches where it is utterly impossible for us to see a trace of our former passage.

One Samoyed male from the Abruzzi expedition was returned to England. This dog was Houdin. Houdin was shown and used at stud, and left a good mark upon the breed. Russ, another dog that had been purchased in Tobolsk by Trontheim for this expedition, also eventually made his way to England, and is in early Samoyed pedigrees.

Carsten E. Borchgrevink, a Norwegian who lived in Australia, led an English expedition to the Antarctic, February 17, 1899—February 2, 1900. He had over 100 Samoyeds with him at the start of the trip. While he did not write much about the breed, two dogs from his pack had tremendous impact on the breed. The greatest was Antarctic Buck, left in the Sidney Zoo after the expedition, and in 1908 imported to England by Mr. and Mrs. Kilburn-Scott. The other dog was Trip, who ended up on the Ernest Shackleton expedition, and was returned to England by Lieutenant Charles Adams. Borchgrevink handed over 27 of his dogs to Dr. Douglas Mawson in 1911 for another Australian expedition.

Sir Ernest Shackleton, on his 1907-1909 Antarctic expedition, had a few teams of dogs from other expeditions that had been left in Australia. He was a strong advocate of the use of ponies for sledge work in the Antarctic, but the problems created by their weight and the need to provide food for them made it necessary to destroy all of them.

Captain Robert Falcon Scott followed in the pattern of Shackleton, and used many men and ponies, with but few dogs, for his expedition in

Members of the Shackleton Expedition returning on the "Nimrod." The Samoyed "Trip" was brought to England and Mrs. Kilburn-Scott by Lt. Adams of this expedition.

Borchgrevink and dogs on an ice ledge in the Antarctic.

Dogs of the Borchgrevink Expedition. Borchgrevink's notes state, "Dogs were sheared before crossing Equator on way to South Pole."

1911. Why he did not use dogs as a main plan in dashing to the South Pole is not clearly known. Perhaps he did not care to use them in the customary cannibalistic way of the other explorers, or he may not have trusted them. This is particularly puzzling in that he was a good friend of E. Kilburn-Scott, who did so much to establish the Samoyed breed in England. In fact, E. K. Scott gave his friend the dog Olaf, a son of Antarctic Buck, to take on the expedition, Captain Scott did take 33 dogs with him to the Antarctic, but planned to rely upon 20 ponies and men to pull the sledges. The ponies broke through the snow, sweated, and froze, and eventually all became snowblind. The freezing of the ponies was due to the fact that they sweat through their hides, while dogs sweat through their tongues and pads of their feet. Someone docked the tails of one team of Scott's dogs, and they died of pneumonia within three weeks because of the lack of the thick bushy tail, which is a great protection to the dogs while sleeping.

Scott made his dash to the South Pole with six men laboriously pulling the sleds. From his diary, found after his death, we have learned that he did reach the pole, only to find it covered with paw prints of dogs and a note from Roald Amundsen giving him greetings dated a month before.

Roald Amundsen, first to reach the South Pole (planting the Norwegian flag there on December 14, 1911), was the most successful "dog man" of all the explorers. His accounts of the training and selection of his sledge dogs are outstanding. He acquired 97 dogs for his expedition, and after much training used 52 of them and four sledges for the dash to the pole. As planned, they returned with the four men, one sledge, and 12 surviving dogs. The round-trip covered 1,860 miles in 99 days, and the first animal over the pole was an all-white Samoyed lead dog. Twenty-seven of Amundsen's dogs were given to Douglas Mawson for an Australian expedition in 1911, and the rest returned as pets of the crew.

The points made by Luigi Amadeo had been proven. He had written, "Dogs are undeniably the most useful animals for man in his expeditions with sledges over the ice of the Polar Sea. They have this advantage, too, that unlike horses or reindeer, they readily eat their fellows. Their weight is small, and they can be easily carried on light boats or ice floes. Their loss represents but a small diminution of motive power in comparison with that which results from the death of a horse or reindeer."

On each of these expeditions, except the ill-fated Scott expedition, the Samoyed played a major part. Almost all Samoyeds today can be traced back to expedition dogs.

Although the utility of the dogs was the main concern, the warmth of their personalities was frequently noted by the explorers. Samoyed admirers of today will recognize their dogs in such comments as: "and the white dogs crowded around to be petted" (by Fridtjof Nansen); "At night we could tell the white dogs, as they poked us with their noses to get attention" (by James Murray, biologist for Shackleton); and "We found that at night the best way to thaw our sleeping bags was to spread them out, for the white dogs would jump right on them" (by Roald Amundsen). In his book *First on the Antarctic Continent*, C. E. Borchgrevink wrote: "It was curious to watch the marked difference in the habits and manners of the Greenland dogs to that of their brethren from Siberia. The former were much more wild and seldom or never mixed with the other dogs, nor did they attach themselves as much to man as the Siberian dogs did."

While not an explorer in the sense of the polar expeditions, **W. B. Vanderlip** in 1898 made a two-year trip through Siberia, and left us a detailed account of travel by dog sled. Frequent references to the Tungoos, Uraks, and Koraks show us that he covered much of the land where Trontheim collected dogs for the explorers. From the book *In Search of a Siberian Klondike* we quote:

> The reader may well ask how the natives can use both dogs and reindeer if the very sight of a deer has such a maddening effect on the dogs. The explanation is simple. The two never go together. There is the dog country and the deer country, and the two do not impinge upon each other. Even among the same tribe there may be a clear division. For instance, there are the Deer Koraks, and the Dog Koraks. In some of the villages of the former, there may occasionally be seen a few low-bred curs which are not used for sledging and have been trained not to worry deer.

Need we ponder further on the background of our beautiful breed? Were our Samoyeds hunters, draught dogs, or reindeer herders? No matter, for they all had the common faculty of being the "right hands" of their masters, and the means of survival in the cold bleak land.

One common reference weaves a thread through all the accounts of travel in Siberia—note of a white dog that breeds white. This dog is always living inside the *chooms* or *combes*, the houses, with his master. He is continually referred to as a friendly likeable dog, very unlike the wild creatures.

Thus, while the true origin of our breed is lost in antiquity, we *do* know that the Samoyed came from a general area east of the Urals, near the Arctic Circle, and we *do* know that the generic dogs which were combined were selected from Bjelkiers, the white animals that breed white. We know, too, that any black spots or markings have been a disqualification in the breed in England for 80 years. Nature must be telling us that fallible humans have allowed the one true dominant strain to come through loud and clear—the white dog that breeds white, or white and biscuit, or biscuit.

2

Beginnings in England

OF the first dogs of the breed in England, only a few came from western Siberia. Later imports were from the Ural Mountains and the Island of Novaya Zemblya and were likewise limited in number. Most numerous of the original dogs, and most influential in the establishment of the breed in England, were the dogs from the expeditions, which Alexander Trontheim had originally obtained from the area east of the Yenisei River, stretching to the Olenek. All of these were imported prior to 1914. A very few were brought to England in the mid-1920s, and since then—none.

The first importers, and establishers of the breed in England, were Mr. and Mrs. Ernest Kilburn-Scott. Mr. Kilburn-Scott was a member of the Royal Zoological Society, and in its cause had made a trip to the Archangel in 1889, from which he had brought back a dog. This was Sabarka ("the fat one" in Russian) and he was chocolate-brown in color.

Sabarka was not from the same district in Siberia as Fridtjof Nansen's dogs. He came from at least 900 miles west of the Olenek River. Mr. Kilburn-Scott had sympathetically bought Sabarka to save the young puppy from providing the natives a "feast." He was said to be typical in many good points of the breed such as head, stand-off coat, curled tail, and good carriage.

Soon after this, Mr. Kilburn-Scott brought in the famous cream-colored bitch, Whity Pechora. The mating of Sabarka and Whity Pechora produced a daughter Neva, who went to Lady Sitwell, newly interested in the breed.

Earliest mention of the breed seems to be an advertisement placed by Mr. Kilburn-Scott in 1891, under the *Foreign Dogs and Various* classification in the English papers. It read:

> Lovely white Russian (Samoyed) sledge dog pups, like small polar bears, most gentle and affectionate. Splendid coats and tails. Very rare. Parents imported.

Samoyeds were first shown at the Leeds show in 1893 in the Foreign Dog class.

31

Lady Sitwell later imported a snow-white dog named Musti from northern Russia. When Musti was mated with Whity Pechora in 1901, the white proved dominant, and the litter was the beginning of the all-white Samoyeds in England. It included the famous dog Nansen, who swept the shows in 1903, and the great bitch Olgalene. A third dog, Rex Albus, did not affect the breed as much.

The mating of Musti and Neva produced Ch. Olaf Oussa, important behind pedigrees of today.

When the Kilburn-Scotts wanted more stock, they went through Alexander Trontheim, who had obtained Nansen's dogs in 1894. In 1899, while selecting dogs for the Duc d'Abruzzi, Trontheim chose Russ for the Scotts. This dog was bred to Kvik, the bitch brought back by Dr. Kotelitz when he was the physician on the Jackson-Harmsworth expedition in 1897. This breeding produced Ch. Pearlene, famous for her beautiful head and ears, and for her progeny.

Major F. G. Jackson, who brought back many dogs in 1897, had given seven to Kilburn-Scott, and one (the male, Jacko) to Queen Alexandra. Major Jackson and Mr. Kilburn-Scott worked together in the early years, and joined in the proposal of a standard for the Samoyed. (Both judged the breed in England until the mid-1920s).

Jacko, the Queen's dog, was shown in the first class solely for Samoyeds, in 1902. Six dogs were judged by Mr. Kilburn-Scott: Jacko was Winners, defeating among others the Honorable Mrs. McLaren Morrison's Peter the Great, bred by the Scotts. Queen Alexandra had other Samoyeds, notably Sandringham Pearl.

Nansen bred to Ch. Pearlene produced Kviklene in 1902, carrying on the whites for her grandmother Kvik of the Jackson-Harmsworth Expedition.

When Antarctic Buck was released from quarantine in 1909, he was bred to Kviklene and Olgalene. Olgalene's mating with Buck produced Kaifas, Kirchie, and Bucklene, all whites. When bred to Jacko, Olgalene produced Ivanoff, a fine biscuit specimen.

But it was the all-male litter resultant of the breeding of Antarctic Buck with Kviklene that was to have the profoundest influence on the breed. In that one litter, Kviklene produced Southern Cross, South Pole, Fang, Mezenett and Olaf. This was the same Olaf that Captain Robert Scott took to the South Pole in 1911. And without Southern Cross and South Pole, there would not be many show Samoyeds today.

Antarctic Buck was a dazzling white dog standing 21½" (measured at the shoulder, rather than at the withers), and 35" long from tip of his nose to tip of his tail. He died in 1909, at ten years of age, having contracted distemper after being shown at Redhill, England. From this epidemic, only seven of his famous puppies survived.

Trip, another dog originally from the Borchgrevink Expedition, made

Ernest Kilburn-Scott with Prince Zouroff, one of the dogs from the litter pictured below.

A 1902 litter, by Jacko ex Olgalene, bred by Mrs. Kilburn-Scott. A dog of this litter was presented to Queen Alexandra.

Ch. Pearlene, bred in 1901 of dogs of the Jackson-Harnsworth Expedition (Russ ex Kvik). Pearlene introduced the pure white and thicker type of plush coat, rounder tips to ears, and very black eyes and nose.

his way to England in 1911. He was brought there by Lieutenant Adams of the Shackleton Expedition. Trip appears in some pedigrees, but not in as many as Houdin from the Abruzzi Expedition.

Mrs. Helen Harris, whose Snowland Kennels was so prominent on the American scene in the 1930s, once summed up the early Siberian imports: "There are twelve dogs of importance to the pedigrees of American Samoyeds: the Kilburn-Scotts' *Sabarka*, *Whity Pechora*, *Russ*, *Houdin* and *Antarctic Buck*; Lady Sitwell's *Kvik*; Queen Alexandra's *Jacko*; *Trip*; *Ayesha* (brought in in 1910 by Gordon Colman, and sold to Mrs. Cammack); and from Russia in 1925, *Pelle of Halfway* and *Yugor of Halfway*, imported by Mrs. Grey-Landsberg."

Mrs. Kilburn-Scott had refused to buy Ayesha because she did not like the "Spitz-like face, a faulty foreface, and slightly prominent round eyes." Mrs. Harris concluded her summation with: "The credit really goes to the bitches for launching this breed, and the most influential bitches were Kvik and Whity Pechora."

The breed received some wide attention in 1911 as a result of the Glasgow Exposition. As part of the show, a group of Lapplanders were on display with their tents and reindeer. Spectators began asking, "How do you herd your reindeer?" Of course, the Scots used the Collie for their sheep, and expected to see some type of work dog. But the Lapplanders had not brought the smaller Renvall-type dogs which they used.

When the director of the Exposition discussed this with Mr. Kilburn-Scott, the latter offered some of his Samoyeds to be put on display as reindeer herders with the Lapplanders. Many of the English newspapers photographed the dogs and publicized them as reindeer herders.

Will Hally, a long-time dog columnist and Samoyed breeder and judge, questioned the Lapplanders as to the similarity of the white Samoyed to

34

Antarctic Buck, imported to England by the Kilburn-Scotts from the Borchgrevink South Pole expedition.

Houdin, imported to England by the Kilburn-Scotts from the Duc d'Abruzzi's North Pole expedition.

Nansen, bred in 1901 by Mrs. Kilburn-Scott. Nansen, who lived to be 16 years of age, was of the Musti-Whity Petchora breeding that was the beginning of the pure white Samoyed in England.

Lapphunds, the original reindeer herder of the Lapps. When we judged in Sweden, the Finnish people told us they preferred using black dogs to herd in the snow.

their herd dogs, and they were most emphatic in stating that there was no resemblance. But *reindeer herder* would not be an altogether wrong classification for the Samoyed, for they are indeed an all-purpose dog. Basically, the Samoyed was a hunting and guard dog for the family, but where occasion demanded he became a herd and draught dog for certain tribes. Joe Stetson, writing in *Field and Stream*, once summed it up "The Samoyed is a three-H Dog . . . Hunting, Herding and Hauling."

Initially the Samoyed was shown in the Foreign Dog class in England, and labeled Samozia Sledge Dogs. But by 1909, Mr. Kilburn-Scott's choice of name for the breed, the Samoyede, had become the established designation, the Samoyede Club had been founded, and a standard formulated. Beginning in 1912 the Kennel Club ruled that Samoyedes should be classified separately.

The Samoyede Club as originally formed had excluded women, so in 1912 the Ladies Samoyede Association was founded. In this same year, the Samoyed and the Laika were combined for show purposes, but only the dominant white was to survive as a breed and type.

The year 1912 also saw the coming on the scene of a breeder who was to become one of the legendary figures in the development of the Samoyed. Miss J. V. Thomson-Glover acquired her first Samoyed, Snow Cloud, from the Kilburn-Scotts. Miss Thomson-Glover was a strong influence in guarding the quality of the Samoyed for many years, and was particularly influential in maintaining the typical smiling expression in the breed. She played an important part in the founding of the Samoyed Association of Britain, which absorbed the earlier Samoyede Club and the Ladies Samoyede Association in 1920.

With importation halted by the cessation of the expeditions and the rumblings of World War I, the breeders of England took over on their own.

36

The immortal Eng. Ch. Kara Sea.

Eng. Ch. Polar Light of Farningham.

37

Scotland contributed mightily to the breed when in 1915 Miss E. Marker bred Antarctic Bru (by Southern Cross out of Zembla). She followed with Mustan of Farningham, a great sire.

But the greatest was yet to come. Ch. Kara Sea, by Mustan of Farningham out of Ch. Zahrina (later to become Ch. Zahrina of Norka in the United States), was whelped on February 7, 1924. Kara Sea was bred by Mrs. D. Edwards. He was shown to a fabulous record that included 21 Challenge Certificates.

But even more than for his extensive winning over a long period, attention must be paid to Ch. Kara Sea for his importance in the concentration upon all-white dogs by certain breeders. His first generation descendants included: English and American Champion Tiger Boy of Norka, Eng. Ch. Kara Queen of the Arctic, Eng. Ch. Leader of the Arctic, and Am. Ch. Siberian Nansen of Farningham of Snowland. Second generation offspring of note included: English Champions White Fang of Kobe, Ice Crystal (also Am. Ch.), Surf, Riga, and Greta of the Arctic; Kosca of Kobe; and Am. Ch. Norka's Moguiski.

Another Scottish breeder, Mrs. Simon, bred the winning Polar Light of Farningham (Polar Sea out of Ch. Snowy) in 1923. This dog, owned by Mrs. Kilburn-Scott, not only won Best of Breed at Crufts Dog Show for five years, 1925 through 1929, but also contributed greatly as a sire.

Climaxing all of the activity in breeding and showing was the first Samoyed Club show in England in 1923. In the same year, the Samoyed Club of America was formed across the Atlantic.

In closing out the story of these beginning years, we think all Samoyed owners and breeders will find interest in the observations on size, type, and consistency over the first forty years of the breed, expressed by Will Hally in this 1934 commentary:

> The first fact is that we have not made the Samoyed bigger. I saw every one of the original importations, and I saw all the dogs which were secured from the polar expeditions. Now that takes me back to the first days of the 1890s, to the very, very beginning of Samoyeds in this country (England), and I say emphatically that Samoyed size has not altered in the very least during all that period.
>
> Then, too, in my travels as a young man, I saw the genuine Spitz in various countries, and no one who really knew the two breeds could possibly say that they were one and the same. The true Samoyed (and I am not writing of the white dogs, and dogs which have not been white, that have been paraded as Samoyeds) is radically and fundamentally different from the Spitz. The Samoyed is a product of the Samoyed people, and this is corroborated by every traveler and explorer who has gone into the matter deeply and intimately.

A statement such as this is very reassuring to Samoyed breeders today, for few owners of other breeds can look at pictures of their breed of 80 years ago, and see in them present-day show winners.

3

The Samoyed
in the United States
(1906-1965)

FROM origins steeped in mystery in the frozen far reaches of north central Siberia, the Samoyed was brought to the attention of Western civilization by a Nobel Prize winner (Fridtjof Nansen) and a king's cousin (the Duc d'Abruzzi), and supported in England by their Highnesses, Queen Alexandra and King Edward VII. It was only fitting then that it should be introduced into America by royalty, and this it was through the Princess de Montyglyon.

Mercy d'Argentau, a Belgian countess and the daughter of a royal favorite of the Court of Napoleon II, was also a hereditary princess of the Holy Roman Empire. The Princess was one of the great beauties of her day. Her world was what today would be termed "cafe society." Despite her upbringing and contacts with royalty, she met and married Captain John Bonavita, a well-known lion tamer. Captain Bonavita was to be written up more fully in the story of Lillian Russell's life than in the Princess' own autobiography.

1906-1923

Princess de Montyglyon had the first Samoyed registered in the American Kennel Club Stud Book (December 1906). The dog was the Russian Champion Moustan of Argenteau, #102896. Moustan was obtained in 1902 in St. Petersburg, Russia, from the Grand Duke Nicholas, brother to the Czar.

The reported story of how the Princess became the owner of Moustan is quite a romantic one.

At the time, the Princess owned Collies and Chows, and exhibited them quite often throughout Europe. In St. Petersburg, as she was leaving the show grounds for refreshments, she found at her heels one of the string of Samoyeds being shown by the Grand Duke. In her book she describes the dog as being a big, square-headed, good-tempered beast dragging his chain. The Princess took his chain and led him back to the bench. Next day she paid a visit to the bench to see the dog, and he followed her again. This time the Grand Duke was there as she returned him and said, "You seem to like Moustan very much." She replied, "I would give anything in the world to have him, but I hear none of this breed can be obtained. I well know that this one is not for sale."

Nicholas replied, "Oh, surely not for sale—but to give anything in the world for him? Is it not a reckless offer? I must think it over." All this with a smile and a drawl so filled with meaning that the Princess hastily dropped the subject.

The next few days and nights were filled with parties and court balls. As her departure approached, the Grand Duke asked her the date of leaving. When the Princess arrived at the station, she saw one of the Imperial Coaches on the train. She was informed that the Grand Duke had put his private car at her disposal. In the drawing room, she found a huge basket heaped with roses and orchids. When she began to remove them, there emerged the shaggy white head of the Russian Champion Moustan, with a card from the Grand Duke tied to his collar. "Moustan is not for sale," it read, "no price could buy him, but it will be a favor to him and me if you will graciously accept him."

The Princess came to America in 1904, two years after obtaining Moustan. She brought with her four Samoyeds, two Collies, and two Chow Chows—all of which she exhibited in the shows of the day (as remembered and related to us by the late dean of American judges, Alva Rosenberg).

Registered in 1906, Moustan of Argentau (#102896) holds honor as the first Samoyed in the AKC stud book. Moustan has at various times been rumored to be from the Fridtjof Nansen Expedition (1894-1897). This would have made him 10 to 12 years old when he began siring litters. Some books have attributed him to Antarctic Buck of the Borchgrevink Expedition, but Moustan's own son, Ch. de Witte of Argenteau, was born in 1900—the date of the expedition.

Even without known parentage, Moustan's name appears behind many of our Samoyeds of today. In the 1940s, one veteran remembered him as being "a large powerful dog and of sturdier build than many of the breed seen today".

Moustan's son, Ch. de Witte of Argenteau, whose dam Sora of Argenteau was also of unknown ancestry, became the first American champion Samoyed of record in 1907.

40

Of the four Samoyeds that the Princess had brought to America, only Martyska of Argenteau had known parentage. She was by Houdin out of Olgalene. Moustan, Sora, and Siberia of Argenteau were all shown as unknown. Siberia became an American Kennel Club champion in 1908.

Another almost unknown dog of the Princess' was the dog ETAH, which was given to her in 1913 by a member of the Amundsen Expedition. ETAH was one of the Samoyed lead dogs of the expedition. The Princess dedicated her autobiography to ETAH, and a picture of him at 11 years of age is included in it.

The only get by Moustan of note and impact on the breed was Czarevitch, who was out of Martyska. Czarevitch and a grandson of Moustan, Ch. Zuroff, won constantly in the early days, but were shown largely against their kennelmates.

Early competition for the Argenteau dogs was provided by the Greenacre Kennels of Mrs. Ada Van Heusen, who (as Mrs. E. E. Lincoln) had imported the two full sisters Volga and Tamara, along with Soho and Katinka—son and daughter of Southern Cross, in 1912. Tamara became the first bitch of the breed to win American championship.

The mating of Czarevitch and Tamara produced Zuroff. Czarevitch also sired Ch. Greenacre Kieff and Evalo. Ch. Greenacre Kieff was the grandsire of Champions Zanoza, Kazan of Yurak and Fang of Yurak.

New owners and exhibitors were appearing upon the scene. However, we must bear in mind that they faced problems that the great advances of veterinary medicine have pretty much erased. Many dog owners of this era, and indeed up until the mid-thirties, would not exhibit because of the distemper problem.

In 1908, Miss Elizabeth Hudson obtained her first Samoyeds, Togo and litter sister, Alice, acquired from Mrs. King Wainwright of Bryn Mawr, Pennsylvania. Twenty and thirty years later Miss Hudson was to import two great ones, but we'll talk of them in their time cycles.

Mrs. Sidney Borg and her sister Mrs. Cahn imported Samoyeds from Mrs. Cammack and Mr. Common of England, to compete at the shows with the Princess and Mrs. Van Heusen.

As could and does happen (even today), with the large kennels importing dogs to improve the breed, an individual bitch brought in as a gift to a schoolgirl by her father had some of the greatest impact upon the early dogs. Miss Ruth Nichols was given the bitch Wiemur in 1914, which was registered in 1918. Mated to Czarevitch, Wiemur produced the Champions Malschick and Shut Balackeror, as well as the uncrowned Boris. (Shut Balackeror, born on April Fools' day, was named after the last Court Jester to the Czar.)

As we look back, these early days were discouraging, for type and quality were rather ignored. Beauty to the eye of the individual was the sole criterion. There was great discrepancy in size and a standardized type had not really been settled upon. Few dogs survived in pedigrees. But isn't this true of other breeds as well? Many early dogs have been lost in oblivion after brief show careers, and the breeds have been carried on by just a few.

In all, from 1906 through 1920, exactly 40 dogs had been registered with the American Kennel Club. There had been 15 imports with well-authenticated English pedigrees traced by Catharine Quereaux, plus two imports from China, three from Russia, and one from France. The breed had seven champions of record.

The end of World War I was a turning point in breeding in both England and America. This new era got its start on this side of the ocean with the import of Tobolsk by the Yurak Kennels of Mrs. Frank Romer. Tobolsk (by Fang ex Vilna) was obtained by the handler-broker, Percy Roberts, who later became an all-breed judge.

Tobolsk was heralded as the greatest Samoyed of all time in America, and at the same time condemned as leggy and ungainly. No matter, for Champion Tobolsk #285263 proved to be a magnificent dog and a good sire. He produced the constancy of size needed in the breed, and together with later imports Ch. Donerna's Barin and Ch. Yukon-Mit was vital in giving America back the type of dog from which Trontheim had made selections for the expeditions.

Ch. Tobolsk, when mated with Otiska, sired a great line of winners including Ch. Toby of Yurak II, Nanook II, and Nanook of Donerna. (Ch. Toby of Yurak II won until he was 12 years of age, and in fact was Best of Breed at Westminster at that age.) Tobolsk mated with Sunny Ridge Pavlova produced Champions Fang of Yurak and Kazan of Yurak. (Kazan, who had difficulty making his championship because he was 26″ tall, was a large heavily-boned dog, shown from 1922 to 1927.)

Many daughters of Tobolsk were excellent specimens and good producers. They included: Queen Marie, Queen Zita, Ch. Patricia Obi, Donerna's Nara, and Champions Valeska, Semstra, and Snow Cloud of Yurak.

Ch. Draga, litter sister to Tobolsk and imported at the same time, was bred to Shut Balackeror and Zev of Yurak, and produced Ch. Kritelka of Yurak, Boy Yurak and Toby of Yurak.

The Frank Romers were active in the breed for 21 years until 1937, when their Yurak Kennels was transferred to Eddie Barbeau. The Romers (and Barbeau too) were active sledding enthusiasts.

Returning to 1920, we note the importation by Miss Mildred Trevor Sheridan of Hasova #292683, a seven-year-old dog from Russia, and Loree #294040, a bitch from England. They are best remembered as the sire and dam of Lady Olga, #320651, born 1920. Lady Olga was the dam of Ch. Icy King, who became the sire of such big winners of the 1930s as the litter brothers, Ch. Icy King Jr., Siberian Icy King Duplicate, CD, and Ch. Prince

Kofski. Miss Sheridan, now Mrs. Mildred Sheridan Davis, owns Park-Cliffe Kennels, still in operation as of 1984—over sixty years later.

Two notable kennels were added in 1921. The F. L. Vintons' Obi Kennel continues through the Obi suffix found in today's pedigrees. The other was Mr. and Mrs. Harry Reid's Norka Kennels. In 1929 the Reids were to give great impetus to the breed with their importation of Ch. Tiger Boy.

In this continued period of imports, the years 1922 and 1923 brought the Romers' Yurak Kennels the great bitch Olga of Farningham (by Antarctic Bru, a grandson of Antarctic Buck, out of Olga, a granddaughter of Buck); Trip of Farningham (by Antarctic Bru out of Miss Muffet); and Yurak's Fox Laika—all from Mrs. Kilburn-Scott. To Yurak also came Donerna's Kolya of Farningham and Donerna's Tsilma, a litter sister to Donerna's Barin. To Louis Smirnow came Nico of Farningham, who was on the small side, as were his progeny. Miss Grafton of England sent Polas of Farningham to the W. B. Donahues. Mr. and Mrs. James L. Hubbard of Howardsville, Maryland, imported Olaf of Farningham, another son of Antarctic Bru out of Nish Nish (thus the grandfather was again Mezenett of Antarctic Buck's famous litter).

The second of the three pillars of the American Samoyed was imported at this time by Mr. and Mrs. Alfred Seeley for their Donerna Kennels at the foot of the George Washington Bridge in New York. He was Ch. Donerna's Barin, a son of Eng. Ch. Kieff out of Ivanofva, bred by Mr. Pitchford of England.

It is interesting to note that Barin was sent to this country in place of Snow Crest when the American Kennel Club waived the three generation rule for Ch. Tobolsk. Barin, you see, went back to the expedition import, Antarctic Buck in just two generations. He was himself an able sled dog and proved a great worker in the sled teams of the Donerna Kennels.

Ch. Donerna's Barin had 120 registered sons and daughters. Therefore, by sheer numbers, he had great influence on the breed, an influence that was especially positive for size and coat. Barin was a measured 22″ and 60 lbs. Some of his get were larger, but judging from the picture of him in this book at his tenth birthday, he reproduced his size.

Donerna's Kolya was influential because 60 of his progeny soon appeared in the Stud Book, mostly bred in the Midwestern States. Bred to Polas of Farningham, Kolya produced Pollyanna and Princess Illeana. Pollyanna, who died in 1940 was the dam of Ch. Duke of Norka and the great winner Ch. Norka's Lubinlay.

The 42 Samoyeds registered in 1922 equalled the total registration of the previous 15 years of American Samoyed history. In this last year before the formation of the parent club there were six large kennels: Donerna, Yurak, Top O' The World, Obi, Park-Cliffe and Wingbrook.

43

It was a year of turmoil for Samoyed owners, breeders and exhibitors. Some dogs, both registered and unregistered, imported and homebred, were being denied ribbons or were being excused from the rings because of their inferior quality and discrepancies in size and type. Lack of a standard and lack of any uniformity in the classes caused further loss of status to the breed. In Cleveland, the show committee had provided for the Samoyeds in the Miscellaneous Class, with the designation of dogs of 25 pounds or over. Still in 1922, judge J. Muss-Arnolt had a very nice entry of 12, and placed Nico of Farningham to Winners Dog, and Kazan of Yurak as Reserve. Both dogs had been refused ribbons at earlier shows.

1923-1944

The Samoyed Club of America was formed on February 14, 1923. But even with so auspicious an event, the day was a shocker for Samoyed exhibitors. At the Westminster Kennel Club show of the same day, the judge, J. Willoughby Mitchell of London, England, provided a skyrocket sendoff. He withheld the awards for Reserve Winners in both dogs and bitches. Mr. Mitchell declared they were apparently not true Samoyeds because of their small size and flattish lay-down coats. Three of the animals involved were newly imported from the kennels of Mrs. Kilburn-Scott in England.

Catharine Quereaux later wrote "Whether this was a back-handed slap at English breeders or indigestion, it assuredly was decidedly in error, and even today we speak of the wrath of the 1923 Westminster!"

Will Hally, veteran Samoyed columnist for the English publication *Our Dogs* wrote:

> That remark of the London judge has created a lot of indignation amongst the Samoyed's supporters in the States, and with reason, I think. While I am not able to speak of all the exhibits at New York, the authenticated British pedigrees of most of them are the surest proof that Mr. Mitchell is mistaken. I noticed that Mr. Smirnow refers to the New York Winners dog, Billy Boy of Yurak, as a flat-coated dog of good character, and perhaps it is that flat coat which led to Mr. Mitchell's criticism. Such a coat is faulty, but it by no means indicates a Collie influence. The American fanciers, from what I know of the stock they now own, are on the right road, and if they breed to the standard, they need not worry over what one or two judges say of their exhibits.

Nevertheless, following the judging at the Westminster show, the serious exhibitors and breeders of the Samoyed met in the club rooms of the Madison Square Garden of the day, and organized the Samoyed Club of America. The club's stated purposes were to promote the breeding of purebred Samoyeds; to urge adoption of this type upon breeders, judges, dog show committees, etc., and to bring to the notice of the general public the wonderful characteristics and affectionate dispositions of these superlative dogs.

Eng. Ch. Kieff, sire of Ch. Donerna's Barin and Ch. Donerna's Tsilma. Kieff was noted for throwing good coat to his progeny.

H.N. Pinkham with the Laika Kennels' team at South Poland, Maine, in 1929. Included are three show champions (Ch. Donerna's Illinishna, Ch. Laika Natiya, and Ch. Donerna's Barin).

Styles may change but Samoyeds stay constant. Miss Katherine Morey, who later became Mrs. H.N. Pinkham (Laika Kennels) is shown wearing a suit made of Samoyed combings in this 1929 photo. The dog at left is Ch. Donerna's Barin, at ten years of age.

They adopted the English breed standard, adding the words "black or black spots to disqualify" and a description of disposition. This standard was adopted as the sole standard for excellence in breeding and awarding prizes of merit to Samoyeds by the American Kennel Club when it approved the Samoyed Club of America for membership in the AKC on May 15, 1923.

Thus the Samoyed Club of America was formed out of an emotional realization of the concrete need for a parent club to guide and standardize the breed beyond all doubt.

In 1923, there were less than 300 Samoyeds in the United States, and at least half of these were in just five kennels. The Samoyeds were being shown in the Non-Sporting Group with the Collies, Doberman Pinschers, French Bulldogs, Great Danes, Maltese, Old English Sheepdogs, Boston Terriers, German Shepherd Dogs, St. Bernards, Toy Poodles and Yorkshire Terriers. Registrations in the 1923 Stud Book were the heaviest yet, with 74 recorded.

The breed was beginning to move across the United States. Princess Montyglyon had moved to La Jolla, California, and new owners were showing elsewhere in that state.

Publicity for the breed was provided by A. H. Seeley when he wrote a feature article for the *American Kennel Gazette*, February 1925. This article was entitled, "Dogs that See the Midnight Sun," and gave a history of the breed and a plea for research to aid in gathering more facts. As he stated, "The breed history was indeed lost in antiquity."

Mr. Seeley was killed in an automobile accident shortly thereafter and many of his dogs were acquired by Mr. and Mrs. H. N. Pinkham for their Laika Kennels in Ipswich, Mass. Among them was the famous Ch. Donerna's Barin. Mr. Seeley had been a sledding enthusiast, and Mr. Pinkham too was an avid believer in the working ability of the dogs. He wrote three feature articles for the *American Kennel Gazette*: July 1930, "The Dog Nobody Improved"; a series article in November and December 1930, "The Gamest Dogs In the World"; and in February 1932, "The Real Way to Raise Dogs."

Mr. Pinkham kept his dogs in the north woods and gave them immense runs of twenty acres. He retained the desired disposition in his dogs, and they were able to run together. The Laika Kennels' winter home was twenty miles from a traveled road and all supplies were transported by dog team. These desired traits were passed to California in 1935 when Mrs. Agnes Mason of Sacramento, California went to the Pinkhams for Dasha of Laika, with aim of breeding dogs with sledding ability, conformation, and good Samoyed dispositions. Both the Pinkhams and Masons bred for show dogs that could work.

The most influential import in 1925 was Yukon Mit, imported by Morgan Wing, first Samoyed Club of America delegate to the AKC. Mit passed on his style and true Samoyed type to his get. His dominance in producing style, Barin's in improving coat and gait and Tobolsk's in establishing size, gave America back Samoyeds of the type of the original expedition strains.

The mating of Yukon Mit to Barin's daughter, Nona of Donerna, produced the great Ch. Gorka. Gorka was the pet of Mrs. Horace Mann, who was urged to "support" a show with her eight-year-old dog. She walked off with the wins, including Best of Breed and the Working Group at Trenton. Ch. Gorka ideally fulfilled the dual role of pet and show dog. Yukon Mit, mated to another Barin daughter, Nanci, owned by Catharine Quereaux, produced Ch. Mitboi, who belonged to Dr. and Mrs. William Bridges of Maryland, and Tarquin (who sired Ch. Tarquin II), owned by the Very Reverend Monsignor Robert F. Keegan.

The distinguished Yukon Mit and Barin lines were carried on through Tarquin, Ch. Tarquin II, Ch. Prince Igor, and Ch. Dobrynia in the kennels owned by Monsignor Keegan, who showed and bred Samoyeds from 1928 to 1948. Ch. Dobrynia, son of Ch. Norka's Lubiniey, was Best American-bred in the Working Group at the Westminster Kennel Club, 1936. Following the show, *The New York Times* reported, "Upon seeing the Samoyeds for the first time, there is no more beautiful dog in the world."

Msgr. Keegan was featured in the *American Kennel Gazette* in February 1937 in an article by Arthur Frederick Jones, which pictured his dogs, kennels, and home in the Adirondack Mountains. Msgr. Keegan was a believer in raising dogs in the natural state, and never kept them in heated buildings.

By the year 1929, the breed had arrived at some semblance of solidarity and the *American Kennel Gazette* stated, "The growth of the breed has been both conservative and constant, and augurs well for the future. The Samoyed is an established fixture in American dog circles, and becoming more popular in the right direction for the future of the breed."

The first specialty of the parent Samoyed Club of America was held with the Tuxedo Kennel Club show in September 1929. An early summation of the progress of the breed was given by Louis Smirnow, first club president, prior to his judging of the Specialty:

> The progress of the breed depends largely on careful breeding. Those of us who have seen Samoyeds know we are apt to see some specimens shorter in body than others, and unless a short-bodied Samoyed is bred to a longer-bodied one, the results will be undesirable from the viewpoint of the standard of the breed.
>
> A careful breeder will try to eliminate the various faults of his dogs by breeding to a dog who is strong in the characteristics that this breeder is endeavoring to correct.
>
> Occasionally we see an excellent dog, big boned, excellent coat, proper size with a small head. Precautions should be taken to breed a dog of this type to one where the head condition will be improved.

47

The real champions in England and the old champions in this country, such as Tobolsk, Olga of Farningham and Nico of Farningham, all had fine heads. Unless a champion has a real true head there cannot be the proper expression, which is a very strong point in the beauty of the Samoyed.

The fact that a breeder may have 20 dogs among which are a half-dozen bitches and three or four studs is no reason why this breeder should not endeavor to breed outside his kennel, if by so doing, the proper characteristics will be had.

It seems to me and to some of the old timers that too much stress is being laid on size. I need hardly emphasize the fact that the large dog lacking other features will not do as well in the ring as the smaller dog with good head. One of the largest dogs ever bred in the history of the breed is Snow Crest of English fame. I have seen many photographs and read many discussions of this dog, but he was too long in the muzzle for me; his head has the appearance of a collie. Yet the owner of this dog, by careful breeding, bred the finest champions of English fame. (The breeder referred to was Miss Thomson-Glover.)

This first specialty had an entry of 40 for Mr. Smirnow's judgment. With only 40 Samoyeds registered between 1906 and 1920, such a large entry less than a decade later was remarkable. Tiger Boy of Norka, owned by the Reids, only three weeks in America from England and reported by Miss Thompson-Glover as taller than most English dogs, made his debut and was Best of Breed.

People as well as great dogs are needed to weld a breed together. Such a person was Mrs. Catharine S. Quereaux of Long Island and New York City. She joined the breed in 1926, and by 1929 was collecting pedigrees and information of the breed. As the parent club secretary and/or publicity director, Mrs. Quereaux disseminated this information to all, largely at her own expense, for the period 1929 through 1951. Her importation of dogs and bitches to aid the breed were generously placed with breeders throughout the country.

Mrs. Quereaux wrote a history of the Samoyed breed which was never published in its entirety. Parts of this, titled "Dog of the Ages," appeared in a few magazines and club bulletins, but the complete twenty chapters were still unprinted at her unexpected death in 1952. For many years, her columns in the *American Kennel Gazette* aided owners. With permission of Mrs. Serena A. Bridges, her sister, the authors were given access to Mrs. Quereaux's vast files when first compiling the early history for this book.

In the late twenties, Miss Elizabeth Hudson, an enthusiast since 1908, visited Russia. She reported, "There were no Samoyed dogs in Moscow or Leningrad, nor could I get any information about the breed. All apparently had disappeared in the Revolution. Undoubtedly, if the breed is preserved in Russia it was in the original habitat, with the Samoyed tribes." She brought back with her from England the influential Ch. Storm Cloud in 1929. Storm Cloud, was by Ch. Sea Foam out of Ch. Vara. He too, was reported taller than most in England and weighed slightly over 60 pounds. In America, he became the sire of Ch. Tucha, owned by Mrs. Helen Harris.

Later (1939), out of the great bitch Morina of Taimir, he sired Vida of Snowland, the foundation bitch for Mrs. Harris' Snowland Kennels. Ch. Storm Cloud won the second parent club specialty, held in 1930 at the Morris and Essex Show.

Early in the 1930s, Mrs. Helen Harris began her famous Snowland Kennels at Merion, Pennsylvania, by importing Pedlar of the Arctic. She and her daughter were on a trip to Europe and in a park in London, became acquainted with a Samoyed dog. Her daughter, Faith, simply "had to have one" and so Pedlar was obtained. Unfortunately, this puppy contracted distemper and blindness resulted. This did not prevent Pedlar from enjoying a full and long life until 1942. The stories of the other dogs acting as his "seeing eye" are amazing; he seemed to rule the sighted dogs. Another trip to England followed, and Mrs. Harris purchased Sabarka of Farningham, and tried valiantly but unsuccessfully to obtain Kara Sea from Mrs. Edwards. In 1936, Mrs. Harris returned to England for a puppy of Ch. Kara Sea. This is the event which put so much of the bloodline of Ch. Kara Sea into America. Mrs. Harris requested a litter by Kara Sea and Pinky of Farningham. Due to the age of Kara Sea, 13 years at the time, it required some discussion. She agreed to take the entire litter home to America. The entire litter consisted of two, Siberian Nansen of Farningham of Snowland and his litter sister Martyska of Farningham. Both were brought to America, but the bitch died at an early age. Nansen proved to be a great stud dog. He sired many champions, even at the age of eleven years. Thus, we find Ch. Kara Sea on the paper of modern pedigrees spanning a period of 24 years. Included in his later progeny were Champion Pinsk of Snowland, owned by the Ralph Oateys, and Ch. Staryvna of Snowland, owned by the authors. These dogs were showing as late as the 1950s. This is truly a remarkable span of time in dog bloodlines.

Mrs. Harris had earlier purchased Vida of Snowland (Ch. Storm Cloud out of Morina of Taimir), Tucha of Snowland, Ch. Sprint of the Arctic, and Ch. Moscow of Farningham of Snowland. When she bred Nansen to Vida, she had her remarkable "N" litter—Champions Nim, Nadya, Norna, Nianya, and Nikita. There is scarcely a Group-winning or Best in Show dog of the breed that does not have one of these as an ancestor. These great examples of the breed were successfully shown by famous handler J. Nate Levine.

The pride of Mrs. Harris' kennels, Ch. Nadya, in turn, became the dam of Ch. Novik of Snowland, owned by the Ruicks. Ch. Nianya of Snowland, owned by the Masons, became the dam of Ch. Chum, Cleo, Soldier Frosty of Rimini and was behind many, many other famous Pacific Coast champions.

Mrs. Harris once wrote to us of meeting a French painter named Jacques Suzanne while at Lake Placid. He seemed to know the Samoyed breed well, and said he had painted the dogs and horses of the late Czar. He

Morina of Taimir (1933-1948), bred in England by Miss E. Creveld and chosen by Miss Thomson-Glover to be sent to America and Miss Elizabeth Hudson. Morina's mating with Storm Cloud produced Vida of Snowland and had great impress upon the breed.

A lineup of champions at Snowland Kennels: Ch. Siberian Nansen of Farningham of Snowland (a Kara Sea son), Ch. Nim of Snowland, Ch. Nalda of Snowland, Ch. Nadya of Snowland and Ch. Norna of Snowland. Nim and his sisters, Nadya and Norna, were of the famous "N" litter sired by Nansen out of Vida of Snowland.

Ch. Starvyna of Snowland, a Ch. Kara Sea granddaughter. The first bitch to win the SCA National Specialty (in 1947), Starvyna was acquired as a puppy by the authors from Helen Harris.

had traveled to Siberia and had something to say on the size of the Samoyed dog. He related that the majority of the native dogs were not as large or so beautiful as the good grooming and feeding provided by our society seems to make them. He believed that in their native habitat they were stunted by the infrequent feedings, for they varied in size, while the Samoyeds owned by the Czar were all beautiful big specimens. He presented Mrs. Harris with a picture of three puppies which came from the kennels of the Czar.

Headlines in Boston on May 21, 1930, read "Famous Champion is Host to Byrd Dogs on Birthday." Ch. Donerna's Barin observed his 10th birthday surrounded by seven sons and four daughters and friends. Barin was pictured with Dinney and Torgnac, who served with Admiral Byrd's South Pole expedition.

Mrs. J. C. McDowell of La Crescenta, California founded the Khiva Kennels in 1928, and for the next decade was active on the show scene. She imported Ch. Snow Frost of the Arctic, who in 1935—at 7 years of age—became the first Samoyed on the Pacific Coast to win the Working Group. But it was Mrs. Agnes Mason with her skill in selecting bloodlines and organizing that gave the big push to Samoyed popularity there from the late 1930s through the 1950s.

Mrs. Mason, as a girl in Alaska, was very familiar with dogs, as her father had sled teams. Renewing her work with dogs, in 1935 she purchased a Samoyed for her daughter Aljean from M. D. Robison of Oakland, California. He became Ch. Czar Nicholas Lebanov. His dam went back to Ch. Snow Frost of the Arctic and his sire was by Nico of Farningham. Mrs. Mason gathered breeding stock from many States and England. Her English imports, Silver Spark of the Arctic (litter brother to Chs. Sport and Sprint of the Arctic) and Ch. White Way of Kobe were imported in 1938. These added the bloodlines of Arctic and Kobe (through English Chs. Snow Chief of the Arctic and White Fang of Kobe) to West Coast pedigrees. Further, she combined her West Coast and English bloodlines with an infusion of the Snowland Kennels of Pennsylvania by obtaining Ch. Nianya of Snowland. With the addition of Dasha of Laika from the Pinkhams, she had the best in American bloodlines.

Mrs. Mason and her daughter, Aljean Mason Larson, owned and finished 14 champions and bred 22 champions. Many more would have finished, but for her preoccupation with other activities and strong interest in sled work and sled races. She wanted to prove that show dogs had stamina and endurance and that sled dogs are not vicious. She did.

World-wide publicity was received by the breed when the Masons' sled team of champion Samoyeds performed at the World's Fair on Treasure Island at San Francisco, California. Their daily performances encouraged much picture taking and exposure to the public for attention and petting. Further publicity occurred when the picture of Ch. Sprint of the Arctic, Ch.

51

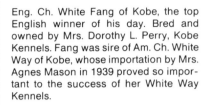

Eng. Ch. White Fang of Kobe, the top English winner of his day. Bred and owned by Mrs. Dorothy L. Perry, Kobe Kennels. Fang was sire of Am. Ch. White Way of Kobe, whose importation by Mrs. Agnes Mason in 1939 proved so important to the success of her White Way Kennels.

Ch. Prince Kofski (1934-1946), owned by Mr. and Mrs. Samuel K. Ruick. Kofski's many wins included Best of Breed at Westminster in 1944, at almost 10 years of age.

Eng. Ch. Kosca of Kobe, owned by Mrs. Dorothy L. Perry, England. Agnes Mason commented on this photo: "Good front legs, good stifles, feet, tail. Well-balanced dog. Head well set."

Wendy, C.D., whelped 1940. Bred by Msgr. Robert F. Keegan and owned by Miss Margaret Schlichting, she was the foundation in establishment of Mrs. Schlichting's White Barks Kennel. Dam of Chs. Peter Pan and Barrie.

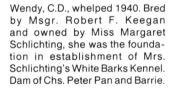

Moscow of Farningham of Snowland, and Ch. Siberian Nansen appeared upon the cover of *Western Kennel World,* which began a tradition of the Samoyed as the "Christmas Dog" on the cover each December.

The get of Ch. Tiger Boy of Norka were proving themselves in the East, for at Westminster in 1937 Best of Breed was the Winners Dog, 4½-year-old Norka's Viking (by Tiger Boy ex Norka's Dutochka). This dog was of the same large type as Ch. Norka's Moguiski, who won the 1938 parent club specialty under the breeder-judge Msgr. R. F. Keegan, at the Morris and Essex show.

Contributions to the breed by Miss Juliet Goodrich were many and valuable. Not only did she import, breed, and show, but she was a pioneer in the field of eradication of hip dysplasia in the mid-1930s. Her Snow Shoe Hill Kennels was situated upon 5,000 acres of beautifully wooded land, complete with lakes, at Land O'Lakes, Wisconsin. Here the dogs Jack Frost of Snow Shoe Hill, her first, and Keena (by Ch. Kandalaska Yena of Marne), had runs of several acres each if they so desired.

When the new field of Obedience entered the dog shows in 1937, the first Champion and C.D. obedience titled Samoyed, Ch. Alstasia's Ruka-vitza, C.D., was owned by the well-known breeder judge, Mrs. Anastasia MacBain of Ohio. Mrs. MacBain was a pioneer member and founder of the Inter-State Samoyed Club. Rukavitza won the 1941 parent club specialty show at the Morris and Essex Kennel Club. He was shown 42 times and won 33 Bests of Breed with 13 Group placings.

The Inter-State Samoyed Club held the first separate specialty show for the breed in 1938 on the Friday before the Western Reserve Show. Ch. Jack Frost of Sacramento was Best of Breed.

Dogs with very close type to that of the American Snowland Kennels were developed by Mrs. Ruth Bates Young of Ohio. She bred her Olga Pogi of Obi to Natalie Rogers' import Ch. Sport of the Arctic, a brother to both Sprint and Spark of the Arctic. One of the puppies from this litter, Snow Chief, became the sire of the Poiriers' International Champion Kola Snow Cloud of Loralee.

The year 1940 was a banner one for Samoyeds, for they placed 17 times in the Working Group. Three won Companion Dog degrees: the MacBains' Ch. Rukavitza, the Kroepils' Ch. Icy King Duplicate, and the Burnettes' Polar Sea. The Cleveland Western Reserve Show had 56 Samoyeds with eight champions. Mr. Harold Danks, of Wisconsin, had his sled team on exhibition at the show and gave children rides in the Cleveland auditorium.

With 1941 came the war years. Breeding and showing were curtailed, but there was some activity. The pioneers—the Romers, the Reids, the Pinkhams, the Seeleys, Mercy Argenteau, and the Van Heusens were gone, but the breed was reaching out to all parts of the country.

The Samoyed Club of the Pacific Coast held a Specialty in 1941 in conjunction with the Oakland Kennel Club. Best of Breed with an entry of 41 was Agnes and Aljean Mason's Ch. Petrof Lebanof.

Bloodlines were beginning to reach back and forth across the land. Mrs. Mr. Perrin Wintz of Indiana purchased a bitch from Mrs. McDowell, a double granddaughter of Ch. Snow Frost of the Arctic. She believed that bitches should be more of the size of the males, and owned the imported Ch. Kandalaska, who was 22½ inches tall and weighed 68 pounds with a four-inch coat.

The traveling during the war moved some other dogs around, a widening that greatly aided the breed. Captain and Mrs. Ashley were the breeders of a litter sired by Nikita of Snowland out of Ch. Nova Sonia of Kobe, that placed Ch. Echo of Kobe of Breezewood in Indiana. Then, while the Ashleys were stationed in the state of Washington, they bred Nikita with Niarvik of Inara, owned by Mrs. Edna McKinnon. This produced the males Sooltan and Am. and Can. Ch. Snohomish of Oceanside, who began siring new bloodlines in the Seattle area. Lewis and Claire Bajus in Milwaukee had the influential Ch. Yeinsei's Czar Nicholas II in their kennels. Their nephew, Joe Scott, brought Queen Senga of Lewclaire to the West Coast.

One of the outstanding sires of the breed appeared in 1943, and marked the introduction of the authors, Bob and Dolly Ward, to serious Samoyed showing and breeding. The great sire was Ch. Starchak, C.D. (Ch. Herdsman's Chattigan ex Ch. Silver Star of White Way), bred by the Masons' White Way Kennels. "Chatter", as Starchak was affectionately called, was an outstanding winner of 32 Bests of Breed. He sired 16 champions, was grandsire of over 40 champions, and won the parent club Stud Dog Trophy in 1956.

His mating with Ch. Starvyna of Snowland (personally selected for the Wards by Mrs. Helen Harris, and Best of Breed winner at the 1947 SCA Specialty) was to have an especially strong influence on the breed. Out of the mating came Ch. Starchak Witan, Ch. Starchak Witangemote and the bitch, Ch. Starchak Warnistura.

Witan sired, among others, Ch. Starctic Storm, who became implanted in hundreds of pedigrees through his son Ch. Kazan of Kentwood, and his grandsons, top-winning and producing Ch. Karshan and Ch. Sayan of Woodland.

Ch. Starchak's Warnistura, called Sissy, went to Mrs. Mason and produced Ch. White Way's Silver Streak, a many time Group winner.

Ch. Starchak's Witangemote, and Ch. Princess Startinda, a daughter of Ch. Starchak ex Princess Tina of Tonia, went to Mr. and Mrs. Kenneth Bristol of Thousand Oaks, California and were the start of their Startinda Kennels. Witangemote sired a dozen champions; out of his mating with Startinda came three champions in one litter: Talnik, Sarana and Chrinda. In 1956, Ch. Startinda's Talnik, handled by Lloyd Bristol, was second only

Ch. Starchak, C.D., ("Chatter") notable winner and sire (16 chs.) of the 1940s. Bred by the Masons' White Way Kennels and owned by the authors.

Ch. Rainier (1947-1959), a Starchak son. Bred by Elizabeth Wyman, trained and owned by the authors. "Raini" broke the ice in the West with his win of the Group at Sun Maid in 1949, first for a Samoyed in 16 years.

Ch. Starchak's Witan, by Ch. Starchak, C.D. ex Ch. Starvyna of Snowland. Noted for tremendously powerful gait and agility.

Ch. Starctic Storm (1950-1961) by Ch. Starchak's Witan ex Mazzi's Duchess (linebred to Starchak). At his first show Storm went BOB from the classes over SCA-supported entry at Los Angeles, 1954.

to Ch. Yurok of Whitecliff as the top winning Samoyed on the West Coast. While very active in shows, the Startinda Samoyeds became best known in sled dog racing. For many years the Bristols entered two full teams of five to seven dogs in many races from Donners' Pass, California to Williams, Arizona.

Another influential Starchak son was Ch. Rainier, bred by Miss Elizabeth Wyman and owned and trained by the authors. Ch. Rainier was the second Samoyed to win a Working group on the Pacific Coast. His progeny included the Int. Ch. MacGregor of Glenstrae, winner of four championships in Europe and the C.A.C.I. B. award.

Mrs. Pamela Rhanor (California) had her Petsamo bloodlines carried on extensively when she sent Snow King of Petsamo to Mrs. Betty Arneson in Seattle in 1944. That same year, Tynda of Petsamo went to Mrs. Margaret Tucker and was the start of the now famous Encino Kennels when she was bred to Ch. Starchak, C.D. to produce Ch. Kun To of Encino.

In the years 1939 to 1943, an annual average of only about 195 all-breed and 150 Specialty Shows were held. Today, there are over 1,000 all-breed shows each year. In this connection, a point should be made that many fail to take into account when discussing great winners. Prior to 1950, a dog to win 20 or 30 Best of Breeds had to be a flyer, and shown extensively. For example, English Champion Kara Sea had 22 Challenge Certificates and was a hallmark of the breed. American Champion Donerna's Barin, a pillar in America, had only approximately nine Bests of Breed in the 1920s. Ch.

Alijean Mason Larson, breeder-owner, handling Ch. White Way's Silver Streak to his win of the Group at Glendale KC.

At left, Ch. Martingate Snowland Taz, important winner and sire of the 1950s. Originally owned by Dr. William Ivens, later acquired by Mrs. Elma Miller. At right, Am. & Can. Ch. Tazson (1946-1958), first of Taz's notable progeny. Tazson, bred and owned by Mrs. Ashbjorn Ulfeng, won two SCA Specialties and 55 BOBs. Sire of Ch. Nordly's Sammy (4-time Specialty winner).

Alstasia's Rukavitza U.D. earned 33 BOBs in the late 1930s and early 1940s. Ch. Starchak C.D. obtained 32 Bests of Breed in the late 1940s. One must learn to judge a record by the competition and the availability of shows.

1945-1950

To begin the post-War era, Samoyed enthusiasts had a new parent club structure to aid in promoting the breed. The club had expanded from an Eastern group into a national club with three areas or divisions to promote more local activity and interest.

In 1946, Dr. William Ivens, of Pennsylvania, who had been showing and breeding Samoyeds since 1937, imported Ch. Martingate Snowland Taz, an import that made a permanent impression on the breed in the Eastern section of the country.

Ch. Martingate Snowland Taz was selected personally for Dr. Ivens by Miss Thomson-Glover, through the efforts of Miss Ruth Stillman, who was visiting in England. Imported at the age of two years, Taz enjoyed a glorious show career through the years 1946 to 1950, garnering 50 Bests of Breed out of 54 times shown including four in succession (1946-49) at Westminster, 3 Group Firsts and 19 other Group placements. In 1951, at age of seven, Taz was purchased from Dr. Ivens by Mrs. Elma Miller, Elkenglo Kennels.

Taz brought much substance and heavier heads to many of the bloodlines. He was quite in demand as a stud, and was the sire of 28 champions and 29 champion grandchildren. His mating with Mrs. Bernice E. Ashdown's Eng. and Am. Ch. Princess Silvertips of Kobe produced a litter of five champions that included two Best in Show winners—Ch. Silver Spray of Wychwood and Ch. Silvertips Scion of Wychwood.

The Glendale Kennel Club show in 1947 had a special significance, for it was agreed to test the American Kennel Club rule which permits the entry of any dog over six months of age in Open class. Of this, Catharine Quereaux wrote:

> This show was a test show where members were privileged to enter champions in the classes, contrary to our usual custom. The Wards' Champion Staryvna of Snowland was entered in the Open Bitch Class and was Winners Bitch in stiff competition with Snow Queen of White Way and Khatanga of Snowland among others. Though the Winners Bitch was beaten for Best of Winners by the yet untitled son of Ch. Starchak, Kun To, the win was a fact. True this one show proves nothing, but the day must come in this country that if champions are to be considered worthy of the title, they must be entered in the classes. It has always been done in England. This procedure is not unknown to America, for the Reids, when owners of the Norka Kennels, entered champions in the classes. Long before, Tobolsk must have been entered many times in the classes after gaining his title. We are told Tobolsk won five championships. The more exhibitors brave wrath by doing this, the better for the breed, for better dogs will be found to defeat any one dog too long in a winning streak. Further, at big shows we often have five or six champions entered for Specials Only. One may be chosen Best of Breed, but there is no placement for the others. They may be infinitely better than the dogs entered in the classes, or may not be as good, but there is no rating given. In England they know their top ranking champions, their seconds, their thirds, and the day must come when we have the same knowledge of our own here. Mrs. Ward felt she could not, as President of the Pacific Coast Division, ask any one to make the test if she did not do it herself. Thus, taking it as a club matter rather than a personal one, she welcomed the win of the Winners Dog from her stud; this being the very thing which proves the desirability of such entries of champions. Perhaps after the 1947 SCA National Specialty Show at Pasadena another test will be made, and the example should be followed by other divisions of the Samoyed Club of America.

The Pacific Coast Division hosted the parent club specialty with the Pasadena Kennel Club in June 1947 and Ch. Staryvna of Snowland topped the entry of 47, the beginning of multiple Best of Breed awards for bitches.

Not all dogs receive a Good Conduct Medal, but Soldier Frosty of Rimini (by Ch. Petrof Lebanov ex Ch. Nianya of Snowland), was awarded his with the Victory Medal. Frosty was presented the medal in a ceremony at Camp Stoneman, California. During World War II, he was number P-254 in the K-9 sled dog Corps. He served in Attu, Iceland and in Greenland as a lead dog to take supplies to marooned fliers. The ceremony and presentation was interesting in that it took place at a special luncheon in the Officers'

Club. Frosty was given an honorary commission as a Colonel in the Reserve Corps. When luncheon was served, his was roast beef and a pan of water, but his mistress, Miss Barbara Stewart, wouldn't let him eat at the table where he was seated. While age and time did not offer him a show career, his progeny gave him an added medal for his record. He left a mark as the sire of Ch. Omak, and thus the grandsire of the outstanding winner Ch. Yurok of Whitecliff.

Another son of Soldier Frosty that performed splendid public service was Ch. Samoyland's Vojak U.D., owned by Chloe and Tom Witcher of San Francisco. Vojak was the first Samoyed to make this dual championship on the West Coast, and was one leg away from his Tracking title when death came at the young age of six years. Ch. Vojak U.D. performed for television, service organizations, hospitals, for handicapped children and the March of Dimes, as well as for several years leading a team with Santa Claus into the Shriners' Hospital in San Francisco, where the children always enjoyed him and his teammates.

An historic recognition was brought about in 1949 by the first Best in Show award to a Samoyed in the United States. The award was made by judge Mrs. Marie Meyer at the Toledo Kennel Club Show, April 10, 1949. A beautiful puppy bitch, Sweet Missy of Sammar, owned by Mr. and Mrs. J. J. Marshall Jr., came up from the classes under the breeder judge Mrs. Anastasia MacBain, who also did the Group. Sweet Missy was sired by Ch. Martingate Snowland Taz out of Ch. Frolene of Sammar.

Sweet Missy of Sammar, puppy bitch from the classes, winning the first all-breed Best in Show by a Samoyed in the United States, at Toledo Kennel Club, April 10, 1949. Judge was Mrs. Marie Meyer and Missy was handled by her breeder-owner, Mrs. Joseph J. Marshall.

Ch. Silvertips Saba
of Wychwood.

1950-1965

In the wake of this first Best in Show in 1949, the Samoyed rose to great eminence in inter-breed competition in the 1950s. Spearheading this rise were the dogs of the Wychwood Kennel, owned by Mrs. Bernice B. Ashdown, and trained and shown by Charles L. Rollins.

Although Mrs. Ashdown owned Samoyeds as far back as 1930, it was not until about ten years later, when she acquired Rimsky of Norka, that she became seriously interested in breeding and showing. Obedience training was then still in its infancy, and Wychwood became one of the pioneers and missionaries for that phase of the sport. Rimsky became the first champion U.D.T. Samoyed.

With the importation of Eng. Ch. Princess Silvertips of Kobe in November, 1949, Wychwood winning went into high gear. Instrumental in securing Silvertips for import to this country was the eminent breeder-judge, Miss J. V. Thomson-Glover, who considered her "probably the finest Samoyed in Great Britain today." Princess Silvertips had been undefeated in England with nine Challenge Certificates to her credit. She was embarked on her American show career in 1950, at just a few months short of her sixth birthday. After completing her championship, she was temporarily retired to rear what was to be a historic litter by Ch. Martingate Snowland Taz, and then was returned to the ring in 1951 to begin her show career in earnest. Her American record included 48 Bests of Breed in 49 times shown (the one defeat being to her daughter, Ch. Silvertips Saba of Wychwood), 33 Group placements including 14 Firsts and two Bests in Show. The first Best in Show, won at seven years of age, made her only the second in the breed to have gone BIS. Her second was won at nine years of age. Her winning is all the more remarkable when it is realized that her career was interrupted four times for the bearing of litters.

Ch. Silver Spray of Wychwood, one of the five champions born of the mating of Silvertips with Taz, established what was then a record for the

Ch. Silver Spray of Wychwood.

Charles L. Rollins watching Ch. Rimsky of Norka, first Samoyed U.D.T. titlist, jump over kennelmates Bettina of Wychwood, C.D., Ch. Marina of Wychwood, C.D.X. and Ch. Ballerina of Wychwood.

61

breed with wins of five all-breed Bests in Show and a Best American-Bred in Show. Spray made his championship in just 34 days, finishing at but nine months of age. Undefeated in the breed after completing his title, he was Best Samoyed at Westminster four years in succession, matching the achievement of his great sire. He twice placed in the Group at Westminster.

In December 1956, Wychwood brought over another star. This was the young English Ch. Americ of Kobe. Americ's introduction to the American show rings in 1957 was most sensational. At his first show, he went from Open class to Best in Show. This was followed by four successive Working Group Firsts, thus completing his championship undefeated by a Working dog of any breed. In all, Americ was shown in the United States 33 times, was undefeated in the breed, scored 29 Group placements including 19 Firsts, and four Bests in Show.

The contribution of Wychwood in bringing the Samoyed to favorable all-breed attention was tremendous. One of its Samoyeds was Best in Show in every year from 1951 through 1959 (except 1956), and in 1953 it was the only kennel of any breed in America to win Best in Show with three separate dogs. Much of this winning was done in a period of outstanding Working Group competition that included such all-time greats of their breeds as the Doberman Pinscher Ch. Rancho Dobe's Storm, and the Boxer Ch. Bang Away of Sirrah Crest. In 1952, when Spray placed third in the Group at Westminster, Storm was first (and on to Best in Show) and Bang Away was second.

The 1950s were to see the establishment of another of the all-time great show records of the breed. A strong strain had been started in 1948, when Mrs. Jean Blank of Fremont, California, began her career with Cheechako and Chumikan, completing their championships in 1949. She raised a few litters, and with Percy and Lena Matheron, co-owned Yurok of Whitecliff.

"Rocky," as Yurok was known, was by Ch. Omak out of Kara Babkrah of White Frost. Handled exclusively by Mrs. Blank, Yurok was an outstanding dog and stayed in remarkable coat, which permitted continual campaigning. In the five-year period from 1956 through 1960, he acquired 136 Bests of Breed, 98 Group placements including 26 Firsts, and 5 all-breed Best in Show awards. Yurok's most monumental win was of Best in Show at Harbor Cities Kennel Club show in 1959, when judge Percy Roberts placed him tops in the entry of 2,500 dogs. It was Percy Roberts who—as a dog broker—had been instrumental in the important importation of Tobolsk back in 1920.

A combination of the new breeders and owners, the lifting of prior limitations from the war years, and the holding of only three parent club specialties since 1943, started a rebirth of Samoyed activity. Entries skyrocketed in Southern California, which hosted the largest benched specialty ever held for the Samoyed Club of America with an entry of 110 individual dogs at the Harbor Cities Kennel Club in 1950. After the

Ch. Yurok of Whitcliff (1955-1970).

showing, the judge, Christian Knudsen, jokingly hoped he would never see another white dog. The Best of Breed, Shirley Hill's Cinderella dog, Ch. Verla's Prince Comet, was placed fourth in the Working Group. Agnes and Aljean Mason's brace was second in the Working Brace at this 2,500 dog entry in the Long Beach Civic Auditorium. This twelfth Samoyed Club of America Specialty was a resounding success in both numbers and geography, drawing dogs from many parts of the country, plus England and Canada. Samoyed owners enjoyed a nationwide togetherness, seeing dogs and meeting owners from far away places, and talking with the 114 persons at the pre-show banquet. This number was greater than the total ownership of 20 years before.

An unusual exhibition marked the 13th Specialty Show of the parent club held at Bay Meadows Race Track in California in 1952. Following the judging, 25 Samoyeds were taken off the bench to give a demonstration of sled work and races. Five teams competed in a short race with drivers: Tom Witcher with Ch. Vojak U.D. at lead; Bob Ward with Ch. Starchak C.D.; Lloyd Van Sickle with Rex of White Way; Charles Burr with Ch. Nick of White Way; and Ken Bristol with Ch. Starchak's Witangemote. Each team consisted of five dogs. Later, an exhibition of a 25 dog hook-up was given with a Ford convertible as ballast. A specially selected team of 15 was chosen for a demonstration for television and motion picture cameras. This team, led by Rex of White Way and including eight show champions,

The memorable hookup of 24 Samoyeds taken off the bench after the 1952 Specialty at San Mateo. At lead, Rex of White Way.

coursed the mile track, executing right and left turns and complete about turns.

Joining the list of proud owners of Samoyeds in this period were Major General Roderick Allen and his wife Maydelle. Their bitch, White Frosting, completed her championship at the 1953 Westminster Show, and their Ch. Narguess of Top Acres was Best Opposite Sex, ably handled by Len Brumby, Jr. The General also imported the English bitch Ch. Janet Jan Mayen.

Ch. Narguess of Top Acres came from a notable litter sired by Ch. Martingate Snowland Taz out of Ch. Sparkle Plenty of Arbee. This famous litter consisted of five sisters, named by the late Shah of Iran, who at that time was the house guest of Major General Allen, then stationed at Ft. Knox, Kentucky. The Shah said they should be named for lovely white flowers: 1. Narguess or White Narcissus. 2. Pratika or White Rose. 3. Hadesse or White Myrtle. 4. Yasmin or Jasmin. 5. Sosanna or White Lily.

Narguess, Pratika, and Hadesse became champions. Yasmin of Top Acres was taken to Japan. Ch. Narguess of Top Acres also went to Japan, and whelped one litter there. Yasmin was returned to the States, where she whelped one litter sired by Ch. Bunky of Lucky Dee. It was later possible for Dr. and Mrs. Wm. Herbst of Inglewood, California, to acquire from the Lucky Dee Kennels a son of Int. Ch. MacGregor of Glenstrae out of Heather of Glenstrae who had a German champion father with a granddam that was a Japanese champion.

A new kennel owned by ardent sledding enthusiasts appeared in 1954—the Woodsam Kennels of Mr. and Mrs. Robert Wood in Chittenago, New York. The Woods worked their teams at Oneida Lake. Other advocates of working dogs, both as sled dogs and as packing dogs, sprang up in the far Northwest. The positive effect of these Northwest breeders was still felt in the 1960s.

64

Famed TV star Lucille Ball with Ch. Modoc of Lucky Dee, initial winner of the Charles Tucker Brood Bitch Trophy in 1954. Bred by Mr. and Mrs. B.P. Dawes and owned by Mr. and Mrs. Roy Long.

Ch. Kazan of Kentwood ("Clancy"), wh. 1959, bred by Laura and Elva Edwards, and owned by the authors. One of the linebred dogs behind Ch. Quicksilver's Razz Ma Tazz.

Ch. Stormy Weather of Betty Blue and Ch. Misty Way of Betty Blue, owned by Martin and George Gleason. Stormy Weather, a Group winner, was the Wimundstrev Stud Dog Trophy winner for 1958.

Am. & Can. Ch. Kapegah Okanok of Nichi (1957-1968), a Best in Show winner in Canada. Owned by Mr. and Mrs. Clifford Collins of Seattle, Washington.

Ch. Joli Knika (1959-1965) pictured winning the breed under author Dolly Ward en route to Best in Show at Colorado, 1963. Bred by John and Lila Weir, Joli Knika was owned by Helen and Cliff Cabe of Oregon.

Mex. and Am. Ch. Danlyn's Silver Coronet, wh. 1963. Winner of the Arctic Breed Olympiad at San Fernando KC, 1968 under the famous sled dog authority, Mrs. Milton Seeley. Owned by Louis Torrez.

In the mid-50's, Mr. and Mrs. Robert Bowles' Ch. Noatak of Silver Moon and Ch. Silver Moon won the Stud Dog Trophy and the Brood Bitch Trophy three years in a row. They are behind the Best in Show winners Ch. Sam O'Khan's Chingis Khan, Ch. Sam O'Khan's Tian Shan, Ch. Karasea's Silver Nikki, Ch. Karasea's Silver Kim and the Ch. Maur-Mik's Kim. John and Lila Weir's breeding program with their "Happy," Ch. Tod-Acres Fang and Ch. Kobe's Nan-Nuk of Encino, produced the influential Best in Show winner Ch. Joli Knika, and his grandson Ch. Star Nika Altai of Silver Moon, a Best in Show winner in 1967.

The second parent club Specialty of 1956, held at the Mason Dixon Kennel Club, brought to light a winning dog that dominated the Samoyed circles for the next four years. Judge Marie Meyer awarded Best of Breed to Ch. Nordly's Sammy, owned by Mr. and Mrs. John Doyle of Doylestown, Pennsylvania. Butch, as he was known, was sired by Mrs. Ashborn Ulfeng's Am. and Can. Ch. Tazson out of Bluecrest Karenia, and was a grandson of Ch. Martingate Snowland Taz. Champion Nordly's Sammy won four parent club specialties in succession in four sections of the nation. In 1957 at Monmouth, New Jersey, he was Best of Breed under judge C. A. Swartz and 1st in the Working Group, as well as Best American-Bred Dog in Show under James Trullinger. The largest entry of Samoyeds he topped was 71 at the specialty at Santa Clara Kennel Club under judge Major Godsol, where he went on to 2nd in the Working Group. Sammy retired the Club's perpetual trophy (White Bark Kennels' Ch. Barrie Memorial Trophy) and was retired from competition.

Ch. Nordly's Sammy, winner of four successive SCA specialties, 1956 to 1959, inclusive. Owned by Mr. and Mrs. John Doyle of Pennsylvania.

Am. & Can. Ch. Noatak of Silver Moon, wh. 1960. Top winning Samoyed for 1963 and Wimundstrev Stud Dog Trophy winner for four successive years—1965 to 1968. Bred and owned by Mr. and Mrs. Robert Bowles.

Am. & Can. Ch., Sam O'Khan's Tian Shan, wh. 1963, by Am. & Can. Ch. Noatak of Silver Moon ex Am. & Can. Ch. Sam O'Khan's Tsari of Khan. Best in Show winner in Canada, and a Group winner in the U.S. Bred and owned by Mr. and Mrs. George Fitzpatrick.

Dominating bloodlines were created in the state of Washington when the George Fitzpatricks of Richland, Washington, produced Sam O'Khan's Tsari of Khan. Sired by Am. and Can. Ch. Zaysan of Krisland C.D. (1957-1967) out of Whitecliff's Polar Dawn, Tsari was destined to prove a Best in Show and Brood Bitch Trophy winner. They also owned Ch. Sam O'Khan's Tian Shan, and bred the five-time Best in Show winner, Ch. Sam O'Khan's Chingis Khan. Full brothers and sisters include the dogs Am. and Can. Ch. Sam O'Khan's Khyber Khan, owned by the Richard Woods of Wenatchee, Wash.; Ch. Sam O'Khan's Temushen O'Dudinka, owned by Bill and Ann Miller of Milford, Conn., and Pat Morehouse's Ch. Sam O'Khan's Kubla Khan in southern California.

Donna Yocom and the Colorado group were inspired to prepare another outstanding Samoyed showing in the spring of 1963. The judge, Mrs. Dolly Ward, had a geographical representation of 37 including Best in Show Samoyeds. The quality was excellent and Best of Breed was Ch. Joli Knika, bred by John and Lila Weir and owned and handled by a 17-year-old boy, Cliff Cabe, from Oregon. Knika climaxed his win by taking the Group under George Higgs, and going on to Best in Show under Louis Murr. The show was held on a floor over an ice rink. Prior to the first Group judging at this show, the automatic ice-making equipment "turned on". As the air and floor became colder and colder, judge Donia Cline was heard to comment,

Ch. Sam O'Khan's Chingis Khan, wh. 1963, winner of 5 all-breed Bests in Show. By Ch. Noatak of Silver Moon ex Ch. Sam O'Khan's Tsari of Khan, bred by Francis C. Fitzpatrick and owned by James and Joan Sheets. Winner of the A.E. Mason trophy, awarded to the top Samoyed winner, in the last three years it was presented (1966, 1967 and 1968) and winner of the Juliet Goodrich award for top winning Samoyed in the first two years it was presented (1969 and 1970).

"It ought to be a good night for the Samoyed, for if it gets any colder he will be the only one that can take it."

In this period, the long-time advocate of the Samoyed in the South, the Snowdrift Kennels of the W. R. Ingrams at Prattville, Alabama, imported the American and Australian Ch. Kobe Holm Storm. Mrs. Ingram introduced Mrs. Rita Bowling of Virginia Beach, Virginia, to Samoyeds, and Mrs. Bowling also acquired White Krystal's Luba and Startinda's Rabochi.

In 1964, the breed was still 32nd in number of registrations, but recognition at the shows was becoming apparent with 28 Samoyeds receiving 45 Group placings, and four winning Best in Show, Ch. Saroma's Polar Prince, Ch. Bazuhl of Caribou, Ch. Karasea's Silver Nikki and Ch. Winterland's Kim.

A new era and the end of the old system by which the parent club had always held a Specialty show in conjunction with an all-breed show, took place in 1964. Samoyed owner Richard Breckenridge was selected to be show secretary, assisted by Lloyd Bristol. They operated without a professional show superintendent. Show chairman was Robert Ward. The show was held on the beautifully landscaped grounds of the Mira Mar Hotel at Montecito, Santa Barbara, California. Albert E. VanCourt, who had placed the first Samoyed male to a Best in Show, judged the 92 entries present, including 21 champions. He chose the beautiful open class bitch, Shondra of Drayalene, owned by Joe Dyer of Idaho, as Best of Breed.

The authors were proud to assist in the engineering of this breakthrough for separate specialties for the Samoyed Club of America. Such an event had not taken place in the 41-year history of the Club. The advantage of having the show separate from all-breed shows is that it allows special events spotlighting the breeding efforts within the breed, such as Best Puppy and Best-Bred-by-Exhibitor. A futurity match or a best puppy sweepstakes is best when held with an individual specialty show. Best of all, it is *always a Samoyed that is Best in Show.*

Am. & Can. Ch. Lulhaven's Snowmist Ensign ("Tiki"), winner of 8 AKC all-breed Bests in Show and 16 in Canada, with over 100 BOBs. Owned by Ott Hyatt and Sonny White of Bellevue, Washington, and handled by Pat Tripp.

Ch. Sayan of Woodland, four-time Specialty winner. Wh. 1964 by Ch. Kazan of Wentwood ex Snow Heather Radant. Owned by Joseph and Evelyn Kite and handled by Jack Dexter.

70

4

The Samoyed in the United States Today

WE come now to Samoyed development between the two editions of this book, from the late 1960s through to the present.

It begins with the restructuring of the Samoyed Club of America. The SCA had been formed in 1923 following the Westminster show, and had few members in its early years. In the 1940s, as membership grew, the club began to establish Divisions, each comprising several states. At the end of the 1950s, there were four such Divisions, each headed by a Vice-President.

By 1965, interest had grown to such strength that there were three parent club Specialties in 1965, two in 1966, and three again in 1967, whereas there had been only ten in the first 25 years of the SCA.

In 1965, the American Kennel Club suggested that a new constitution and a revised organizational set-up of SCA that would allow more local activity was in order. It was felt that information and education on the breed could be provided better at the local level.

Accordingly, the members reorganized into a structure that retained the parent SCA as a member club of the AKC, with provision that many independent local clubs—each with their own exclusive territory—could be formed, and could hold AKC-licensed matches and championship point Specialty shows.

Under the Division structure, everyone had belonged to the parent club. Now, under the new structure, local club members did not automatically become members of the SCA.

The first president under the new structure, in February 1969, was author Robert Ward. There were four Vice-Presidents: Tom Tuttle, Clifford Collins, Donald Hodges and Anne Snee. Nancy Alexander was Secretary, Lila Weir was Treasurer and Peggy Borcherding was Publicity Director. Mrs. Margaret Tucker was named Honorary President.

The first years of the change were turbulent ones. Some groups tried to hold on to the past, and to the power they had enjoyed as Divisions. Also, the growth did not develop as the AKC had expected.

As of mid-1985, there are now eleven independent Samoyed clubs licensed by the AKC in the United States:

The Samoyed Club of San Diego (1965)
The Samoyed Club of Los Angeles (1966)
The Samoyed Club of Washington State (1968)
The Potomac Valley Samoyed Club (1971)
The Greater Milwaukee Samoyed Fanciers (1975)
The Samoyed Club of Houston (1978)
The Northern California Samoyed Fanciers (1982)
The Metropolitan Atlanta Samoyed Club (1982)
The Chicagoland Samoyed Club (1984)
Samoyed Association of Minneapolis-St. Paul (1985)
The Minuteman Samoyed Club (1985)

The first independent group to conduct a Specialty was the Samoyed Club of San Diego, which (in 1965) was the first local Samoyed club licensed by the AKC. The show, held in February 1967 in conjunction with the Silver Bay Kennel Club, drew 73 entries. The club has held a Specialty each year since, attracting 100 to 150 entries, and in 1980 they hosted the SCA National Specialty.

Started in 1955 by John and Anne Butler, the San Diego club's membership has included: Kathy Horton, Art Mandale, Vic and Angie Monteleon, Norm and Ruth Mary Heckeroth, Gail Milburn Stitt, Don and Myrna Dougherty, Joe and JoAnn Marineau, Diane Williams, Carol Barnum, Cathy and Mark Walsh, Dick and Chris Higley, Myra Price, Rudy Munoz, Patty Amshey and Maggi Simmons. Maggi was approved by the AKC to be a show secretary.

The 1970s brought many new people and changing perspectives to the Samoyed scene. In the 1900 to 1920 era, there were few breeders but most of them owned 10 to 30, or sometimes 30-40 dogs. In the late 1920s, these larger kennels became outnumbered by owners of one to four dogs. Then the "Terrible Thirties" of the Depression era reduced the larger kennels still further, to virtual non-existence.

Now, strangely, beginning in the late '60s and developing even more so in the '70s and '80s, we again have kennels owning 5 to 20 dogs. Perhaps, the reason is that the anti-dog laws of the large metropolitan areas are moving dog owners out to where larger kennels are more feasible.

So, while we note some successful one or two dog owners over recent years, the strongest impact has been made by about a dozen or so owners of larger Samoyed kennels, with serious and well thought out breeding programs. These programs are as technical as any in our sophisticated society.

72

Am. & Mex. Ch. Midnight Sun Kimba,
BOB at the SCA National Specialty, 1972.
By Ch. Sho-Off's Czar of Whitecliff ex
Nicola of Shondi. Owned by Kathi Horton
and Art Mandale. Pictured with handler,
Jim Manley.

Ch. Pushka Czar of Snowcliff, 1967-1980, by Ch. Sho-
Off's Dorok of Whitecliff ex Ochi Chernya of Snowridge.
Owners, Lois and Randolph Wendelin. Pushka was
shown to championship by 11-year-old Lori Wendelin.
Lori excelled both in Junior Showmanship and in the
center ring competition with the "big guys." In October
1972, at Two Cities KC (1,554 entries) Lori showed
Pushka to Group I under Robert Ward, and on to Best
in Show under Louis Murr.

Ch. Czar's Kobe-Wah of Whitecliff (Ch.
Sho-Off's Czar of Whitecliff ex Howyks
Snowfury). One of the Top Ten of his
time. Best of Breed at San Diego and
Washington State Specialties, 1973. Sire
of Ch. Shawndi of Midnight Sun, BOB at
SCA National Specialty 1980. Owners,
Kathi Horton and Art Mandale.

Left, Ch. Antares Danila of Darius and Ch. Larissa of Taymylyr. Right, Ch. Antares Tatiana. Owners, Jo and Jo Anne Marineau, Antares Samoyeds.

Ch. Belaya Sergeant Pepper, wh. 7/24/72, by Ch. Kondako's Sun Dancer ex Ch. Belaya Taiga Lily. Bred, owned and handled by John and Carol Chittum. Pictured winning BOB at 1976 SCLA Specialty over 92 entries. The trophy sash being presented by judge Robert Ward was offered by Ron and Dot Clarke of Australia.

Sheer numbers do not a good kennel make, but where more litters are handled, more selection is available for combination of bloodlines, and more championships can be earned. However, it remains—large operation or small—that the moral obligation of all breeders is to place what they produce into conscientious, proper caring hands.

No couple could be more conscientious than Joe and JoAnne Marineau of Antares Samoyeds. They began in 1970 with Antares Danila of Darius, a son of Ch. Darius Karlak Cheetal, 1970 SCA Specialty winner, owned by LaVera and Dan Morgan.

Their first female was Larissa of Taymylyr, acquired from Tom and Margi Tuttle. The Tuttles also bred her mother, Ch. Holly of Taymylyr and Ch. Ivan Belaya of Taymylyr, C.D. from their Ch. Trina of Taymylyr, sired by Ch. Kazan of Kentwood, and thus in a direct line to Ch. Starctic Storm, Ch. Starchak's Witan and Ch. Starchak, C.D. All were known for their outstanding gait, soundness and superb temperament.

In 1973 the Marineaus bred Larissa to Ch. Midnight Sun Kimba, owned by Kathy Horton and Art Mondale. From this breeding they kept Antares Tatiana and sold her sister, Great Sitkin's Midnight Magic for Dick and Chris Higley's breeding program.

Larissa was bred to their Danila after she completed her championship going Winners Bitch at the Samoyed Club of Los Angeles Specialty. This litter had special significance as Birgit Hillerby, of Stockholm, Sweden, had ordered a female puppy. Shatazah of Antares was selected to be sent to Birgit's Explorer Kennels in Sweden. Shatazah became a Swedish Champion and two of her daughters are Nordic Champions. One, Ch. Explorer's Lady JoAnn, is now an International Champion. (To be a Nordic Champion, one must be titled in Norway, Sweden and Finland. In addition, Finland requires the prospective champions to be certified free of hip dysplasia before receiving the title.)

Ch. Larissa of Taymylyr, at the age of 7 years, won Best Opposite Sex at the Samoyed Club of Los Angeles Specialty in an entry of 119 with 29 champions entered. The importance of having bitches that are sound, both mentally and physically, for your breeding program is inestimable.

The Samoyed Club of Los Angeles was the remnant of the former Pacific Coast Division of the Samoyed Club of America. It was organized into an independent club in 1966 when the AKC required the SCA to eliminate its four divisions. With Ed Adams as its first president, among its members were the Wheelocks, Billy Tucker, Ed and Gertrude Adams, Dianne Miller and Margie and Tom Tuttle. The club continued to hold events for the SCA, and added its own Specialty. The first SCLA independent specialty was held with the California Associated Specialty Clubs at Inglewood, California in September 1968 (judge Mrs. Anastasia MacBain had an entry of 69, with 13 champions), and there has been an annual SCLA Specialty ever since.

A spectacular national SCA specialty was held in September 1969 at Thousand Oaks, California. Show chairman was Tom Mayfield, and the show was acclaimed by many to be a model for separately-held specialties. A splendid entry of 94 (including 14 champions) competed under breeder-judge Joyce Cain of Wisconsin. Best of Breed, scoring his fourth Specialty win and tying Ch. Nordly's Sammy's record, was the Kites' Ch. Sayan of Woodland, handled by Jim Manley.

A major highlight of the show was the publication by the parent club, for the first time, of a catalog which incorporated the breed history, the official standard, illustrations including the authors' "Fault Finders," pictures of great Samoyeds of past and present representing bloodlines from coast to coast, and a directory of all local clubs.

In 1969, the SCA published a Standard Illustration of the breed, as prepared by Mrs. Gertrude Adams and her committee after over twenty years of discussion. This work was dedicated to Mrs. Agnes Mason, White Way Samoyeds, who first promoted the idea in 1948.

The SCLA qualified the breed for obedience, and this privilege was transferred to the Samoyed Club of America when the SCA National Rotating Specialty was held in the East, West, Midwest and Northwest. An added region to provide for the South will take effect in 1985, which action by the SCA Board has also split California into two sections.

The SCLA was the first club to initiate the Tournament event. It was they, too, who gave the parent club the idea of holding the Futurity, designed to encourage better breeding. The breeder nominates a planned litter, and then (before they have reached the age of 4 months) selects the most promising puppies to be shown at the next SCA Specialty, wherever it may be in the United States. Winners are judged in the competition at the "National," and money prizes go to the puppy owners (who do not necessarily have to be the breeders themselves).

The SCLA Specialty always includes a Sweepstakes event, which is usually judged by a breeder approved by the AKC specifically for the event. It is open to puppies from 6 to 18 months in age, and winners receive trophies, rosettes and prize money divided per the rules of the day. Its purpose is also to encourage better breeding and what could be more delightful than a ring full of puppies, competing according to their ages? Usual classes for both dogs and bitches are 6-9 months, 9-12 months, 12-18 months, Best Puppies, Best Juniors, and a final Best Puppy in Sweepstakes. These same exhibits are also entered in the regular classes of the Specialty show.

SCLA activities include meetings with suitable programs, social parties, practice match shows, B-OB matches with obedience, and the annual Tournament. One of the most productive achievements during Jim Osborn's presidency was the making of a film to educate fanciers on the breed. Cameramen were Jim and Ken Berry, commentator was Carol

Chittum and assisting in the myriad of things were Marian Osborn and Marie Berry. Six Samoyeds (3 males, 3 bitches) were judged for the camera by AKC judges Howard Dullnig, Lowell Davis and Robert Ward, who then commented on why they had placed the dogs 1-2-3. The film was shown at the seminar held in Denver for the SCA National Specialty in 1984.

The SCLA has retained many of its charter members through the years. In 1985, Mrs. Robert Ward is president, Carol Chittum is Vice President, Sue Fulps and Norma Binkley are Secretaries, and Kathy Hernandez is Treasurer. Past President Teena Deatherage, John Chittum, Pat Morehouse and Gini Addamo, editor of the newsletter *Paw Prints*, are on the Board. Altogether, a slate that is an ideal mixture of age and youth, men and women, novices and oldtimers in dogs.

In the 1960s, Kondako, a "company" of good Samoyed breeders— Connie (Kon) and Dave (Da) Richardson and Company (Ko)—was located in Maryland.

Their first bitch came from the Weltzins in British Columbia, Canada and was Kombo's Lucky Star of Kondako. Next was Ch. Oni-Agra's Silver Bunny from the Ralph Wards of New York. Thus they started with bloodlines from the East and the West. Kondako developed a bloodline that has been bred and shown successfully on both coasts. Silver Bunny almost became the first Sammy to have an OFA number, but her X-ray was lost. Bunny was bred to Ch. Nachalnik of Drayalene in 1968 during a driving snow storm. The two dogs and Doris McLaughlin became a snowdrift in the 40-minute mating. The litter produced Ch. Kondako's Dancing Bear ("Ruff"), who became the titular head of Kondako. You will find him in pedigrees from coast to coast.

Ruff produced a total of 27 champions including his sons: Ch. Kondako's Sun Dancer, winner of the 1974 San Diego Samoyed Club and the Samoyed Club of Los Angeles Specialties; Ruth Homan Stevenson's Ch. Kondako's Snow Bear, Winners Dog at the 1972 National Specialty; the Quigleys' multi-Group winning Ch. Winterway's Beowulf; Audrey and Gregg Lycan's Ch. Winterway's Mr. Wonderful, that Gregg as a Junior Handler took to a number of Group placings; and Jean Gerst's (AKA Anderson) Ch. Plyzha's Dancing Magic, winner of several Group Firsts and Best of Breed at the 1978 SCLA Specialty. Ruff's Ch. Kondako's Anybody's Girl won Winners Bitch at the 1975 SCA National Specialty, and his son Ch. Kondako's Nightwatch achieved his title by taking Winners Dog at both the Houston and San Diego 1980 Specialties. Ruff was SCA's Top Producing Dog in 1972 and 1975.

Kombo's Lucky Star of Kondako was bred to Helinski's Ch. Wynterkloud of Silver Moon and produced Ch. Kondako's KoKo-Lossal. Koko-Lossal was bred to Ch. Kondako's Dancing Bear five times, producing 26 puppies. Nine became champions and six others won points. Koko and Ruff were mates for life and died two months apart in 1980.

Ch. Kondako's Sun Dancer achieved a total of 20 champions including: Sue Skrobiszewski's Ch. Banquo's Pride of Chuckataw, a Group-placing dog who died before his career was really started; John and Carol Chittum's Ch. Belaya Sergeant Pepper, twice winner of the San Diego Specialty and Best of Breed at the 1976 SCLA Specialty; and Jack and Helen Feinberg's Ch. Northwind's Running Bear, one of the top five winners (all breeds) in 1981. At last calculation, the three generations—Nachalnik, Dancing Bear, Sun Dancer—had produced 89 champion offspring!

(One of the most rewarding judging experiences realized by the authors was in 1972, when they judged the three Arctic breeds at Westminster in New York. Thirty-three Samoyeds were entered and Dolly Ward awarded Best of Breed to Ch. Kondako's Sun Dancer, owned by the Richardsons.)

In 1972, Kondako relocated a total of five Samoyeds from Frederick, Maryland to the Los Angeles area city of Fullerton. Here, Connie, Dave and Company reported that they found an extraordinary level of competition present in Southern California that required an adjustment in their thinking on breeding, showing and presentation. The adjustment was successfully made.

Between 1966 and 1980, Kondako produced 17 homebred champions through five generations and were breeding participants in creating some 53 or so champions. With Ruff and KoKo gone and Sun Dancer in active retirement, the mantle has fallen to Ch. Kondako's Sundance Kid, Ch. Kondako's Nightwatch, Ch. Kondako's Rising Sun, and Anybody's daughter, Kondako's Busybody.

Dr. Mary Ellen and Joe Torrez started their Statusam Kennels with Tasha of Snowflower (from Carmen Way) and bred her to Ch. Kondako's Rising Sun to give them the two males they kept—Ch. King Kody of Kondako and Ch. Statusam's Troublemaker, and their bitch, Ch. Statusam's Lollipop, whelped 2-3-83. The kennel name Statusam obviously develops out of her profession (which is psychology) and the status of the Sam. Cheryl Cates, PHA, handles their dogs.

Statusam Troublemaker won an Award of Merit at the SCA Specialty in Denver in 1984, and the SCLA Tournament in June, 1985, judged by Werner Degenhardt from Brazil, Karen McFarlane (Kansas) and Linda Jordan (California). We predict that this is a kennel to watch for the future.

Sue Skrobiszewski (Chuckataw Kennels) caught the Samoyed fever in 1968 and continues to this day with Ch. Laugh 'N Chuckles, a grand-daughter of her Ch. Sayan's Chuckataw Tymba.

Her first dog was from Verla Davis' Igloo Kennels of Los Angeles. While attending a Samoyed Club of Los Angeles Specialty, Sue was impressed with the famous Ch. Sayan of Woodland, four-time winner of SCA Specialties, owned by Bob and Evy Kite. She purchased a son of his out of Candida Princess Lorenza. He became Ch. Sayan's Chuckataw Tymba and finished at the age of 22 months. Tymba (owner-handled) won 32 Bests

Ch. Nachalnik of Drayalene, wh. 9/16/61, by Ch. Rokandi of Drayalene ex Drayalene's Clarisse. "Chief" sired 45 champions, until 1984 tops for the breed. Owners, Harold and Doris McLaughlin, "Silveracres," Colorado.

Ch. Kondako's Dancing Bear, 1968-1980, by Ch. Nachalnik of Drayalene ex Ch. Oni-Agra's Silver Bunny. "Ruff" sired 27 champions, and won Top Producer Award (SCA) in 1972 and 1975. Bred, owned and handled by Dave and Constance Richardson.

Ch. Kondako's Sun Dancer, by Ch. Kondako's Dancing Bear ex Ch. Kondako's Koko Lossal. Sire of 21 champions. Winner of two Specialties and a Tournament. Owners, Dave and Connie Richardson.

of Breed and several Group placings. At the age of nine he was brought out of retirement and won Best of Breed over youngsters. He was Best Veteran Dog at the 1976 SCA Specialty in Denver, and Best Veteran and an Award of Merit winner at the Samoyed Club of Los Angeles in 1978.

Tymba sired Ch. Nootka's Dream of the Snows, owned by Catherine Wilcox, and Champions Luvumuch O'Nootka and Nootka's Chuckataw. Chuckataw Kennels also produced Ch. Banquo's Pride of Chuckataw out of Frost River Kola and Ch. Bianca Snow Bear of Chuckataw, who is a joy to watch at her home in Utah with the Rogers.

The 1970 parent specialty was hosted by the Washington State Samoyed Club, and established a then record high of 150 entries (122 actual dogs). Judge Joseph Faigel selected Ch. Darius Karlak Cheetal, owner-handled by Dan Morgan, as Best of Breed.

The Samoyed Club of Washington State, Inc. was founded as the Northwest Division in 1952 by the Collins, the Gleasons and the Beals. The Stefaniks joined in 1959 and in 1964, Joyce and Joe Johnson were typed on the roster. The club was licensed to give independent Specialties in 1968. On August 16, 1969, SCWS held its first Specialty (with the Olympic KC); the entry of 47 was judged by Kurt Mueller, and Best of Breed was Ch. Lulhaven's Nunatat, owned by Lulham and Spaugh. The club hosted the annual rotating SCA Specialty in 1956, 1965, 1970, 1974, 1978 and 1982. The fifth area of the SCA that was formed in 1984 now includes Washington with the northern half of California.

By the 1970s it had become apparent to Samoyed breeders in the Northwest that hereditary eye disease in the form of Progressive Retinal Atrophy (PRA) was a problem threatening the breed. "Vision for the Future" was the theme of the 43rd National Specialty, which the SCWS hosted in 1974. SCWS also sponsored an in-depth Eye Research Project under the direction of Paul V. Dice III, V.M.D., M.S. Rosemary Jones and the late Ethel Stefanik were co-chairmen. The results of the research were published in the September 1979 SCA *Bulletin*. SCWS remains a supporting member of the Canine Eye Research Foundation, Inc. (CERF).

In Colorado, the Silveracres kennel has stood the test of time very well. Beginning in 1952, and still producing winners, Silveracres is located 17 miles southwest of Denver high in the mountains and on a running stream named Critchell Creek. Harold and Doris McLaughlin began with forty rough, uncleared acres of boulders and trees and established a home and successful hobby. At first, along with their original Samoyed, Ch. Fancy of Critchell Creek, they raised silver foxes and quarter-horses.

It took 12 years to obtain the kennel name, "Silveracres," as the American Kennel Club turned them down time and time again because of the word "silver." There were many Northern breeds using silver in their names.

Ch. Sayan's Chuckataw Tympa, 1968-1981. By Ch. Sayan of Woodland ex Candida Princess Lorenza. Tymba was Best Veteran at SCLA 1977 Specialty. Owner, Sue Skrobiszewski, Utah.

Ch. Los Laika's Belaya Traicer. (Wh. 2/13/70, by Snow Ridge's Ruble of Tamarack ex Ch. Belaya Anja Padrushka.) SCLA Sweepstakes winner, 1970; SCLA Tournament winner, 1975. Sire of Ch. Sassillie's Merlyn of Vicrian, Best Veteran at 1983 SCA Specialty. Great, great grandsire of Ch. Quicksilver's Razz Ma Tazz. *Ludwig*

Ch. Silveracres Diamond Marquise, by Ch. Silveracres Trademark ex Ch. Silveracres Jinni O'Frostfire. Reserve Futurity Winner at 1978 SCA Specialty. Owners, Dennis and Katherine Metter, Colorado.

Ch. Kondako's Nightwatch, wh. 4/15/78 by Ch. Kondako's Dancing Bear ex Snowflower Bluff of Silver Blue. Winners Dog at SC of Houston and SC of San Diego 1980 Specialties. Bred by Geraldine Klosson and Carmen Way. Owned by Dave and Connie Richardson.

The amazing story of a problem they encountered was related to us by Harold: "We had a breeding problem for many years at this location. Lots of years we sold from three to ten puppies all year. Our puppies became champions but we did not have many puppies to sell. We finally cleared up the breeding problem by hauling all drinking water for the dogs all the way from Denver. Our well water is so pure that it has no trace minerals. You do not produce animals without trace minerals. Today we have large healthy litters. Same breeding stock, just different water."

The dog who was to become the shining star at Silveracres was Ch. Nachalnik of Drayalene (whelped September 16, 1961). "Chief," who was acquired at the age of nine months from Helene Spathold, became the top Samoyed sire in the history of the breed with 45 champion offspring—a total that stood as the all-time high in the breed until 1984. The McLaughlins also obtained Ch. Cnejinka from Helene Spathold, and she and Nachalnik formed the foundation stock from which they linebred and inbred to develop the Silveracre line.

In 1981 the McLaughlins added Ch. St. Croix's Batu Khan O'Sam O'Khan as their almost outcross stud. He was obtained from Mrs. Florence V. Watson of Minnesota. The 11 current Silveracre Sams live with them and have worn out three doggie doors going in and out, but Harold and Doris don't mind as each dog has its own place to sleep in the house.

Iris M. Clough and Johnnie M. Rogers of Denver, Colorado began with Samoyeds in 1969. Their Karana Samoyeds are based on Kobe and Silver Moon lines. Their first dogs were acquired from Kobe of Encino Kennel (Margaret Tucker) and the Snomesa Kennel (Jean Brown of Colorado).

Karana dogs have done exceedingly well in Obedience. Ch. Karana's Diko Apollo, U.D. was their first homebred champion and U.D. winner. Their other champions have included Am. & Can. Ch. Sir Khan's Ian of Karana (Ch. Sam O'Khan's Khyber Khan ex Ch. Scherazade of Kubla Khan), Ch. Kalmarli's Lord N' Master and Ch. Travois Penelope. The breeding of Lord N' Master to Penelope produced Karana's Aspenglo Razzmatazz, winner of the 1978 SCA Futurity, and Best of Winners at Westminster in 1979.

Conscientious breeders often require investigative clearances from potential buyers out of their own areas. Or they may ask for recommendations from fellow club members. This was the procedure before Mrs. Francis Fitzpatrick allowed a Sam O'Khan male to go to Pat Morehouse, now located in the Van Nuys, California area.

Mrs. Morehouse has been a supporter of the breed for twenty years. One of her early champions was Ch. Icelandic Princess Zoe, sired by Ch. Kazan of Kentwood. In 1967 she acquired a male puppy from Mrs. Fitzpatrick, from a repeat breeding of Ch. Noatak of Silver Moon ex Ch. Sam O'Khan's Tsari of Khan. The puppy became Ch. Sam O'Khan's Kubla Khan, and Kubla Khan became the name of Mrs. Morehouse's kennel.

Ch. Sam O'Khan's Kubla Khan, twice Top Producer of the Year (SCA and *Kennel Review* Awards). Wh. 6/18/67 by Am. & Can. Ch. Noatak of Silver Moon ex Am. & Can. Ch. Sam O'Khan's Tsari of Khan. A specially selected Sam who came from the Northwest to California and fulfilled his destiny. Breeder: Francis Fitzpatrick. Owners, Pat and Carolyn Morehouse.

Ch. Silveracres Trademark, by Ch. Nachalnik of Drayalene ex Ch. Silveracres Jinni O'Frostfire, a father to daughter mating. Bred by Harold and Doris McLaughlin, "Silveracres," Colorado.

Kubla Khan was dominant for his excellent front, good bone and lovely head, and has made a most significant contribution as a sire. He became the sire of 31 champions and twice earned the Top Producer Award (*Kennel Review*). His Northwest bloodlines produced in his first litter: Ch. Sam O'Khan's Chingis Khan, Am. & Can. Ch. Sam O'Khan's Tian Shan and Am. & Can. Ch. Sam O'Khan's Khyber Khan. Six of his get won Group placements and an additional six were Winners Dog or Bitch at large Specialties. Khan won the Stud Dog class at the SCA Specialty in 1972, a year in which nine of his get completed their championships.

The Aladdin Samoyeds, owned by Joe and Joyce Johnson of the state of Washington, have contributed importantly to the breed in the Northwest. They have carried on some of the older Northwest bloodlines and have added some of the good lines from other areas to supplement their planned line breedings.

As so many dog people do, they began with an unsuccessful first dog. This does not deter real dog people. Their next bitch was Kapegah's Nelata of Nichi, a good combination of Tod Acres, Stormy Weather and Polar Prince lines. When this bitch was bred to Ch. Chu San's Silver Folly, who was a remarkable producer of strong-moving get, they obtained their foundation brood bitch, Ch. Aladdin's Silver Snow Shadow. Shadow was Best of Winners at the 1970 Samoyed Club of America Specialty. An outstanding producer, she has delivered three litters with fine champions in each litter. Her litter with Ch. Ivan Belaya of Tamylyr, C.D. gave the Johnsons Ch. Lightfoot Lass, who is the mother of their current winner, Ch. Aladdin's Dominator. Dominator has consistently placed in the Top Ten of current winning Samoyeds, and in September 1984 was Best in Specialty at the Northwest Samoyed Club show. Dominator's son, Ch. Neaderlander's Dutch Treat, is fast establishing himself as a top stud for the Johnsons.

In 1981, the Johnsons added a new bloodline to their stock, acquiring a puppy from Lynette Hansen's Polar Mist Kennels. The dog, now Ch. Polar Mist De Icer of Aladdin is by Ch. Iceway's Ice Breaker ex Ch. Polar Mist Ain't She Foxy, and is co-owned by S. Hill.

The first champion for Polar Mist Samoyeds, owned by Lynette Hansen of Libby, Montana, was Ch. McKenzies Polar Mist Nikke, in the early 1970s. She was a granddaughter of Ch. Rokandi of Drayalene. Lynette's second bitch (Polar Mist's Baerstone Nisha) lacked the temperament for showing, a factor that is so important and one that many exhibitors neglect to take into account. However, she had many good qualities and Lynette bred her to Mrs. Peggy McCarthy's Ch. Silver Raffles of Misty Way, a Best in Show dog and a good dominant sire. This produced Am. & Can. Ch. Pepsi Kola of Polar Mist, who became the dam of the Best in Show winner, Ch. Polar Mist Dr. Pepper. A litter sister, Ch. Polar Mist's

Am. Can. & Bah. Ch. Polar Mist Dr. Pepper, the top winning owner-handled Samoyed in the history of the breed. Wh. 2/9/78, by Ch. Belaya's Sergeant Pepper ex. Ch. Pepsi Kola of Polar Mist. Winner of 7 all-breed BIS, 5 Specialty Bests, and over 100 Group placements. Co-owned by John and Kathy Ronald with Lynette Hansen (breeder), Dr. Pepper is shown going BIS at River Valley KC (Minn.) 1984 show under Robert Ward, with John Ronald handling.

Ch. Aladdin Dominator, BOB at the 1984 Samoyed Club of Washington State Specialty. Wh. 1/22/78, by Ch. Knight Nicholas ex Ch. Aladdin's Lightfoot Lass. A Top Ten winner with many Group placements. Owners, Joseph and Joyce Johnson, Washington.

Polar Mist Naughty Angel, at 6½ months. Sired by Am. Can. & Bah. Ch. Polar Mist Dr. Pepper ex Polar Mist Heartbreaker, Angel was bred by Pam Richardson and is owned and handled by Lynette Hansen. She was BOB and placed in the Group in her first three shows.

Ain't She Something became a foundation bitch for Timberline Samoyeds, owned by Stephanie Kroel.

Lynette Hansen became good friends with Peggy McCarthy, who had two Best in Show dogs. Kohoutek became Can. & Am. Ch. Kohoutek of Polar Mist, C.D.X., and bred to Ch. Polar Mist's Ain't She Something produced 3 champions from the first litter. Kohoutek was Best of Breed at the Washington State Samoyed Club Specialty in August, 1981. One of his sons, Ch. Polar Mist King Khan, was BOB at the Washington State Specialty in 1979 and another son, Am. & Can. Ch. Timberline's Lord Tikal, was Best of Winners at the Potomac Valley Samoyed Specialty in 1979 and Winners Dog at the 1980 Canadian National Specialty.

Lynette decided that since she lived in such a remote area, her dogs needed to have greater exposure. So, after Polar Mist's Dr. Pepper scored Winners Dog at the 1979 SCA National Specialty, she formed a partnership with John and Kathleen Ronald, who owned a dog she had bred—Ch. Timberline's Sparkling Kayta. John Ronald then went on to handle Dr. Pepper to wins in the 1980s that have made him the top owner-handled Samoyed winner to date. Am., Can. & Bah. Ch. Polar Mist's Dr. Pepper's record now includes 10 all-breed Bests in Show, 5 Bests in Specialty, and over 100 Group placements, all owner-handled. In 1984, he won the Canadian National Specialty under Thelma Brown.

Pepper is proving himself as a sire, too. One son is a Canadian champion and winner of a Canadian Best in Show. Another son, Timberline's Justin Tyme was Best Puppy at the 1981 SCA National Specialty and Best Puppy in Sweepstakes. A daughter, Ch. Silver Echo's Mahalo Pepper (out of Grey Ghost's Teesha Astarte, won the Group at Kalamazoo 1985, owner-handled by Patti Carden.

For Lynette Hansen, "Quality comes first at all times." Lynette wants her dogs to have driving rears and very good extension in front. She feels that the breed as a whole needs improvement in the front quarter. She is scheduled to judge the Sweepstakes at Rio Hondo following the 1986 SCLA Specialty.

Don Hodges, the Samoyed Club of America delegate to the American Kennel Club and his wife Dot, Kipperic Samoyeds, began in 1968 with the purchase of three Samoyeds. One male became Ch. Astro of Rivido; and another became Ch. Ku Techi, C.D., known as Kipper. He was a descendant of Mel and Miriam Laskey's Suruka Orr Samoyeds. Kipper was ninth rated Samoyed by the Phillips System in 1969.

In 1970, the Hodges obtained two females. One, sired by Ch. Saroma's Polar Prince and bred by Charles and Evelyn James, became Ch. Kipperic D'Lite of Frost River. The others became Ch. Kipperic Kandu of Suruka Orr, C.D., also bred by Mel and Miriam Laskey. Kandi was sired by Ch. Nachalnik of Drayalene ex Ch. Kuei of Suruka Orr, C.D. Both foundation bitches did well in the show ring and the whelping box; each produced four champions and each produced a Group First winner: Ch. Orion of Kipperic out of D'Lite and Ch. Kipperic K.C. Heritage out of Kandu.

Am. & Can. Ch. Kipperic Kandu of Suruka Orr, C.D. Whelped 1970, by Ch. Nachalnik of Drayalene ex Ch. Kuei of Suruka Orr, C.D., Kandu was bred by Mel and Miriam Laskey and owned by Don and Dot Hodges. Winner of 2 all-breed BIS, she is pictured winning the 1973 SCA Specialty under Phil Marsh. Handled by Don Hodges, SCA's delegate to the AKC. Kandu, dam of 4 champions, is the only bitch to have been top winning Samoyed (in 1974).

Am. & Can. Ch. Nordic Wynter Sunniglo winning BOB at the 1978 SCA National Specialty under judge Derek Rayne. Handled by Don Hodges. Presenting trophy, club president Mrs. Duvella Kusler. Sunni, an all-breeds BIS winner, was whelped 1973, by Tsiulikagta's Wynterwynd ex Ch. Nordic's Ketsie Tu. Bred by Dick and Gail Mathews, and co-owned by Gail Mathews, Mr. and Mrs. LeRoy Anderson and Don Hodges.

Ch. Kipperic Kandu of Suruka Orr, C.D. was Best of Breed at the 1973 National Specialty and a few weeks later won Best in Show all breeds. In 1974, Kandi was Top Winning Samoyed in all rating systems, defeating over 5500 dogs, and gaining another Best in Show. Kipperic's next Best in Show dog was Am. & Can. Ch. Nordic's Wynter Sunniglo, co-owned by Gail Mathews and her parents Leroy and Betty Anderson, and the Hodges. Sunniglo was Best of Breed at the 1978 SCA National Specialty in Portland and Best in Show that weekend at the Vancouver, Washington show.

Dot and Don Hodges have owned or bred 21 Champions and 5 Group winners. They are the only owners in the Samoyed breed thus far to own two Samoyeds that have won both Best in Show all-breeds and Best of Breed at a National Specialty.

In 1972, on way to Westminster, the authors attended the famous Crufts Dog Show in the old Olympia Building, London, England. There we spotted a young dog being shown by his owner, Gerald Mitchell, that was a "dead ringer" for our Ch. Starchak of 30 years before. Even his pedigree approximated Starchak's—i.e., 1/2 Snowland, 1/4 Arctic and 1/4 old Kobe. Of course he was not for sale.

Returning to the USA we counted all of the Challenge Certificates that had been awarded Samoyeds for the period 1950 through 1970 and realized that 83% had been awarded to ancestors in his pedigree. While such statistics do not guarantee champions, it does increase your chances. (Challenge Certificates are not easily acquired. All champions are shown in the Open Dog class, and not all shows are accredited for CC's. Also, a judge may only judge the breed once in a 12-month period.)

We returned six weeks later to judge at the Golden Jubilee of the Irish Kennel Club (on St. Patrick's Day!) and afterwards went to Chesterfield, England determined to talk the Mitchells out of the young dog—Kiskas Karaholme Cherokee, "Painter." This time we succeeded—Painter was exported a few months later at the age of 18 months. Sired by Cavalier of Crensa ex Lisa of Crownie, Painter had been bred by Mr. and Mrs. Tom Stamp. His sire, Cavalier, was not shown much, but was a litter brother of Ch. Grenadier of Crensa, whose win of 43 Challenge Certificates stands as an all-time record for the breed in England.

Being judges, we did not campaign "Painter" after his championship, but did occasionally show him at National Specialties. He was shown 14 times, handled by Barbara Humphries, and won 9 Bests of Breed and 3 Group placings as he completed his American championship. Shown in five National Specialties, he won Stud Dog 3 times, Best Veteran and Award of Merit 3 times.

Painter was awarded the Samoyed Club of America Stud Dog of the Year honors in 1980 with 15 champions, sired out of 12 different bitches. The wins scored by his progeny have done much to give notice to other breeds that the Samoyed is on the dog show scene.

Ch. Kiskas Karaholme Cherokee, Top Stud Dog (SCA Award) 1980. "Painter," pictured at 6 years of age, was an English import from the kennels of Gerald and Kathy Mitchell, and was owned by the authors until his natural death in 1984.

Am. & Can. Ch. Snowblaze Linc'n Continental, Winners Dog at the 1981 WSSC Specialty. Sired by Ch. Kiskas Karaholme Cherokee out of Dr. John Meyer's (Idaho) Ch. Christori's Paka of Vellee. Co-owned by the Meyers with Dave and Marguerite Seibert of Arizona.

Ch. Boreas Blue Velvet Paint ("Blue"), by Ch. Kiskas Karaholme Cherokee ex. Ch. White Velvet of Sawinjaq. Multi Group winner and one of the Top Ten Samoyeds in the mid-70s. Now a magnificent veteran. Breeder-owners: Frank and Claire Schlegel.

Am. & Can. Ch. Cherokee's Kazan of Bouquet ("Clancy"), wh. 11/8/73 by Ch. Kiskas Karaholme Cherokee ex Ch. Sayan's Bouquet of Chatique. A companion and motor home traveler for his breeder-owners, Bob and Evelyn Kite.

Three sons, Ch. Ice Way's Ice Crush, Ch. Ice Way's Ice Breaker and Mex. & Am. Ch. The Hoof 'n Paw White Knight became Best in Show and major Specialty winners. (Their stories are told in the accounts of the Ice Way and Hoof 'n Paw Kennels that follow.)

Another son, Ch. Tsuiligata's Skagit, owned by Bert and Gloria Ramos of Texas, was BOB at the Houston Samoyed Specialty and had multiple Group placements.

A daughter, Ch. Starctic Aukeo, was Best of Opposite Sex at the SCA National Specialty in 1978 in an entry of over 300. Another daughter, Ch. Nanank's Bathzarah, was Best of Breed at the New England Specialty and had multiple Group placements.

Painter sired his last litter at the age of 12½, as did his father and uncle in England. He passed on in his sleep at the age of 14 years one month, never sick a day in his life.

Ice Way Kennels began modestly in California, but with purpose and plan. Ch. Powered Puff of the Pacific was raised by Bobbie and Michael Smith in 1969. Puff was a granddaughter of the 1965 SCA National Specialty Best of Breed winner, Ch. Danlyn's Silver Coronet. Her dam was by Ch. Barceia's Shondi of Drayalene out of a Ch. Rokandi of Drayalene daughter. Puff was a beautiful bitch with excellent coat and structure and excelled in showmanship. She had the attitude that dominates a class, and passed this quality to her descendants.

In 1975, Puff was Best of Winners at the Samoyed Club of Los Angeles Specialty, defeating 110 exhibits. Bred to Snoline's Apollo of Sassillie, she produced the Smiths' first champion, Ch. Ice Way's Honey Bear, and the top producing bitch, Ice Way's Angel. Angel produced Can. & Am. Ch. Ice Way's Bialow Mishka, a multiple Group winner, for owners Doug and Pat Gilliam of Tucson, Arizona. Bred to Ch. Kiskas Karaholme Cherokee, Angel produced Mex. & Am. Ch. The Hoof 'N Paw White Knight for Mardee Ward. Bred to Int'l Ch. (C.A.C.I.B.) Snoline's Joli Shashan, C.D.X., she produced Ice Way's Sunshine Mardee (a successful lead bitch on Mardee Ward's racing sled team) and her litter sister, Ch. Ice Way's Ice Cube.

Ice Cube ("Cubie") exemplified the qualities the Smiths are maintaining at Ice Way—good neck length, long upper arm, and 45° shoulder layback. As the Tournament winner of the Samoyed Club of Los Angeles, "Cubie" was sent to the SCA National Specialty in Washington state, and was Best of Winners. Later she was WB at the San Diego Samoyed Specialty. The following year she was Best Opposite at both the San Diego and the Greater Milwaukee Samoyed Fanciers specialties. In 1976, she was the first bitch in 20 years to win a Working Group 1st at Del Monte KC, and followed with a Group 3rd at Santa Barbara KC, the largest dog show in the United States for that year.

Cubie's outstanding litter with Ch. Kiskas Karaholme Cherokee

Ch. Ice Way's Ice Crush (Ch. Kiskas Karaholme Cherokee ex Ch. Ice Way's Ice Cube), bred by Michael and Bobbie Smith, and owned by Ann Bark, Massachusetts. Crush, handled by his owner to 7 all-breed BIS, is pictured winning the 1981 SCA National Specialty under judge Mrs. Peter Gunterman (371 dogs in competition, 75 Specials). Handled here by Mike Zollo. The sled was one of the trophies. Crush was unfortunately victim of an accidental death at an early age.

Ch. Ice Way's Ice Breaker (Ch. Kiskas Karaholme Cherokee ex Ch. Ice Way's Ice Cube), bred and owned by Michael and Bobbie Smith of Mountainburg, Ark. A 1981 BIS winner, Breaker is pictured being handled by Bobbie to a Group win under T.D. Jones. Breaker has become the eminent sire of the breed with 58 champions to his credit in early 1985.

Ch. Andromeda Tugger of Crush (Ch. Ice Way's Ice Crush ex Sherica's Kalestina O'See Onee.) Tug examples superb type and movement. Bred by Ann Bark and Dawn Tomevi and co-owned by Mardee Ward.

At left, Ice Way's Ice Chip, sired by Ch. Ice Way's Ice Breaker ex his sister, Cherokee Sun O'Somar—in-bred to stamp type and structure. Chip is owned by Sherry Webster of Memphis, Tennessee. At right, Ice Way's Oso Blanco, Best Puppy in Sweepstakes at the SCLA Specialty. Oso is by Ch. Ice Way's Ice Breaker ex Ice Way's Heavenly Body.

Ch. Ice Way's Sun Stryker, finishing to his championship in May 1984 with BOB over 7 Specials (on to GR3) at Sioux Empire KC. By West Free's Calif Honeymoon ex Ice Way's Ice Show, a super-seven in-bred female bred to a son of Ch. Honey Bear. Owners, John and Jina Haikey, Oklahoma.

produced the Best in Show winning brothers, Ch. Ice Way's Ice Crush and Ch. Ice Way's Ice Breaker.

Crush, owned by Ann Bark of Boxford, Massachusetts, was Best of Breed at the 1980 SCA National Specialty over an entry of 370 including 79 champions (the Specials class alone took over four hours to judge), and scored 7 all-breed Bests in Show and many Group Firsts before his untimely death in December 1983. Crush's son, Ch. Andromeda Tugger of Crush, was Winners Dog at the Samoyed Club of Los Angeles 1983 Specialty with 131 entries, and completed his championship the same month at the Northern California Samoyed Fanciers Specialty, handled by his co-owner Mardee Ward. Tug is retired to stud with Terry and Shelley Mumford.

Ch. Ice Way's Ice Breaker, owned by the Smiths, was Best of Breed at the San Diego Specialty over an entry of 160, and again at the Greater Milwaukee Specialty.

Breaker has become one of the most influential producers in the history of the breed. In his first four years on the Top Producer charts, he sired 58 champions in the United States and Canada. At 7 years of age in 1984, he is proving that a stud dog genetically intensified for producing correct structure and temperament can have a significant and positive influence on the breed.

Breaker was the No. 1 stud for the breed in Canada in 1983, and at this writing is the front runner stud in both Canada and the United States for 1984. His son, Can. Ch. Orenpac's Chenna was the top winning Samoyed in Canada for 1983. Another son, Can. Ch. Orenpac's Mogul is a Best in Show winner in western Canada.

Bobbi and Mike Smith produced the ultimate in inbreeding when they mated Breaker with his litter sister, Ice Way's Cherokee Sun O'Somar. This was both to intensify a gene pool, and to prove a point regarding genetic faults. The litter, now called the "Super Seven," have all cleared an eye check for progressive retinal atrophy. First of the litter to finish his championship was Ch. Ice Way's Flash Cube, owned by Christina Deatherage of California. Flash Cube was Best of Breed at the SCLA 1983 Specialty over an entry of 211. Four of the litter finished before the age of two. Breaker's influence is being further enhanced by the outstanding winning of his grandchildren. It is comforting to know such an influential stud will be available to the breed through the sperm bank.

Hoof 'n Paw Samoyeds was established in 1970 as a continuation of the ideals and principles established over the past forty years by Mardee Ward's parents, Robert and Dolly Ward. The kennel name Hoof 'n Paw was derived from Mardee's interest in both dogs and Morgan horses. The goal continues to be to perpetuate the Samoyed as a dual purpose dog for work and show. Mardee is also an AKC approved judge of the Arctic breeds.

Mardee blended the English lines of Ch. Kiskas Karaholme Cherokee and Ice Way's Angel (he was the number 1 SCA Stud Dog in 1981 and she the number 2 brood bitch in the same year), and they produced Am. & Mex. Ch. The Hoof 'n Paw White Knight. "Knavioux," or simply "K" as the White Knight is called, won 110 Bests of Breed, 48 Group placements and a Best in Show All-Breeds, with Marna Pearson (P.H.A.) handling. He won three Specialty Bests of Breed, each with entries of over 100, and managed at the same time to work in harness with Mardee, and compete in over 40 sled races in Colorado, Oregon and California. "K" was not shown until he was three years old, nor bred until he was over four. His first champion get were three bitches by three dams: Ch. Anja's Bound for Glory, owned by Linda Mueller-Lashley, Ch. Hoof 'n Paw White Cloud owned by the Abilas in California, and Mardee Ward's Ch. Tasha of Sacha's Knight, known as Teka. Teka was unusual for a bitch of any coated breed in that she finished her championship by winning Group First at the age of 14 months. She was campaigned from the age of 2½ years and acquired 45 Bests of Breed (including Westminster K.C.), 14 Group Firsts and 30 Group placements. With these wins Teka won the SCA Parent Club Award for #1 show bitch for 1981 and 1982. In addition, she has won three Specialty Bests in Shows: at the Samoyed Club of Houston, the Samoyed Club of San Diego and the Samoyed Club of Los Angeles. In San Diego, Teka retired the perpetual trophy for Best of Breed which had been won twice previously by her sire, Ch. The Hoof 'n Paw White Knight. (*Note: Perpetual trophies are often donated with the provision that they must be won by the same owner three times, not necessarily with the same dog. This trophy was donated by the Samoyed Club of San Diego and initially won by Skip and Nancy Alexander, with Ch. Blizzard of Snoline.)

While Mardee, like other breeders, strives for the standard and dual purpose dogs, she insists upon outgoing, animated personalities which are indeed part and parcel to the Samoyed breed type. She likes to do her own handling but has called on Pam Stage or Marna Pearson, both P.H.A.

In 1984, one of K's new champions is Ch. Desert Knight O'Candida, aka Patrick, owned by Terry and Shelley Mumford. Patrick finished at two years in exciting competition and displays much potential. He is another Samoyed of superior temperament and is a fine companion for the Mumfords' small children.

In the late 1970s Teena Scherer Deatherage joined the Samoyed scene and obtained Hoof 'n Paw's Rain Dance (Ch. The Hoof 'n Paw White Knight ex Starctic SnowBasin Sioux, C.D.). For Rain Dance's first mate she chose Ch. Ice Way's Ice Breaker. Teena, an advocate of style, movement and substance, selected one male puppy and successfully won a Specialty Match and then his first points at eight months. A tragic accident cut his show career short but she believed in her breeding program and continued with Crizta Wamp-Up Whitekloud (Ch. Kiskas Karaholme Cherokee ex Ch. Hoof 'n Paw White Cloud) and in 1980 with young senior puppy male,

Am. & Mex. Ch. The Hoof 'n Paw White Knight, BIS winner. Wh. 3/10/74, by Ch. Kiskas Karaholme Cherokee ex Ice Way's Angel. Breeders: Mardee and Dolly Ward. Owners: Mardee and Lindi Ward. Handler: Marna Pearson. "Knavioux" was nationally rated in the Top Three during his entire Specials campaign from 1978 through 1981. His wins included 1 all-breed BIS, 3 Specialty BOBs, 48 Group placements (13 Firsts) and 110 BOBs.

At left, Am. & Can. Ch. Tasha of Sacha's Knight ("Teka"), owner-handled by Mardee Ward, winning under judge Hayden Martin. "Teka" was the top winning Samoyed bitch in the nation for 1980, 1981 and 1982. She was linebred to the authors' English import, Ch. Kiskas Karaholme Cherokee. At right, Am. Ch. Hoof 'n Paws Drifting Snow ("Smurf"), bred, owned and handled by Mardee Ward, is pictured finishing to his championship at Cheyenne KC in 1984 under judge Irene Bivin. Whelped 8/18/82, Smurf is by Danish Ch. Sir Jonah of Banff ex Hoof 'n Paw Has Klout.

Lynthea's Kimba (Ch. Ice Way's Ice Breaker ex Lynthea's Miss Conduct). Kimba finished quickly after winning Best of Breed from the classes under judge Robert Lentz and a Group 2 under judge Robert Ward.

Mrs. Deatherage's next dog, now Ch. Ice Way's Flash Cube, was one of the famous "Super Seven" litter, the brother-sister breeding by the Mike Smiths that has produced four champions (before the age of two) to date. Ch. Flash Cube was Best of Breed at the 1983 Samoyed Club of Los Angeles under judge Howard Dullnig with an entry of over 100 Samoyeds, and was sire of two puppies who were exported to Japan under Teena's kennel name of Critza.

Down in Ensenada, Mexico, March 12, 1972, the Mayfields' Int. Ch. Snowline's Joli Shashan, C.D.X., won Best in Show under judge Virginia Miller. "Shawnie" was handled by Jim Manley, P.H.A.

In April 1972, there were pages of Memorial Tributes to Ch. Shondi of Drayalene, (1960-1972), written by friends and owner Elliot Colburn, who mourned the nine years separation until they were reunited in December 1981.

Another important dog was retired from the ring in 1972. Am., Can., & Bda. Ch. Lulhaven's Snowmist Ensign (Tiki) ended his show career for owners Ott Hyatt and Sonny White with 8 American Bests in Show, 16 Canadian Bests in Show, 100 Bests of Breed and 47 Group placements. He was handled by the Canadian handler, Mrs. Pat Tripp.

In 1972, The Potomac Valley Samoyed Club held its first Specialty Show with the Rock Creek K.C. at Gaithersburg, Maryland. The entry was a good one of 95. This group had its beginnings in 1966 in Virginia with Lillian Crist, Art and Elsie DaCosta, Win and Marilyn Orr, Dave and Connie Richardson and Jim and Joan Sheets.

After several years of "Fun Matches" and B Matches the club neared recognition by the AKC with their A Match in 1971 at Silver Springs, Maryland with an entry of 48. This was the first A Match for Samoyeds ever held on the East Coast. Gaithersburg has been the site for all their Specialties since, and in 1980 the entry was 108.

Under the leadership of their president (1979-80) Stirling Rasmussen, Potomac Valley membership was increased and interest promoted. The club conducted Information Fairs, at which they demonstrated handling techniques, obedience training and grooming, and dispensed information and advice to novice and prospective owners. The club issues a bulletin, *Samantics*.

Samoyeds of Seelah Kennels, owned by Major General (Ret.) Merrill B. Evans and his wife Rowena of Prole, Iowa, was officially started in late 1971 with two puppy bitches. These puppies were carefully selected and they became the Evans' foundation bitches; their bloodlines emphasized both the Kobe (Tucker) and White Way (Mason) heritage. Both bitches,

96

Ch. Ice Way's Ice Cube (Am. & Mex. Ch. Snowline's Joli Shashan, CDX, CACIB ex Ch. Powered Puff of the Pacific) winning Group under judge Howard Dullnig. Ice Cube was WB, BOW and BOS at the SCA National Specialty, 1974. Owners, Mike and Bobbi Smith.

Ch. Ice Way's Flash Cube, wh. 1/11/80, by Ch. Ice Way's Ice Breaker ex Ice Way's Cherokee Sun O'Somar (Breaker's sister), winning Best of Breed at the SCLA supported entry at Orange Empire Dog Club show, 1984 under judge Mrs. Arlene Davis. A multi-Group placement winner, Flash Cube won the Stud Dog class at the Northern California Samoyed Fanciers Specialty, 1984. Bred by Mike and Bobbi Smith, and owned by Teena Deatherage.

Snowfire's Bo Peep and Snowfire's Miss Muffet, were shown to their championships and Companion Degrees in obedience.

The first planned breeding of Bo Peep was to Ch. Oakwood Farm's Kari J'Go Diko. This combined the lines of Silvermoon, Drayalene, Kobe and White Way. From this December 1974 litter, they selected a male puppy, Di Murdock of Seelah. Rowena showed him some as a puppy. Then in September 1977, Di Murdock was placed with Jerry Kesting, a professional handler, and was off to glory.

Murdock finished to championship in February 1978 with a Working Group 1st award. Then, extensively campaigned over the next three years, he became the top winning Samoyed in the nation (SCA) for 1979 and 1980, compiling a coast-to-coast record of 216 Bests of Breed, 100 Group placements including 16 Firsts, 2 all-breed Bests in Show and 2 Specialty Bests of Breed. He was the Top Stud Dog (SCA) for 1982.

Ably taking over after Murdock has been Ch. Murdock's Marauder of Seelah, "Bucky," whelped May 22, 1979. Bucky began at 7 months of age on the Florida circuit with three majors, and finished at 9½ months with a Best of Breed. In the fall of 1981, he won 13 of 14 Bests of Breed and 6 Group placements within a five-week period. In 1982 he was the top winning Samoyed (SCA and all systems), registering 83 Bests of Breed during the year. In February 1984, his record stood at 169 BOBs, 5 all-breed Bests in Show, and 75 Group placements including 20 Firsts.

In 1973, the Samoyed Club of Los Angeles decided to try a new idea to select a top specimen of the breed to send to the annual national specialty. Borrowing largely from the Collie Clan of Southern California, they initiated a "Tournament." This is a competition between dogs of all ages and titles. It is judged by three judges; one a breeder, one a breeder-judge and one an AKC Working Group judge. The winner receives air fare for dog and owner to the SCA National Specialty. In 1973, Ch. Southern Star of Lynthea, owned by Jim and Marion Osborn, was the winner. The Specialty which they attended was held at San Leandro, California and the entry was 233, which was the 15th largest specialty show of all breeds in the AKC in 1973. In 1975, Ch. Los Laikos Belaya Traicer, owned by the Edwin L. Adams, won the trip to Maryland with his handler, Jim Manley. Other Tournament winners are named under their kennel records.

The Northwest area had a notable loss in 1974 with the passing of Ch. Shaloon of Drayalene, 1962-74. He was the sire of 15 champions and Best of Breed at the 1963 SCA National Specialty. The owners Lee and Sandy Wacenske, long time Samoyed breeders and professional handlers, continue to aid and support the breed.

Greater Milwaukee Samoyed Fanciers is the only licensed Samoyed Specialty Club in the Midwest. They have been holding independent

Ch. Di Murdock of Seelah, Top Winning Samoyed (SCA award) for 1979 and 1980, Top Stud Dog for 1982. BIS and Specialty winner. Wh. 12/14/74, by Am. & Can. Ch. Oakwood Farms Kari ex Ch. Snowfire's Bo Peep. Breeder-Owners: Dr. Merrill and Rowena Evans.

Ch. El Sol's Lucky Prynce ("Tony"), son of Ch. Tsiulikagta Kara Sun, winning Group at Baton Rouge KC 1980 under judge Vincent Perry. Breeder: Nancy Foster. Owners: Mr. and Mrs. Gerald Langlois.

specialties since 1975. Their purpose when organized in 1969 was to promote the breed and improve quality and showing of Samoyeds throughout the upper Midwest.

The club's first President was Joyce Cain of Samtara Kennels. Secretary was Jeanne Nonhof, Moonlighter Samoyeds, and Treasurer was Joanne Hilbelink of Karalot Kennels. Board members include Judy Berlinger, Marion Seavers and Ruth Tausend.

Greater Milwaukee's educational programs on standards and breeding led to open evaluation clinics to help fanciers understand how their dogs compared to the standard. Harness work and weight pulling contests were sponsored. A newsletter, Howls 'N Growls, is published and exchanged with other groups.

Community events have included educational programs and demonstrations at the Wisconsin State Fair; shopping center programs including spinning demonstrations, pulling contests, conformation and obedience matches. The club feels these have been very successful in educating the public on the breed. Tattoo clinics and numerous programs by veterinarians aid the health of the dogs. Members are aided by handling classes and grooming programs.

In 1981 the club moved to two Specialty shows per year and their group was involved in organizing the 1981 National Specialty, which drew an entry of nearly 450 entries including 79 champions. GMSF is a charter member of the Combined Specialties Clubs of Greater Milwaukee.

The Moonlighter Kennels in Waldo, Wisconsin, are owned by Wayne and Jeanne Nonhof. All of the Samoyeds at "Moonlighter" trace at least once back to the foundation bitch, Moonlighter's Altai Star Mist (line-bred Joli). Misty more than proved her worth in the whelping box. At the time of her death in 1978, her descendants were the #1, #3, and #8 Top Winning Samoyeds in the nation. Dam of 5 champions, Misty was a Top Producing Brood Bitch in '73 (Kennel Review) and the Samoyed Association of the Midwest's Top Brood Bitch.

Probably Misty's most famous son is Ch. Moonlighter's Hallmark (Ike), a multi-group winner. Besides his illustrious show career, Ike did the breed proud in weight pulling contests, with his record pull being 1,400 pounds. Ike was the result of a line-breeding, sired by the BIS winning Am. & Can. Ch. Saroma's Polar Prince. Also produced in that breeding was Ch. Moonlighter's Celestial Hipy, Am. & Can. C.D., owned by Anne Copeland in Chicago. Ike produced a number of champions, most notably Ch. Karalot's Kit 'N Kaboodle, (dam of the BIS winner, Am. Can. & Bda. Ch. Karalot's Jak Frost 'O Westwind) and Ch. West Free's A-Del-Ice-Sar.

Misty has principally carried on through her daughter, Ch. Moonlighter's Ice 'N Spice—a second generation Top Producing Brood Bitch sired by Ch. Kondako's Sun Dancer. Spice is the dam of 10 champions. As

100

Three of the 7 champions from the breeding of Am. & Can. Ch. Moonlighter's Ima Bark Star (pictured on P. 138) with Ch. Samkist's Classy Chassis. Top left, Ch. Samkist's Touch of Class, a Group winner with multi-Group placements. Bred, owned and handled by Sharon Kremsreiter, Michigan. Top right, Ch. Samkist's Super Bonanza, owned by Paul and Betty Powell, No. Carolina. At left, Ch. Moonlighter's Ima Spark O'Bark, Group placing bitch, owned by Randy and Kathy Lensen, Wisconsin.

Ch. Mithril's Star of Earendil, bitch show sparkler, by Am. & Can. Ch. Moonlighter's Ima Bark Star ex Gimli Mithril Cotton, CD. Owner, Tim Trojan, Wisconsin.

Am. & Can. Ch. Moonlighter's Ima Better Bet ("Bettsie"), at 6 years. BOS at Potomac Valley Specialty, 1980. By Am. Can. & Eng. Ch. Delmonte This Is It ex Ch. Moonlighter's Ice 'N. Spice. Owned, trained and handled by Pat Kreif, Wisconsin.

evidence of the producing strength of this bitch line, Ch. Spice was tied for awards with her own granddaughter, Ch. Frostyacres I've Been Samkist, for Top Producing Brood Bitch in the United States for 1982 (*Samoyed Quarterly*). And the link between the two is that Top Producer, Bark Star.

The best known of Spice's babies is the owner-handled Best in Show winner, Am. & Can. Ch. Moonlighter's Ima Bark Star, TT. Bark Star is the winner of a record five Specialties and was *Kennel Review*'s and *Samoyed Quarterly*'s Top Producing Stud Dog for '79. The mating of Spice to Eng., Am. & Can. Ch. Delmonte This Is It which produced Bark Star was very fortunate and produced six champions (Ch. M's Ima Better Bet, Ch. M's Ima Yogi Beara, C.D., Ch. M's Ima Huggi Bear [Group Winner], Ch. M's Ima Moonbeam, C.D. [Tournament winner & SCA Award of Merit '83], and Ch. M's Ima Firecracker, C.D.

With some 50 champions already on the books, Bark Star is leaving his mark on the breed for sound, glamorous, good tempered smiling Samoyeds.

There are a number of breedings that have worked especially well and this information may be of use to breeders in the future. The mating of Bark to that lovely bitch, Ch. Samkist's Classy Classis, which was a line-breeding, produced 8 champions; including the before-mentioned top producer, Ch. Frostyacres I've Been Samkist (McFarlane) and the Specialty winning and Group placing bitch, Ch. Moonlighter's Ima Spark 'O Bark (Lensen). Five champions resulted from the combination of Bark and the Trojan's Gimli Mithril Cotton, C.D., (an outcross to the old Alicrys lines), and four from a litter of five out of Shanda Bear (Winterway), owned by Roanne Harmon, also finished.

The full story of Bark's influence on the breed is still being recorded. Some of his puppies are just starting their careers. Some males who have already made their marks in the Group rings are Ch. Samkist's Touch of Class (Kremsreiter), Ch. Moonlighter's Ima Wescana Guy (Anderson & Nonhof), and Ch. Nuvak's Star Chaser (Harrigan-Rost), who also runs on a racing sled team.

Adding to the strong upsurge of the Samoyed breed in Wisconsin (which surely helped swell the entry at the 1981 SCA National Specialty to somewhere near 450) has been the contribution of Bob and Wanda Krauss of Poynette, Wisconsin. Bob and Wanda had a Samoyed for four years before they became totally involved in all phases of the dog sport. They acquired Ch. Prairiewind's Shanna, C.D. as a young adult from Phyllis Hellems of Kansas. Shanna is an inbred daughter of Ch. Nachalnik of Drayalene. Because the Krausses own horses, their breeding program has been strongly influenced by the need for soundness and good movement in a working animal. In particular, they believe that fronts are the weakest part of the Samoyed breed today; therefore they have placed a strong emphasis on producing a line of dogs with sound fronts.

At left, K-Way's Omen of Destiny, CD, distinguished sire and the grandsire of top winner Ch. Quicksilver's Razz Ma Tazz. By Ch. Sassillie's Merlyn of Vicrian ex K-Way's Mint Julep of Vicrian. Owned by Bob and Wanda Krauss, Wisconsin. At right, the Krauss's Ch. K-Ways Classic Snow Fantasy, pictured at 7 months. By Ch. Snow Fantasy's Main Man ex Ch. K-Way's Touch of Class, Snow Fantasy placed in the Group as a puppy and finished at 16 months.

Ch. Trailblazer Silver Talisman, CD, winning the Working Group at Southern Colorado KC 1979 under judge Glenn Fancy. Breeder-owner-handler, Judy E. Mears.

103

Shanna was first bred to Ch. Kondako's Sun Dancer. This produced two champions, Ch. K-Way's Garmouche, C.D. and Ch. K-Way's Gay Gazelle, C.D. The Krausses felt that these dogs were sound and stylish with good coat and type but did not have the dam's reach and sidegait. To obtain this, they bred to Ch. Ivan Belaya of Taymylyr, C.D., a descendant of Ch. Starchak, C.D. and Ch. Shondi of Drayalene. Here they obtained the champions, K-Way's Touch of Class and K-Way's Wind Chaser, C.D. and their lead dog, K-Way's Jeremiah Johnson, C.D.X. Ch. Gazelle was taken to Ivan and they produced Ch. K-Way's Mickey Finn, C.D. and K-Way's Mint Julep of Vicrian.

The three Ivan daughters, Classy, Chaser and Julie have formed the core of the K-Way breeding program since 1977. Julie suffered an injury after winning her first major points which kept her out of the show ring. Nevertheless, she produced five champions for K-Way, one being Ch. K-Way's Omen of Destiny, C.D. Omen has true proportions for a Samoyed and is passing on his type, balance and movement to his offspring. Classy and Chaser have both been bred to Am. & Can. Ch. Snow Fantasy's Main Man, owned by Frank and Paula Phillips. In 1979 he was a top dog in Canada with 3 Canadian Bests in Show. Main Man is a descendant of 4 generations of BIS dogs on his sire's side; Champions Bopper El Toro of Baerstone; Maur Mik's Kim, Karasea's Silver Kim, and Noatak of Silver Moon.

Omen and Main Man are providing the direction for the K-Way dogs of the 1980s.

It should be noticed that K-Way dogs have obedience titles. Bob and Wanda train and show their dogs in obedience as well as conformation and have also raced a team competitively in Wisconsin for three years. They feel that a truly balanced Samoyed not only moves well but has a title at both ends and can also work well in harness. Their success is proof that the Samoyed is indeed the versatile dog that the standard requires.

Sue and Lou Hoehn entered the field of purebred dogs with a different approach than that of many of our fanciers. For one year they read all they could find about the Samoyed. They visited many breeders and corresponded throughout the United States and Canada. Lou, who later became an AKC approved breeder-judge, explained his objective to us, "We suddenly realized that we were living in an area with two strong and dominant lines and that each had its weaknesses and no one was crossing the lines to complement each other."

One of these lines was Bearstone and the other Samtara. They were largely English Kobe and Snowland, respectively.

Their first champion, bred by Joyce Cain, was a male from Ch. Samtara's Sugay N' Spice, who was a top SCA Top Bitch Award winner, and the sire was Ch. Saroma's Polar Prince, an SCA Top Stud Award winner. This puppy became Ch. Samtara's Suga Koko, who, bred to Silver Sonnett

Ch. Sulu's Mark of Distinction going BOB at 1979 SCA National Specialty. Wh. 1/25/75, by Ch. Sulu's Karbon Kopi o'Baerstone ex Ch. Sassillie's Shasta. Owner-handler, Lewis Hoehn. Pictured, l. to r.: J.D. Jones, judge; Mr. Hoehn; Mrs. Duvella Kusler, then president of the SCA; Jim Koffenberger, v.p.; John Ronald, treasurer; Gene Roberts, show chmn.; and Don Hodges, AKC delegate.

At left, Ch. Sulu's Karbon Kopi o'Baerstone, sire of 28 AKC champions. Top Stud Dog (SCA) for 1976, 1977 and 1978. #2 Top Winning Samoyed in the U.S. for 1973. Wh. 5/22/71, by Ch. Snow Prince of Baerstone ex Silvern Sonnet of Gro-Wil, Kopi was bred by Jean Baer and owned by Lewis and Susan Hoehn. At right, Ch. Blue Sky's Honey Bun, Kopi's daughter ex Snomesa Anastasia of Blue Sky. Honey Bun is the foundation bitch of the Blue Sky Kennels, owned by Dr. P.J. and Elizabeth Lockman Hooyman in Pine, Colo. She is the dam of three Group I winners out of one litter: Ch. Blue Sky's Pound Cake (also BIS), Ch. Blue Sky's Smiling at Me, and Ch. Blue Sky's Rambling Guy.

of Gro-will, another award winning SCA brood bitch, produced a great winner for them, Ch. Sulu's Karbon Kopi O'Bearstone.

The Hoehns were really on their way to fine dogs when they bred Kopi to Tsartar's Somewhere M. Lara, another Top Brood Bitch Award winner, and in three breedings to M. Lara they obtained eight champions, with two of the bitches winning Specialties: Ch. Fascinatin' Rhythm was BOS at the San Diego Specialty and Ch. Que Sera's Karaimee was Best of Breed at the Potomac Valley Specialty and SCA Top Winning Bitch in 1978. A litter sister, Ch. Que Seras Vicki O'Larathor, was Top Winning Bitch in Canada, 1978. Now with their excellent lines combined, they introduced another line which they felt to be dominant for front angulation and overall superior side movement. This was through the bitch, Ch. Sassillies Shasta, whose heritage through her sire, Ch. Ivan Belaya of Taymylr traced to the immortal Ch. Starchak, C.D.

The mating of Kopi to Sassillies Shasta produced their big winner, Ch. Sulu's Mark of Distinction, a multiple Group winner and Best in Specialty Show at the SCA National in 1979 over an entry of 361 including 71 champions at Atlanta, Ga. judged by J.D. Jones.

Mark when bred to Kopi's daughter, Ch. Blue Sky's Honey Bun, produced the great winning bitches: Ch. Blue Sky's Pound Cake, a Best in Show winner owned by Dr. Pat and Liz Hooyman of Denver; and her sister, Ch. Sulu's Fascination Rhythm, who was Winners Bitch at the 1978 SCLA Specialty. Pound Cake won the 1979 SCA Top Winning Bitch Award at 6 years of age.

The Hoehns' success upholds the fact that breeding must have a plan and that to ignore a great and complementing bloodline because of personality conflicts of owners can be a detriment to the Samoyed breed.

Dr. Patrick and Elizabeth Hooyman, Blue Sky Kennel, have carried on the bloodlines of Ch. Sulu's Mark of Distinction. Their breeding of Ch. Blue Sky's Honey Bun to Mark not only produced the Best in Show winner Pound Cake, but also—in the same litter—two other Group winners: Ch. Blue Sky's Smiling at Me and Ch. Blue Sky's Rambling Guy. Further down the line, Liz bred Ch. Blue Sky's Pound Cake to Ch. Ice Way's Ice Breaker to produce Ch. Blue Sky's Breaking Away, Ch. Blue Sky's Piece of Cake, Ch. Blue Sky's Bedazzled, and Ch. Blue Sky's Simply Smashing, owned by Joan Luna.

Using her well established and successful lines to their potential, she bred Ch. BS Smiling at Me to his aunt Ch. Sulu's Fascinating Rhythm. So Barbara Arnaud of Los Angeles has her lovely girl, Ch. Sulu's Mindy on My Mind. Mindy won the 1984 SCA Specialty Brood Bitch Award, and the silverplate tea service donated in memory of Ann Hamlin.

Liz Hooyman became a Samoyed breeder-judge in 1984 and is a welcome addition to the small number that the breed has.

Ch. Blue Sky's Breaking Away, multiple Group winner. By Ch. Ice Way's Ice Breaker ex Ch. Blue Sky's Pound Cake. Bred and owned by Dr. P.J. and Elizabeth Lockman Hooyman.

Ch. Sherica's Lucky Seven Charm, C.D., wh. 10/31/74 by Ch. Sassillie's Tuck In Sherwood ex Ch. Sassillie's Gidget of Asgard, pictured upon her finish for championship with win of her third major at SCLA Specialty 1979. Bred by Lorraine L. Newville and Carole A. Barnum, and owned and handled by Lorraine.

Ch. Kazakh's Albert of Barbicon. Wh. 12/5/74, by Ch. North Starr King's Ransom ex Ch. Weathervane's Genii of Kazakh, C.D. Breeders: Saul and Susan Waldman. Owners: Barbara and Steven Brisgel.

The Samoyed Club of Houston was formed in 1974 and held its first organized meeting in October of that year. A nucleus of about twelve members formed the club but within a year the membership grew to 26. The roster has varied since that time but members of the original nucleus still active include: Archie and Anne Peil, Danny and Chris Middleton, and Don and Barbara Winslow.

Their first Fun Match was in April 1975. They had an amazing entry of 90 dogs which was a record for the South and Texas. The two required B-OB Matches and two A-OA matches were held and then application was made to the American Kennel Club for a licensed show. The club became a member of the Houston Combined Specialties Association, and the AKC granted them permission for a licensed specialty in 1978. This date enabled them to be part of the first World Series of Dog Shows held in the Astrohall. This excellent location has continued and permits them to conduct their Specialty with the Houston Combined Specialties and the three all-breed clubs in the Astrohall in early August of each year.

At the SCA National Specialty in 1975, it was consistent that Ch. Frostymorn's Big Blizzard, owned by Donald Zeeb, was Best of Breed. His sire, Ch. Frosty of Blue Mountain, owned by Norm and Shirley Bartz of New York, won the Stud Dog Class.

By 1975, keeping pace with the increase in breed registrations, the SCA was feeling growing pains. The roster contained 787 names, and the SCA became "computerized" as to membership and mailing lists. Even the Club Bulletin had grown to 84 pages.

The concept of a Futurity had been accepted by the SCA Board of Directors and Dave Richardson was elected Futurity Secretary. As is the practice with other breed Futurities, puppies are nominated prior to birth. At birth, they are further nominated with another fee. Fees keep the nomination in effect during the growing period, and then the individual awards are made at the judging of the National Specialty in which the nominated puppy becomes of eligible age for competition.

After a decade, the Futurity was turned over to Karen McFarlane (Karney Kennels), who adores puppies.

An Award of Merit was instituted. It was to be presented to the Best of Breed and Best of Breed runners-up at the National Specialty, as is the practice of some other breed clubs—notably the German Shepherd Dog Club of America. The German Shepherd club names as "Select" #1 down to a specified number or a limitation based upon 10 to 20% of the champions entered. This enables a champion to be in the top 10 or 20% of 50 to 100 champions, which is quite an honor. The Samoyed system chooses both dogs and bitches. (The Samoyed Club of Los Angeles has been doing this for several years at its Specialty.)

In 1979, Rev. Terry Litton imported, from Betty Moody in England, the 4-year-old Eng. Ch. Novaskaya Silva Khim, winner of 4 CC's and a Group. Jerry Rigden handled Khim to American championship and Group placements. The Littons also imported a bitch, Whitewisp Zaricka, from the Grounds in England.

Ch. Snowdrift Grenadier Kara Sea ("Casey"), in Top Ten SQ System, 1980. By Ch. Chekkalov's Shivago of Valmer ex Hickory Hearth's Mary Margo. Owner, Beth Ingram, Alabama.

Ch. El Sol's Koush Kim O'Whitecliff (at 2 years). Owners, Kathryn Molineux and Wilna Coulter. Whelped in 1977, "Kimmie" was discovered at Nancy Foster's in Texas by Wilna for Katie, and stuck to Katie like moss. Finished to championship at 20 months, he became a Group winner.

109

The Back Yard at Bubbling Oaks, owned by Jack and Amelia Price of Commack, N.Y., have been enthusiastic supporters of the dual-purpose Samoyed since joining the ranks in the early 1970s.

On February 3, 1984, the Bubbling Oaks Samoyed team became the first Samoyeds to complete the Molson-Marmora Classic, the Canadian Long Distance Championship Race. Distance is 68 plus miles and non-stop. All five dogs of the team are home-bred and champion-sired. One of the team (all males) is pictured in this book at completion of the race. He runs at wheel just in front of the sled.

All of the Back Yard dogs live at home and "mostly in the house," according to Amelia. The Prices firmly believe that their dogs must be trained and socialized to be a success in life and in the show ring.

And a success in the show ring they indeed are. Their show records are as enviable as their sledding accomplishments. Star of the kennel has been Am. & Can. Ch. Bubbles LaRue of Oakwood (whelped in 1973, by Park Cliffe Kris Kringle ex Suffolk Princess Kiriv). Bubbles won the 1975 Potomac Valley Samoyed Specialty over an entry of 205. In 1978, handled by Joy Brewster, she was Best of Breed at Westminster and went on to 2nd in the Group, a rare feat for a Samoyed bitch. She won the SCA award for Top Winning Bitch.

Another of their fine bitches, Ch. Me Too of Bubbling Oaks, (whelped 1978, by Ch. Sugar Daddy of Bubbling Oaks ex Kapusta) is a Best in Show winner and was the SCA Award winner for Top Bitch in 1983. She was handled by Nancy Sheehan-Martin.

Nancy Sheehan-Martin went on to handle Cheryl Wagner's Ch. Tarahill's Casey Can Do, the 1985 Westminster BOB under J.D. Jones. Ch. Me Too of Bubbling Oaks, handled by Joy Brewster, was Best Opposite.

A great bitch is truly a pearl without a price. At the 1975 Samoyed Club of Los Angeles Specialty, Skip Alexander judged the club's largest Sweepstakes entry to date (43) and awarded Best in Sweepstakes to Starctic Aukeo, owned by Lindy Ward. She won Best Opposite three years later at the SCA National Specialty in Portland, Oregon in an entry of 220, including 47 champions, judged by Derek Rayne. The authors take pride in that they have won Best of Breed at an SCA National with a bitch, and Best Opposite with two different bitches at National Specialties, plus two Bests of Breed at area Specialties with two other bitches. Ch. Tasha of Sasha's Knight, co-owned with daughter Mardee, has been Top Winning Bitch for three years and won the largest SCLA Specialty ever held in 1985.

Audrey Lycan—Winterway Samoyeds in Huntsville, Alabama— owned a one-of-a-kind bitch, Ch. Kim's Ladybug (May 1967-June 1977). Ladybug whelped 39 puppies and 32 lived. Ten of the 32 became champions and were certified O.F.A. She was bred to four different males, 2 linebred and 2 outcrosses, and produced champions and obedience titlists

A Samoyed does not like to be dirty—look at his face! Jack Price drives the Bubbling Oaks team on Long Island, N.Y., with Ch. Camshaft of Bubbling Oaks. Amelia Price says this backyard "mud grooming" is a long way from the pristine white that their Am. & Can. Ch. Bubbles La Rue of Oakwood exhibited while winning mightily in the '70s. Bubbles' wins included a BIS all-breeds and 2nd in the Group at Westminster.

Ch. Winterway's Mr. Wonderful, Group winner, in the Top Ten for 1979. By Ch. Kondaka's Dancing Bear ex Ch. Kim's Ladybug. Bred, owned and handled by Audrey Lycan, "Winterway," Alabama.

Am. Ch. Crensa Koska, English import sired by the foremost CC winner Eng. Ch. Grenadier of Crensa. His dam is Samovar Melody. Owned by Katie M. Jones and Audrey Lycan, Huntsville, Ala. "Christoff" brings similar bloodlines to those brought by the authors' Ch. Kiskas Karaholme Cherokee over a decade before.

from all of them. Four of these champions became Working Group First or Group placement winners. Ladybug earned the SCA and *Kennel Review* Top Producer Awards in 1973, and the SCA Award again in 1976. She proved to be a credit to her sire, Ch. Maur Mik's Kim, who was from a long line of Best in Show and Top Producer Award winners.

Ch. Winterway's Mr. Wonderful, owned by Audrey, was in the Top Ten of all Working dogs. This quality continued to the next generation. In 1979 at the Samoyed Club of America Specialty, Mr. Wonderful's daughter, Ch. Sax Heartbreak Kid, was Best of Winners. A great grandson of Ch. Winterway's Beowulf, Ch. Ken-Tee's Tarheel Talker of Lyca, was Grand Futurity winner, and his sister, Ch. Lyca's Saucie Sal, was Reserve Grand Futurity winner.

In 1984, Audrey Lycan and Katie M. Jones (Syrius Samoyeds, So. Carolina) imported Crensa Koska from England. "Christoff" is sired by Eng. Ch. Grenadier of Crensa, the record-establishing winner of 43 Challenge Certificates.

North Starr Samoyeds, owned by Dr. Robert J. and Pat Hritzo, of Hubbard, Ohio, is an outstanding kennel of record-establishing dogs. Dr. and Mrs. Hritzo have bred and shown dogs since 1964, and in addition to 48 Samoyed champions, have finished two Papillons, a Pointer, an American Foxhound and a Greyhound to championship.

In March, 1985, Dr. Hritzo, a surgeon, was elected to the Board of Directors of the American Kennel Club.

The Hritzos' homebred Am. & Can. Ch. North Starr's King Ransom, whelped in 1969, was for a time the all-time Top Winning Samoyed. He won the SCA Top Winner Award for 1974, '75, '76 and '77 (he was also Top Winning Samoyed in Canada for 1974), and in 1976 and 1977 was the #5 Working Dog in the USA. His show record included: 10 American Bests in Show, 1 Canadian Best in Show, 1 Specialty Best in Show, 42 Working Group Firsts and 86 other Group placements, and 250 Bests of Breed.

Equally outstanding as a stud, he sired 30 AKC champions, including 4 Best in Show winners and 9 Group winners or placers, and 5 foreign champions.

Ransom's heritage gave him the potential. His sire was Ch. Maur Mik's Kim, a Best in Show winner and the #1 Samoyed in the USA for 1968 and 1970. Kim was himself sire of 29 champions. Ransom's dam, Sam O'Khan's Karelia of Khan, died at the age of 18 months with 12 points and both majors, but was still the dam of 3 champions. She was a littermate to Ch. Sam O'Khan's Chingis Khan, owned by Dr. Joan Sheets, the Top Winning Sam in the USA for 1966, '67 and '69 with 5 Bests in Show. Another in the litter was Ch. Sam O'Khan's Kubla Khan, owned by Pat Morehouse, who was the Top Producing Samoyed sire in 1978 and 1979 (*Kennel Review*).

The Hritzos' great brood bitch was Am. & Can. Ch. Archangel of the North Starr. Archangel stands as the Top Producing Samoyed Bitch of all

Growing up together. Am. & Can. Ch. North Starr King's Ransom was the top SCA Award winner for 1974, '75, '76 and '77 with a record that included 10 AKC and 1 Canadian Best in Show and 42 Groups. Equally outstanding as a stud, he has sired 30 AKC champions, including 4 Best in Show winners. Ransom, then 10 months old, is pictured in his first show (top left) winning BOB over Specials, handled by 10-year-old Kathy Hritzo, daughter of his breeder-owners, Dr. and Mrs. Robert J. Hritzo. Judge was Phil Marsh. At top right, Kathy—then 15 years old—is pictured handling Ransom to Best in Show at Dayton KC 1975 under judge Larry Downey. At right, Kathy is pictured handling Ransom to a Group win in 1976, when she was sixteen. In February 1976, Kathy was Top Junior Handler at the Westminster KC's 100th Anniversary Show. The Junior Handling classes at Westminster represent the cream of the crop—the youngsters have to earn eligibility by placing First in eight or more Junior Showmanship classes during the previous year. Kathy's (now Kathy Heimann) subsequent handling triumphs include showing three Samoyeds from one litter to Best in Show wins.

time, and in 1975 was No. 6 in the list for all breeds. She was the dam of 15 champions (including 2 Best in Show winners) and of 10 foreign champions.

In addition, the Hritzos' daughters—Kathy and Nancy—have been particularly outstanding in Junior Showmanship. Kathy (now Kathy Hritzo Heimann) came first, and won honor as the foremost Junior Handler in the United States by virtue of her win at Westminster in 1976. The Hritzo family's participation in dogs began in Obedience, and they have also sled-raced their dogs over the last few years in Ohio and Pennsylvania.

In 1976, a pioneer supporter and a 51 year booster of the Samoyed passed on. Miss Vera Lawrence of Berkeley, California left her beloved Samoyeds to her sister, Miss Ina Lawrence.

Vera began in our breed in 1925 with a puppy from an unknown breeder in the East, when she lived in Washington, D.C.

Being a true novice with such a rare breed she did not even get the registration papers from the breeder. Her search for information upon this then unknown breed led her to Mrs. Emily Coughlin of the well-known Landover Kennels in Maryland.

Mrs. Coughlin liked Vera's bitch so suggested that she breed to their near Champion Bruoff, a son of Ch. Donerna's Barin. The Lawrences' home was taken by "eminent domain" by the Government for a new Parkway, so they moved to California where the litter of 6 puppies was whelped.

Vera did not show a great deal as the few shows required transportation by electric rail or ferry boat to San Francisco. The threat of distemper was great at that time as there were no inoculations, and often whole kennels were wiped out after shows.

When Vera lost her lovely Lensen of Snowland, obtained from Mrs. Harris, she lost interest in shows. In August 1933, she contacted Al Rosemont with his new magazine, *Western Kennel World,* and became a breed columnist. This she did until 1971, when the magazine ceased publication. Month after month and year after year she publicized the breed and solicited articles from owners with no remuneration. Her satisfaction was in the improvement and betterment of the Samoyed.

The Christmas issues of *Western Kennel World* are collectors items, especially to Samoyed owners. These issues contain ten to twenty pages of prominent dogs of the times and Samoyeds grace every cover.

Vera Lawrence and Mrs. Catherine Quereaux wrote 20 installments of *Dog of The Ages,* hoping some day to produce a book on the history of the breed. This never came to completion, but she pointed the path for others to follow.

Jack and Helen Feinberg, owners of the Northwind Kennels in Bedford, New York, have been very active members of the Samoyed Club of America. Jack is a past president (1980-81).

As *Western Kennel World* columnist from 1933 to 1971, Vera Lawrence did much to publicize the Samoyed. This 1927 picture (submitted to us by her sister, Ina) shows Vera with her first Samoyed, Nannuk.

Ice Way's Crush Velvet, Best Puppy and Sweepstakes Winner at the 1979 Samoyed Club of San Diego Specialty. Owner-handler, Ann Bark.

Am. & Can. Ch. Kendara Czarina of Taiga (Am. & Can. Ch. Czartu of Kendaraland ex Ch. Purjinka of Taiga). Breeder: Jo Carter. Owner, Mary Frederick, Illinois.

Kros Paws Tannhauser. Owners Elva and Fred Libby, Florida, plan breedings at Kros Paws that 20 years later carry the bloodlines of Alesha of Ala Cryss, their original stock.

The Feinbergs have done much to favorably publicize the Samoyed through use of their dogs in advertising commercials and their extensive exhibiting. Their Ch. Northwind's Ivan the Terrible, bred by Al and Karen Hanakahi, was Winners Dog at the first Potomac Valley Specialty in 1973. Ivan worked in harness and was their lead dog. He achieved international fame as "the Helena Rubinstein Dog." Ivan was used as the Helena Rubinstein mascot for a period of five years, and was seen in fashion magazines and in television commercials in the United States, Europe and Japan. His beautiful expression was a credit to our breed.

Ch. Northwind's Running Bear, sired by Ch. Kondako's Sun Dancer ex Troika V, and bred by Alan and Jane Stevenson of North Hollywood, California, was Northwind's big winner. Bear was the No. 1 Samoyed in the country, all systems, for 1981. He was No. 1 Phillips System for 1980, and No. 3 for 1979. His career winnings included 4 all-breed Bests in Show, 22 Group 1, 23 Group 2, 13 Group 3 and 9 Group 4.

The Feinbergs' lovely home-bred bitch, Ch. Northwind's Black Magic (by Ch. Scandia's Kejaare ex Northwind's Ladybug) became a champion in 11 shows, and was an Award of Merit winner at the 1979 Specialty.

Now the banner has been picked up by Ch. Northwind's Robin Hood, whelped in 1981, and bred by Helen and Mindy Feinberg. Robin Hood is co-owned by Diane Chenault and Helen Feinberg, and handled by Jack Feinberg. The No. 2 Samoyed in the nation for 1983 (all systems), he has already won 3 Bests in Show and 15 Group Firsts. Robin lives with Diane in Central Florida when he is not on the road with Jack.

The first New England Samoyed Club of record is now known as the Minuteman Samoyed. It was known by several other names for four or five years. The Minuteman Samoyed Club is a unique specialty club. Its members, as a club and individually, participate in a wide range of dog related activities. Although many members show in the conformation ring and the club has many American and Canadian Champions as well as many obedience titlists, it is not purely a show oriented club. Throughout the fall and winter, there are training sessions with carts and sleds. The culmination is a winter work weekend in Maine or Vermont. Some do sledding for enjoyment. Some are serious participants in sprint and long distance racing.

In the spring and summer, the club shifts into backpacking and hiking. They sponsor hikes, picnics and campouts with their dogs. Members believe that the Samoyed should be recognized as a multi-purpose dog and annually award certificates of merit for conformation, obedience and the various aspects of working. To serve the community, the club holds demonstrations for nursing homes and schools for the deaf as well as exhibits in malls. The club supports tattoo clinics, PRA clinics and has contributed to dog-related institutions such as ADOA and the Morris Animal Foundation.

Alan Katz, president, and Carol Cook, secretary, inform us that this

Am. & Can. Ch. Northwind's Robin Hood winning Best in Show all-breeds at Central Florida KC, under judge George Payton. Robin, by Ch. Northwind's Running Bear ex Ch. Northwind's Black Magic, is owned by Dianne E. Chenault and Helen Feinberg, and handled by Jack Feinberg. Bred by the Feinbergs. Robin Hood was the No. 2 Samoyed in the nation for 1983. His wins include 3 Bests in Show and 15 Groups.

Ch. Northwind's Running Bear finished 1981 as the top winning Samoyed in the nation, all systems. Whelped 5/25/75, by Ch. Kondako's Sundancer ex Troika V. Bred by Alan and Jane Stevenson, owned and handled by Jack and Helen Feinberg. Winner of 4 Bests in Show and 22 Groups, he was retired to make way for his son, Am. & Can. Ch. Northwind's Robin Hood.

group is the only one to hold a "Club" membership in the Organization of Working Samoyeds (OWS).

The Minuteman Samoyed Club held a B-OB Match in September, 1984 with Tim Malueg judging. Best Puppy in Match was Alpine Glo's Tami of Milldam, owned by Gretchen Karlson. Best Pointed in Match was Kovsh' Arabesque O'Crush owned by Ann Bark and Katie Molineux, and Best in Match was Ghostrider's Tabor owned by Dave and Sue Hanson. The Best Junior Handler was Erin Madden. Elaine Marochino was in charge of this qualifying type match that Specialty clubs must hold successfully in order to hold A and A-OA (conformation and obedience matches) in order to become approved as a licensed Specialty Club.

The Minuteman Samoyed Club was licensed by the AKC in the Spring of 1985.

Wayne and Carol MacArthur, from the state of Maine, have winning ways with their dogs. We should say bitches, for they seem to have a preference for quality females. They began with a bitch from Louisiana, purchased from T. J. Dendinger, who became Am. & Can. Ch. Silvertip's Dixie Sensation, C.D. She finished in six consecutive shows, completing with a Best of Breed over champions.

The MacArthurs then acquired another bitch from Dendinger who became Am. & Can. Ch. Silvertip's Dixie Fascination, and specialed her for a while. She produced two champions for them, sired by Ch. Shaloon of Drayalene (out of the state of Washington). Ch. Silvertip's Snow-Mac Heritage, owned by Phoebe Hellem, as a puppy won the SCA National Sweepstakes.

Ch. Silvertip's Dixie Sensation, C.D. was bred to Ch. Nachalnik of Drayalene (Colorado) and produced Snow-Mac's Delta Dawn, who they sold to Francis and Nancy Pace with stipulation that she be bred once and to Ch. Kiskas Karaholme Cherokee (Maine to California). This produced Am. & Can. Ch. Nanank's Bathzarah ("Bonnie"). Bonnie finished very quickly with several Bests of Breed over specials and a Group fourth. In Canada, in four shows, she captured her championship with 3 BOBs over champions and a Group third.

Bonnie won the SCA Top Winning Bitch Award in 1978, and was Best Opposite at the Potomac Valley Samoyed Specialty. She was bred to Ch. Moonlighter's Ima Bark Star, which produced Ch. Snow Mac's Moonlight Serenade. He finished with four majors for owner Elain Marachino. His litter sisters were: Ch. Snow-Mac's Ima Riverview Star (owned by Sandy and Bruce Krupski) and Snow-Mac's Silvertip Fantasy (owned by Wayne MacArthur and T. J. Dendinger), who has three Bests of Breed from the puppy class. Notice the bloodlines in Bonnie's pedigree: Louisiana, Washington, Colorado, California, and England—and she is still quite line-bred!

118

Ch. Chaliph's Lucky Prince (Ch. Chaliph's Sir Kimba ex Silvertip's Song of Praise) BIS all-breeds at Simi Valley KC 1977, his first time out as a Special. Lucky went on to multiple Group wins and was the No. 2 Samoyed for 1977. A son, Ch. SnowKap's Prince Charming, was Winners Dog at the 1980 SCA Specialty. Owner, Barbara Arnaud. Handler, Jim Manley.

Ch. Shawndi of Midnight Sun, BOB at the 1978 SCA National Specialty under judge Virginia Lyne (Canada). By Ch. Czar's Kobe-Wah of Whitecliff ex Sunshine of Midnight Sun. Bred by Gail Milburn Stitt. Owned by Michael and Dianne Hoffecker. Handler, Don Dougherty.

Northern California Samoyed Fanciers began as a social group in 1962. To encourage interest in the breed they conducted matches and clinics for nine years and in 1973 they hosted the SCA National Specialty, held at San Leandro, California.

In 1981 their group finally became a licensed specialty club and held their first show on March 21, 1981. Dr. Malcolm Phelps judged and awarded the Specialty Best in Show to the Evans' Ch. Di Murdock of Seelah.

The Northern California Samoyed Fanciers has produced the popular *Prologue to the Samoyed*. This fine booklet contains many helpful articles on the grooming, breeding and general care of the Samoyed.

A group is fortunate when it has a "steady" member in its ranks so that no matter who comes and goes, the club goes on. Such a person is La Vera Morgan in Northern California. Her husband, Dan Morgan, is a breeder-judge. Others who are currently assisting the Northern California Samoyed Fanciers are Joan and Paula Luna, the Marineaus (who transferred from San Diego), the Walt Kauzlarichs, the John Colomas, the Gittlesons, Ed Altamarino, Kathryn Molineaux, Wilna Coulter, and the late Bebe Hoxey.

The Whitecliff line originated with Percy and Lena Mathaeron and Jean Blank. Their first dogs with the Whitecliff name were the Chs. Cheekako of Whitecliff and Chumikan of Whitecliff and the great winning dog Ch. Yurok of Whitecliff. These dogs were not "Whitecliff" breeding, but were the first to carry the name. Jean Blank showed the dogs and the Matherons raised and bred them. After Jean had shown Yurok to his fabulous record, she retired from breeding and showing and asked Don and Wilna Coulter to carry on the Whitecliff name.

Two sons of Ch. Yurok, Ch. Sho-off's Czar of Whitecliff and Ch. Sho-off's Dorok of Whitecliff, a Best in Show winner, were probably the most prolific of Yurok's offspring. Some of the get are: Mex. and Am. Ch. Elrond Czar of Rivendell, C.D., Mex. & Am. Ch. Midnight Sun Kimba; Can. & Am. Ch. Whitecliff's Ragnar Bjorn, C.D.; Ch. Pushka Czar of Snowcliff, Best in Show winner; Ch. Czar Dorak of Whitecliff; Mex. Ch. Sasha of Whitecliff; Ch. Czar's Kobe-Wah of Whitecliff and Ch. Yeti of Whitecliff.

An all-time favorite of Wilna Coulter's was the bitch Ch. White Star IV. She did not begin her show career until the age of seven. Within a year she was a champion, with several Bests of Breed. Star was co-owned with Karl and Joy Geletich of Shalimar Kennels in Sacramento, California. Star was a natural showman and took the breed or Best Opposite almost every time shown. At the age of ten years she won a Group 3rd under judge Robert Ward. At age 12 she was awarded the Award of Merit and 1st in Veterans at the SCA National Specialty by judge Derek Rayne. The following year, 1979, at the SCA Specialty hosted by the Greater Metropolitan Atlanta Samoyed Club in Georgia, she won 1st in Veteran Bitch Class at the age of 13 years.

120

Ch. Czar Dorak of Whitecliff (1967-1980), winner of two Bests in Show in Texas. By Ch. Sho-Off's Czar of Whitecliff ex Ch. Tyya of Whitecliff. Breeder: Wilna Coulter. Owners: Allen and Pat Walker.

Am. & Can. Ch. Scandia's Kesjare ("Chuck"), Best in Show at Putnam KC, 1978. BOB at Samoyed Assn. of Canada Specialty, 1979. In 1980, the Scovins finished the seventh dog in a litter sired by Chuck out of Ch. Weathervane's Katy-Did, making it an all-champion litter.

121

Michael and Dianne Hoffecker of Huntington Beach, California, purchased a bitch puppy in 1976, bred by Gail Stitt and sired by Czar's Kobe-Wah of Whitecliff ex Sunshine of Midnight Sun. As usual a big win at a puppy match inducted them into the dog show life. This was followed by a Samoyed Club of Los Angeles Specialty B Match where they won Best of Breed in an entry of 62, judged by the well-known breeder judge from Australia, Mrs. Yvonne Sydenham-Clark. Guided and handled by their friends, Myrna and Don Dougherty, the puppy became Ch. Shawndi of Midnight Sun. Shawndi's first time out as a Special was Best of Breed and 4th in the Working Group. The second time she shown as a champion, Shawndi was Best of Breed at the Samoyed Club of America's National Specialty in San Diego, California in August of 1980. The judge was Virginia Lynne of Canada.

The Hoeffeckers philosophical comment was: "Isn't it funny that the dog wins the breed and the awards and has the puppies, and WE take the credit."

New on the show scene, but long time in the breed are Dave and Marguerite Seibert of Phoenix, Arizona.

Dave began with Samoyeds as a young boy in Northern Minnesota when he was given an older Samoyed bitch who had been a lead dog on a team in Alaska. The surprise was that Queenie was pregnant and one night during a blizzard whelped nine Samoyed puppies. Dave trained them into a sled team and ran them on a trap line for years.

The Seiberts' interest turned to showing in 1978. They obtained a puppy from Lorraine Newville (Sherica Samoyeds) that was sired by Ch. Ice Way's Ice Breaker ex Ch. Sherica's Lucky Seven Charm, C.D. This "pick-of-the-litter" put them on the winning way. Ch. Sherica's Ethereal Candida won her first points at 13 months and finished with wins at large Specialty shows. Her line continues with the promising stud, Ch. Hoof 'n Paw Desert Knight O'Candida, known as Patrick, owned by Terry and Shelley Mumford.

In 1985, handled by Pam Stage (PHA), Patrick was BISS at the Samoyed Club of San Diego under judge Robert Lentz. So his name is engraved on the new perpetual trophy as its first recipient.

In 1983, the Seiberts acquired Ch. Snowblaze Linc'n Continental, who was sired by Ch. Kiskas Karaholme Cherokee ex Dr. John Meyers' Ch. Christori's Paka of Vallee. Thus Linc' transferred from Idaho to his new owners in Arizona.

Lorraine Newville obtained her first Samoyed from Carole Barnum of San Diego. She was Sherica's Gidget of Asgaard and her second was Gidget's grandmother, Ch. Sassillies Gidget of Asgaard. Lorraine's homebred Ch. Sherica's Lucky Seven Charm has a strong record in shows finishing her championship with three majors and winners bitch at the SCLA Specialty in an entry of over 130. Her Ch. Sherica's Lucky Break carries on the "Breaker" tradition.

At left, Ch. Sherica's Ethereal Candida ("Candi"), winning bitch, by Ch. Ice Way's Ice Breaker ex Ch. Sherica's Lucky Seven Charm, C.D. Owner-handler, Dave Seibert, Arizona. At right, Candi's son, Ch. Desert Knight O'Candida, sired by Am. & Mex. Ch. The Hoof 'n Paw White Knight. Whelped 1/6/82, Desert Knight was bred by Dave and Marguerite Seibert and is owned by Terry and Michele Mumford.

At left, Ch. Anji Bound for Glori (Am. & Mex. Ch. The Hoof 'n Paw White Knight ex Edan's Cognac Frost Cinandre). Bred by Ann Wenstrom and owned by Linda Mueller, St. Louis. At right, Anja's Princess. Bred and owned by JoAnn Marineau.

Linda Mueller-Lashley of St. Louis joined the ranks of Samoyed fanciers in the mid-70s with a male that was assured to be show quality. Alas it was disqualified at its first show. Linda then determined to obtain a bitch that could be relied upon, and fortunately turned to the late Ann Wenstrom of Zion, Illinois. From Mrs. Wenstrom she obtained a pick of litter female that was to become Ch. Anja's Bound for Glori. Importantly, Mrs. Wenstrom spent hours explaining Samoyed structure, care and the required temperament to her—this is what every conscientious breeder should do—and asked Linda to pass on this same education and expertise to those who purchased puppies from her.

Eugene and Joanne Hilbelink of Oostburg, Wisconsin, cared a lot for Samoyeds. They began their Karalot Kennels in the '70s with a show puppy from Joyce and Louis Cain that became Ch. Samtara's Suga Dandi. Breeding their foundation bitch, Ch. Tsuilikagta's Moya to the Wayne Nonhoffs' Ch. Moonlighter's Hallmark they produced the bitch, Ch. Karalot's Kit N'Kaboodle.

Tim Malueg cared a lot, too, and showed more. In the early '80s he began as the owner of a Kit puppy dog. The dog (soon to be Am., Can. & Bda. Ch. Karalot's Jak Frost O'Westwind) rocketed to fame when as an Open dog he went all the way to Best in Show under Kurt Mueller. Jak's half sister Mindy (Ch. Frosty Acres Noel to Westwind) finished in three months, with wins that included a Group. Both were sired by Ch. Karalot's Hotshot of Windsong.

Malueg boasts a litter, sired by Am. & Can. Ch. Windsong's Yankee Doodle Dandi out of Ch. Karalot's Katy-Did of Westwind, all of which became champions before the age of two: Ch. Westwind's Too Hot to Handle, Ch. Karalot's Jedi Master and Ch. Westwind's Wish Upon A Star. The last named was also High in Trial at the Chicagoland's first Specialty in June, 1984 and again at the SCA National in Denver in September, 1984, with all obedience scores over 197!

Living close to Canada, Tim Malueg has sold puppies there and frequently shows over the border. Jak Frost has three Best in Show sons in Canada. Although devastated by the early untimely death of Jak Frost, Malueg and Buagniet carry on with his son, Ch. Windsong's Jackpot O'Pomirish.

Our 50th State, Hawaii, which has had pure-bred dog fanciers for over five decades, has added the Samoyed in respectable numbers in the past ten years, even though not managing to develop a specialty club for the breed.

We group their breeders together here as they are separated by problems no other Samoyed breeder faces. They not only have 2500 miles of water between us, but they have a four months state-imposed quarantine on the importation of animals. While the quarantine kennels do not prevent

124

Am. Can. & Bda. Ch. Karalot's Jak Frost O'Westwind with owner Tim Malueg. (By Ch. Karalot's Hotshot of Windsong ex Ch. Karalot's Kit 'n Kaboodle.) Breeders: Eugene and Joanne Hilbelink. Jak Frost was a Best in Show winner from the classes. Tim says, "Since Jak was my first show dog, I wanted to do it myself. We made all the mistakes together." Jak Frost tragically died an early accidental death.

Ch. Frostyacres Noel of Westwind pictured finishing at 14 months with win of WB, BOW and BOB over 5 Specials and on to win the Group at Winnegamie DC, 1981, under judge Joe Gregory. Owner, Tim Malueg, Wisconsin.

125

the socialization of dogs, it does make it difficult. It is possible for the owners to visit and train their new imports each day, but it does take much time and effort.

Another facet to the selection and importation of dogs is the fact that animals from New Zealand, Australia, England or any other quarantine country are admitted without the four months at the State kennels.

Shiroi Samoyeds, Clifford and Amy Sakata, began in 1976 with Ch. Orion's Tara of Kubla Khan from Mrs. Pat Morehouse of California. Tara won her championship title in four consecutive shows. This is an unusual feat when you realize that there are only four shows per year on the Island of Oahu where they live.

Tara's son, Shiroi Shogun is on the large side, at 25″ and about 70 lbs. Sata was sired by Ch. Pinehill's Prince Kuragin who was a consistent winner in Hawaii and was the first Best in Show Sammy in Hawaii. Tara's son by Kimchatka Sun Seeker, Shirio Shimakaze Sunski was born 3-3-82, a homebred.

Clifford and Amy Sakata have two recent imports with English bloodlines from New Zealand. They are Kimchatka Sun Seeker and Kimchatka Anatole. Sun Seeker is predominantly Novaskaya bloodlines and Skye is more of the White Wisp lines from England. Mrs. Eli Maitland of the Kimchatka Kennels of Paeroa, New Zealand was their breeder and exporter to the Sakata's. At the Windward DF show in 1984 they finished a new champion—Kimchatka Anatole (by Whitewisp Arrogance ex Novaskaya Tsarina Lafay).

Janice Y. Lau of Oahu, Jahara Samoyeds, had a first dog with Australian and American background. Dukee, registered as Pride N' Joy of Hawaii was 20″, small and compact. His sire was from Australia and his dam descended from Ch. Lulhaven's Snow Mist Ensign and Ch. Joli Tsinuk. Janice turned to a close friend, Ted Awaya, for advice about Samoyeds from the mainland. Ted had been active in the breed and especially involved with training dogs for the deaf and obedience as well as show dogs. (Ted is one of the few Sam exhibitors who is also an obedience judge.) He told Janice of the Ice Way's dogs he had seen at shows. Seven months later Janice obtained Ice Way's Hawaiian Charger from Bobbie Smith. Charger descends from a line-breeding of Int'l. Ch. Snowline's Joli Shashan, C.D.X. One year later Jahara Samoyeds obtained Ice Way's Tropical Delight, sired by Ch. Ice Way's Ice Breaker, and Abakan Maggie Whitehair who is from Ch. Valadimir of Elmfield, bred by Darlu Littledeer of Conconully, Washington. Deedee is co-owned with Ronald Fujihara.

On Oahu also are Pat and Raymond Gibo with their Rain Country Sams called De Gibo Gang. Karl Miyamoto and Barbara Yamasaki co-own a lovely bitch, Sunsan's Kona Kandi O'Rickshaw, sired by their special, Ch. Rickshaw's Top Ace of Sunsan. Barbara Yamasaki previously was a member in Northern California Sam Fanciers.

Ch. Pinehill's Prince Kuragin (Ch. Pinehill's Lord Chattarcy ex Ch. Pinehill's Real Fancy) was brought to Hawaii at end of 1976 by JoAnn Tenorio. Harry Kim became co-owner with JoAnn and Harvey Yamashita was the handler. "Toley" became the first Samoyed to go BIS in Hawaii, top Working Dog (and No. 2 all-breeds) in Hawaii, and No. 6 Samoyed in the nation. During his short time in the islands, he also added several Group placements.

Ch. Orion's Tara of Kubla Khan. The "alpha Sam" at Clifford and Amy Sarata's Shiroi Samoyeds in Honolulu. By Ch. Orion's Thuban of Sir Mishka ex Ch. Orion's Agena of Tsar-Khan.

Shiroi's Sabrina of Magic Isle, daughter of Ch. Pinehill's Prince Kuragin. Owners, Harry and Carol Kim, Alea, Hawaii.

Shiroi Shogan Satara, owned by Clifford and Amy Sarata, Honolulu.

127

Ch. Ivan Belaya of Taymylyr, C.D., wh. 12/26/66, by Ch. Kazan of Kentwood ex Ch. Trina of Taymylyr. Bred by Tom and Magie Tuttle and owned and handled by John and Carol Chittum. Ivan is linebred behind Ch. Quicksilver's Razz Ma Tazz on both sire and dam's side.

Ch. Lynthea's J.C. Whelped 11/23/73, by Ch. Kondako's Dancing Bear ex Ch. Southern Star of Lynthea. Double grand-sire of Tazz's dam. Bred and owned by Jim and Marian Osborn.
Photo, Jim Osborn

Ch. Southern Star of Lynthea. Whelped 10/10/70, by Ch. Ivan Belaya of Taymylyr, C.D., ex White Tundra's Victoria. Bred and owned by Jim and Marian Osborn.
Photo, Jim Osborn

Ch. Lynthea's Kimba. By Ch. Ice Way's Ice Breaker ex Lynthea's Miss Conduct. Breeders: Jim and Marian Osborn. Owner: Teena Deatherage (Crizta Kennels).

Now, in the 1980s, Ch. Quicksilver's Razz Ma Tazz has completely rewritten the record book.

In December 1984, Tazz's record (at only 3 years of age!) includes:

54 Bests in Show, all breeds, under 51 different judges.

202 Group placements, of which 141 were Firsts.

232 Bests of Breed.

Best of Breed at the Samoyed Club of America Specialties, 1983 and 1984.

No. 1 Working Dog (all systems) 1983 and 1984. (No. 1 Samoyed, of course.)

No. 2 Dog all breeds for 1983. No. 3 Dog all breeds for 1984.

Quaker Oats Award for Working Group: 1983 and 1984.

Ch. Quicksilver's Razz Ma Tazz, or "Tazz" as he is popularly known, was whelped August 5, 1981. He is by Ch. Kolinka Quilted Bear ("Hoss") ex Ch. Quicksilver's Lucky Starr, and was bred by Danny and Chris Middleton, Quicksilver Samoyeds, Houston, Texas. The Middletons co-own Tazz with the owners of his sire, Eugene and Joyce Curtis, and he has been handled by Roy Murray.

The universal beauty of "Tazz" is that almost everyone has a "piece of Tazz."

In 1968 Jim and Marian Osborn, Lynthea Samoyeds, entered the ranks of the Samoyed with the purchase of the puppy bitch White Tundra's Miss Mitzi. The Osborns immediately became serious students of the breed and were enthusiastically exhibiting, and planning for future breedings, when Mitzi turned up dysplastic. After serious thinking, the Osborns decided to continue in the fancy and obtained a young adult, White Tundra's Victoria, already X-rayed clear of dysplasia. Vicki thus was their foundation bitch and a fine producer.

The Osborns drew up a breeding plan which expressed the objectives and general philosophy they wanted to follow. More than fifteen years later, they have found no reason to change that original plan. The ideas were fairly simple and certainly not unique. Overall soundness was established as first priority, but each dog was to be evaluated in total. "The whole dog is what counts." They believe in linebreeding, not focusing on any one dog but rather concentrating on a selected group of animals who complement each other in virtues. Linebreed, but never double on a fault, is their golden rule.

White Tundra's Victoria was tightly linebred to Ch. Yurok of Whitecliff. The Osborns' pedigree research had revealed to them that Yurok had produced best in combination with Helene Spathold's Drayalene bitches, especially Ch. Silver Crest's Sikandi. The first stud chosen for Vicki was the young Ch. Ivan Belaya of Taymylyr, C.D., owned by John and Carol Chittum.

From Vicki's first litter by Ivan came Ch. Winterdawn Melody, C.D., who went to Vic and Angie Monteleon of San Diego. Another fine bitch in the litter was Ch. Southern Star of Lynthea, who became the focal point of their breeding plans. As a special, Star was rarely defeated in her sex. In 1979, at 8½ years of age, Star gave the Osborns one of their most satisfying moments by winning Veterans class and Best Opposite Sex at the San Diego Specialty. Her double grandson, Ch. Lynthea's Joshua of Wakan, owned by T. and M. Chavez, was Best of Breed under breeder-judge Madelin Druse.

Star's first breeding was to the Chittums' Ch. Belaya Tony Taiga, C.D., which was a linebreeding to Ch. White Way's Juliette O'Snow Ridge, and thus to all of the original Drayalene dogs. This litter produced Ch. Monique of Lynthea, C.D., owned by Sue Fulps; Kivalina's Sir Ryan of Lynthea, C.D. who won the Sweepstakes at the 1973 SCA National Specialty for owner Ida Mae Huffman, and Ch. Miss Cheevious of Lynthea, also a Sweepstakes winner, owned by the Osborns.

Star's next two litters were sired by Ch. Kondako's Dancing Bear (Ruff), who combined Ch. Ivan Belaya of Taymylyr, C.D., and Ch. Nachalnik of Drayalene in the same pedigree. This proved to be a fine plan; it was also used by breeders Bob and Wanda Krauss, Tony and Maxine Chavez and Sandy Neel, and (redoubled) by Chris and Danny Middleton. Eugene and Joyce Curtis were using some of these lines but linebred on their males' side to Ch. Kazan of Kentwood.

It was the breeding of Star with Ruff that produced the Osborns' important sire, Ch. Lynthea's J.C. The double grandsire of Razz Ma Tazz's dam Ch. Quicksilver's Lucky Starr, J.C. stands as sire of 7 champions to date, including: Ch. Sitkin's Morningstar, owned by Dick and Chris Higley; Ch. Silvercreek's Puddin O'Sitkin, who went to Chris and Danny Middleton as well as Ch. Quicksilver's Red Baron and Ch. Quicksilver's Tiara O'Seamist (out of the bitch, Ch. St. Croix's Miss Hap), co-owned by the Archie Piels.

The Middletons and the Curtises did not just happen upon this great dog. They had had earlier champions, and both breeders had—for several years—a good idea of just what they wanted to produce, and thoughts on where to seek those qualities.

Danny and Chris Middleton became involved in Samoyeds in 1974. Their start was the frequent unhappy one, with two defective bitches. However, they persisted, and in 1976 acquired two fine young bitches. Both finished quickly, at 14 months of age: Ch. St. Croix's Miss Hap and Ch. Lynthea's Yellow Rose of Texas.

After a litter from each of them, the Middletons decided upon Miss Hap ("Missy") as their foundation brood bitch. As a show girl she won 6 Bests of Breed and 3 Group placements. They bred her to Ch. Lynthea's J.C., owned by Jim and Marian Osborn, and obtained Ch. Quicksilver's

Ch. St. Croix's Miss Hap, foundation brood bitch of Danny and Chris Middleton's kennel. By Ch. St. Croix's Batu Khan O'Sam O'Khan ex Tsarstartars Silver Kum Tuppence. Miss Hap is great grand-dam of Ch. Quicksilver's Razz Ma Tazz. Middleton's Quicksilver Kennels.

Ch. Quicksilver's Tiara O'Seamist (Ch. Lynthea's J.C. ex Ch. St. Croix's Miss Hap). Winner of 1978 SCA National Futurity and Best in Sweepstakes, SCLA 1978. Bred by Danny and Chris Middleton and co-owned by them with Archie and Anne Peil (Seamist).

Ch. Seamist's Lavender and Lace. By Yeva's Star Spangled Banner (owner, Bebe Hoxie) ex Ch. Quicksilver's Tiara O'Seamist. Owners, Archie and Anne Peil. She has it all—type, glamour, gait— we saw it at the 1984 National in Denver.
photo, Nugent

131

```
                                           Ch. Snow Ridge's Ruble of Tamarack
                          Ch. Los Laika's Belaya Traicer
                                           Ch. Belava Anja Padrushka
             Ch. Sassillie's Merlyn of Vicrian
                                           Ch. Snowline's Joli Sashan CDX
                          Candace Donella of Sherwood
                                           Ivan's Dame of the Frosty Mist
    Ch. K-Way's Omen of Destiny
                                           Ch. Kazan of Kentwood
                          Ch. Ivan Belaya of Taymylyr CD
                                           Ch. Trina of Taymylyr
             K-Way's Mint Julip of Vicrian
                                           Ch. Kondako's Sun Dancer
                          Ch. K-Way's Gay Gazelle CD
                                           Ch. Prairiewind's Shanna CD
Ch. Kolinka's Quilted Bear
                                           Ch. Starctic Storm
                          Ch. Kazan of Kentwood
                                           Winter Trail's Kazanna
             Ch. Ivan Belaya of Taymylyr CD
                                           Ch. Barceia's Shondi of Drayalene
                          Ch. Trina of Taymylyr
                                           Ellbur's Lady Ilsa
    Ch. Silvercreek's Rustic Charm
                                           Ch. Rokandi of Drayalene
                          Ch. Nachalnik of Drayalene
                                           Drayalene's Clarisse
             Ch. Silvercreek's Ko-Ko
                                           Ch. Sam O'Khan's Kubla Khan
                          Spartans Khan Tika
                                           Ch. Tei Juana Cayenne of Viburnum

                                           Ch. Nachalnik of Drayalene
                          Ch. Kondako's Dancing Bear
                                           Ch. Oniagra's Silver Bunny
             Ch. Lynthea's J C
                                           Ch. Ivan Belaya of Taymylyr CD
                          Ch. Southern Star of Lynthea
                                           White Tundra's Victoria
    Ch. Quicksilver's Red Baron
                                           Am Can Ch. Sam O'Khan's Muhuli Khan
                          Ch. St. Croix's Batu Khan O'Sam O'Khan
                                           Am Can Ch. Se Tahti of St. Croix
             Ch. St. Croix's Miss Hap
                                           Tsartars The Dander Patch
                          Tsartars Silver Kum Tuppence
                                           Kumtu Silke
Ch. Quicksilver's Lucky Starr
                                           Ch. Nachalnik of Drayalene
                          Ch. Kondako's Dancing Bear
                                           Ch. Oniagra's Silver Bunny
             Ch. Lynthea's J C
                                           Ch. Ivan Belaya of Taymylyr CD
                          Ch. Southern Star of Lynthea
                                           White Tundra's Victoria
    Ch. Silvercreek's Puddin O'Sitkin
                                           Ch. Sho-off's Czar of Whitecliff
                          Ch. Midnight Sun Kimba
                                           Nicola of Shondi
             Great Sitkin's Midnight Magic
                                           Klamath Sam of Sayan
                          Ch. Larissa of Taymylyr
                                           Ch. Holly of Taymylyr
```

Pedigree of CH. QUICKSILVER'S RAZZ MA TAZZ
Whelped August 5, 1981

132

Tiara O'Seamist, the 1978 Futurity winner and winner of the 1978 SCLA Sweepstakes. The Middletons co-own Tiara with Archie and Anne Peil of Seamist Samoyeds.

We met Danny Middleton (Chris was off grooming somewhere even then) at the Samoyed Club of America National Specialty in Portland, Oregon in 1978, where "Missy" was awarded Best Brood Bitch by judge Derek Rayne. Danny was shuffling around, talking dogs, asking questions and observing with studious eye every exhibit, the puppies in sweepstakes and the veterans and studs. (It was at this specialty that our Painter won both Stud Dog and Veteran class, and his daughter was BOS to the BOB.) Danny's questions made it clear that the Middletons had a vision—a goal of producing the best—and were studying pedigrees toward that goal.

And then they bred "Tazz"! After linebreeding to produce Ch. Quicksilver's Lucky Starr, the Middletons bred her to Ch. Kolinka's Quilted Bear, also linebred (see Tazz's pedigree herewith) and *voila*—not a surprise flyer, but a vibrant young dog who finished quickly and won his first Best in Show at 14 months, owner-handled. In January 1983, he was placed with professional handler Roy Murray and went on to his history-making record.

Tazz's sire, Ch. Kolinka's Quilted Bear ("Hoss") was bred and is owned by Eugene and Joyce Curtis and Marguerite Baird. He is by the Krausses' Ch. K-Way's Omen of Destiny ex Ch. Silvercreek's Rustic Charm. Marguerite Baird tells of Rustic Charm that, "She did everything I ever asked her to do. Rusty was first and foremost a friend. She asked for little and gave all she had. She was a producer, and as a show dog won top honors at the 1980 Samoyed Club of Houston Specialty." The Curtises and Marguerite bred Rusty to Omen to linebreed back through Ch. Ivan Belaya of Taymylyr to Ch. Kazan of Kentwood, who had sired three National Specialty winners and many Group winners.

Hoss has had quite a career on his own. In mid-1985, his record included 82 BOBs, 35 Group placements including 8 Firsts and 12 Seconds, 1 all-breed BIS, and 2 Bests in Specialty. He won the SCA Sweepstakes in 1980 and the SCLA Tournament in 1983. He topped the SCA Stud Dog class in 1983 and 1984, and won the Top Stud Dog Award in 1984.

Tazz's dam, Ch. Quicksilver's Lucky Starr, is by Ch. Quicksilver's Red Baron ex Ch. Silvercreek's Puddin O'Sitkin, who has two lines back to Kazan of Kentwood, one to Nachalnik, and one to Ch. Sho-Off's Czar of Whitecliff. Starr's grandsire on both sides of her pedigree is the Osborns' Ch. Lynthea's J.C.

To become a truly great winner and campaigner, a dog of any breed must have—in addition to over 90% of the breed standard in his physical attributes—the following:

The ability to show in all climates, on all surfaces, in all types of show ring set-ups, and despite all manner of noises and distractions. The desire to

The history maker Ch. Quicksilver's Razz Ma Tazz, pictured winning one of his early Bests in Show under author Dolly Ward. Handling, Roy Murray. As 1985 begins, we find Tazz being joined in the winning of Bests in Show both by his sire and his son (see facing page).

Above, Ch. Kolinka's Quilted Bear ("Hoss") winning Best in Show at Rio Pecos KC, April 1985, under judge Mrs. Betty Krause. "Hoss" is owned by Eugene and Joyce Curtis and Marguerite Baird, and handled by Mr. Curtis. His wins include 82 BOBs, 32 Group placements including 8 Firsts, 2 Specialty BOBs. Sweepstakes winner at the 1980 SCA Specialty, Award of Merit 1984 and 1985, he was SCA Top Stud for 1983, and is the sire of Ch. Quicksilver's Razz Ma Tazz.

At right, Ch. Kolinka Quicksilver Jazzman, a son of Ch. Quicksilver's Razz Ma Tazz out of Ch. Kolinka's Crystal Reflection. Bred by the Curtises and co-owned by them with Danny and Chris Middleton. Jazzman, handled by Chris Middleton, is also a 1985 BIS winner. A prime example of linebreeding, with his great grandfather on the sire's side (Ch. K-Way's Omen) being the same as the grandfather on his dam's side.

show with animation, never shy, never too aggressive. The ability to eat, drink and maintain all normal functions while traveling. Ring presence. These requisites are not spelled out in the Samoyed breed standard, or in any standard for that matter, but Ch. Quicksilver's Razz Ma Tazz possesses these qualities and 54 all-breed Bests in Show!

Another quality that Tazz had was a pair of dedicated owners and expert handling by Roy Murray, P.H.A. Tazz's owners were so supportive with patience, time and money that after six months of campaigning they formed a roofing company in Houston, Texas with three partners: Danny Middleton, Eugene Curtis, and Razz Ma Tazz. This effort to raise money became very successful when a hurricane moved through Houston, Texas in the fall of 1983. A Kal-Kan television advertising campaign with the Middletons and their dogs aided in the very costly endeavor of travel, entries and handling; thus one could even say that Tazz aided his own cause.

If there is any doubt as to the power of the written word, one need only look at the influence of the SCA *Bulletin*, the official organ of the club. Most of the membership of 1300 Samoyed enthusiasts join specifically to receive the *Bulletin*, having little interest in the business of running the club. This work is accomplished by the Board, who then keep the membership informed through the *Bulletin*. President of the SCA at this writing in 1984 is Ruth Mary Heckeroth, who has been re-elected for 1985. Kathryn Molineau is secretary.

Peggy M. Borcherding has served the SCA *Bulletin* for a full 18 years, and what a job she has done. Today the *Bulletin* stands among the ever-decreasing number of national club publications that are still totally subsidized by club members, and put together by non-professionals on a volunteer basis, and still able to gain recognition as a top quality publication.

The first issue of the SCA *Bulletin* to appear with Peggy's name on it as editor was March 1966. During the next seven years, both the club and its official publication increased in volume and in substance at a rate not experienced before or since. One indication of this expansion: The December 1966 issue of the *Bulletin* contained 50 pages whereas the December 1972 issue contained 217 pages.

Beginning in 1975, the *Bulletin* was entered in the annual writing competition (Best National Club Publication category) held by the Dog Writers Association of America. In 1975, it won Honorable Mention. In 1976, 1977 and 1979 it was judged Best National Club Bulletin. In 1978, it won the Certificate of Merit. In 1981, the DWAA eliminated the Honorable Mention and Certificate of Merit honors, substituting it with a Finalist Certificate, which the *Bulletin* was awarded in 1981 and 1983. In addition, two regular contributors to the *Bulletin* have been honored with individual awards—Ann Hogue and Bill Stanfield.

In 1976, the *Samoyed Quarterly* magazine began publication, providing additional coverage for the breed. However, the *Bulletin* remains the official voice. Managing editor and publisher of the Quarterly is Don Hoflin, based in Wheat Ridge, Colorado. The magazine continues to present the breed fancy with columns of information, and articles by some of the leaders of the breed, and includes Letters to the Editor, always available as a forum for more controversial topics. Oftimes, a different set of advertisers choose the SQ, as it has become popularly known.

Other pen exercises spout spasmodically from the independent clubs. This might be a small newsletter, usually without the benefit of pictures or advertisers, designed to inform the Samoyed fancy of matches and shows that are planned, announcing successful wins of their members, or noting medical problems or articles of strong local interest.

Mrs. Frank ("Gini") Addamo serves as the liaison between the Samoyed Club of America and independent clubs throughout the United States and other parts of the world. She writes a news column in the SCA official *Bulletin* covering world-wide club activities. Her address is: Gini Addamo, 3933 Coronado Circle, Newbury Park, California 91320.

The ups and downs of Samoyed registrations have pretty much followed that for purebred dogs as a whole over the years since 1970. The tremendous growth that took place in the 1960s continued into the 1970s, reaching a peak by the middle of the decade.

The registration total for 1970 was 6,129 Samoyeds, ranking 34th among all breeds. By 1974, it had climbed to 10,203—an all-time high—and the breed ranked 29th. More than 10,000 Samoyeds were registered for three consecutive years, 1974, 1975 and 1976.

The following table records the totals over recent years. The Samoyed holds position as 29th among all breeds in registrations.

1907—1	1970—6,129	1980—8,430
1920—13	1975—10,055	1981—8,307
1940—146	1976—10,147	1982—7,658
1950—660	1977—9,640	1983—7,918
1955—1,066	1978—9,222	1984—8,032
1960—1,249	1979—8,653	

Now we meet the challenge. For all professed breeders, would-be breeders, buyers of show puppies, the challenge is to come up with the next white-water Sammy-Yed (see Page 15) to excite the river—and the spectators.

Am. & Can. Ch. Moonlighter's Ima Bark Star, outstanding winner and sire. Winner of Best in Show and a record 5 Specialties, and Top Producing Stud of 1979 (at 5 years of age). Breeder-owner-handlers, Wayne and Jeanne Nonhof, Moonlighter Samoyeds, Waldo, Wisconsin.

5

Background of the Samoyed Standard

$\mathbf{A}$N EXPLANATION of the whys and wherefores of the breed standards is due the reader who is new to the purebred dog sport.

For each of the 129 breeds recognized by the American Kennel Club, there is an officially approved standard in accordance with which the breed is judged at the shows. The American Kennel Club does not write these standards. They have been propounded and formulated by the parent clubs of the breeds, or adopted by thee parent clubs from standards of other countries.

Obviously, much research and discussion has been required in each case to construct a description of the breed upon which a large majority of the parent club, breeders and owners can agree. In other countries, each breed club does its own policing, and changes in the standards can be effected easier. In the United States, however, after winning the approval of a majority of the parent club (which must be a member club of the American Kennel Club), proposals for change are then submitted to the Board of Directors of the AKC. If the proposal is tentatively approved, it is published in *Pure-Bred Dogs/American Kennel Gazette*, the AKC's official magazine, to bring it to the attention of any owners or breeders who were not aware of the intended revision. After an ample period of time, the proposal is again presented to the AKC Board of Directors for approval.

There are few breed standards which can claim the completeness of the one used to measure and evaluate the Samoyed. As we shall see, only a few changes have been made, and the dog described in the American standard of today could well be the expedition dog that modeled the first standards.

There have certainly been no changes in structure, coat, or disposition. As in his native habitat, the Samoyed remains a friend of man, a hunter, a protector, a herder, a beast of burden, and a draft animal.

The question of the use of the Samoyed has long been a matter of controversy. Is it a herd dog? Is it a sledge dog? Is it a guard dog?

It may be said generally that all work dogs were originally hunting dogs. Certainly this is true of the remaining breeds which are still in their native form, and not reshaped by man. Our research shows that the true Samoyed dog was a hunter for his master. It was not possible for nature to create him as strictly a herd dog. The animals to be herded in his native land were the reindeer, but they did not live in the deep snow country because of the lack of forage and moss. And certainly the Samoyed was not designed as a sled dog by Mother Nature. While his natural attributes lend themselves to draft work, the Samoyed was put to this use by man, and not by birth. When exploration was the "in" thing, the northern dog, used to the climate and lack of food, met a need for the explorers, who lacked other means to conquer the frozen lands.

Early Samoyed breeders met with great resistance to breed popularity when people admiring the "white teddy bear" puppies discovered that they were dogs that had been used for sled work in the arctic lands, and falsely publicized them as "fierce and savage beasts descended from wolves." To counter this reputation, many original breeders felt that the herd dog aspect was the one to foster, as who would ever identify a Collie tending his flock, and nuzzling a lamb, as a "fierce beast"?

There have been many other breeders who have just as loudly proclaimed their Samoyeds' abilities as draft dogs. In the early days in England, even the Kilburn-Scotts trained their dogs as sled dogs until the English laws prohibited it. The sled dog activities were carried on in America and Canada by the majority of early breeders and large kennels. The Reids (Norka Kennels), the Romers (Yurak Kennels), the Seeleys and the Pinkhams all worked their dogs in harness in the early twenties and thirties, and thus bred for sledding abilities. The kennels of Ernie Barbeau, Harold Haas, and Agnes Mason continued to breed for sled work in the thirties and forties. In the forties and fifties, breeders such as the Weirs and Gleasons in the Northwest, the Ralph Wards and the Seekins in New York, Juliet Goodrich and Harold Danks in the Midwest, and the Wards, Witchers, Van Sickles, Burrs, Kepers, Allens, Bristols, King, Goldwater, Tom Witt, and Breckenridge in the West, all trained Samoyed sled teams— leading to the birth of the Organization of Working Samoyeds.

Appreciating this background, a standard was written to include all of the above-mentioned qualities except that of hunting. Mr. Kilburn-Scott cited the Samoyed's ability as a herder and sled dog in his first standard description in 1910, and this description of points has been little changed since. Size is the usual point of difference among breeders and countries, *but isn't size a question in many breeds?*

The Samoyed standard serves the purpose of maintaining a natural, original type of animal. It is not a created breed. Its characteristics have been

140

developed over centuries of living with simple nomadic peoples who had no outside contact with other tribes, and thus no interbreeding of their dogs with others from other areas. The Samoyed was one of the family; he provided an extension of the master's hands and feet. His disposition had to fit into their communal society. His character is as splendid and pure as his shades of snowy white coat.

The Early Standard

Ernest Kilburn-Scott, responsible for so much of the beginnings of the Samoyed in the Western world, formulated a first standard for the breed in the early 1900s. This standard was quite closely followed when the official English standard was adopted in 1909 and 1911 with the formation of the first Samoyed associations in England.

The standard as formulated by Mr. Scott read:

Colour—Pure white; with slight lemon markings; brown and white; black and white. The pure white dogs come from the farthest north, and are most typical of the breed.

Expression—Thoughtful and remarkably pretty in face; fighting instincts strongly pronounced when aroused.

Intelligence—Unusual intelligence, as shown by the many purposes for which dogs are used by the Samoyede people and the ease with which they can be taught tricks.

Size and Weight—Dogs 19 to 21½ inches at the shoulders; bitches 18 to 19½ inches at the shoulders; weight about 40 lbs.

Head—Powerful-looking head, wedge-shaped, but not foxy. Wide and flat between ears, gradually tapering to eyes; stop not too pronounced; absolutely clean muzzle, not too long, with no lippiness; strong jaws and level teeth. The nose may be either black or flesh-coloured.

Eyes—Very expressive and human-like, sparkling when excited; set obliquely and well apart. Eyes should be dark for preference, but other colours are admissible.

Ears—Pricked, set wide apart, and freely movable; set slightly back in contradistinction to the ears of the Eskimo and Chow-Chow, which are forward; shape triangular, and not too large; tip slightly rounded.

Body—Body shapely, but not cobby, with straight back; muscular, with deep ribs; chest wide and deep, showing great lung power; straight front and strong neck.

Legs—Good bone, muscular and not too long; thighs well feathered; forelegs straight; hindlegs sinewy, and set for speed.

Feet—Long, and slightly spread out to get good grip; toes arched and well together; soles hairy and well padded to give grip and protection from ice and snow.

Brush—Long, with profuse spreading hair; carried over back or side when on the alert or showing pleasure; when at rest, dropped down, with slight upward curve at end.

Coat—Long and thick standing well out all over body, especially along back; free from curl; undercoat very soft and wooly; large, bristling ruff; hair on head and ears short and very smooth.

The standard was little changed through the years. There were occasional efforts to expand or change it, such as in 1948 when an attempt was made to require that the coloration of the nose and pigmentation be black, thereby eliminating all throwbacks to the original dogs, which had had light and liver points in many cases. In 1900, Major F. G. Jackson had proposed that "the typical Samoyede should be pure white and have a flesh-coloured nose." In formulating the standard, Kilburn-Scott had not gone as far as that, for they had many good dogs with a little lemon color about the ears, and with black noses. Actually, the black nose and dark eyes add greatly to the expression, making some of the faces of the dogs almost human-like.

It is interesting to see how closely the current English standard, which follows, has evolved from the original Kilburn-Scott standard.

Current English Standard for the Samoyed:

Characteristics: The Samoyed is intelligent, alert, full of action, but above all displaying affection towards all mankind.

General Appearance: The Samoyed being essentially a working dog should be strong and active and graceful, and as his work lies in cold climates, his coat should be heavy and weather-resisting. He should not be too long in back, as a weak back would make him practically useless for his legitimate work, but at the same time a cobby body such as the Chow's would also place him at a great disadvantage as a draught dog. Breeders should aim for the happy medium, viz, a body not long, but muscular, allowing liberty, with a deep chest and well sprung ribs, strong neck proudly arched, straight front and exceptionally strong loins. Both dogs and bitches should give the appearance of being capable of great endurance, but should be free from coarseness. A full grown dog should stand about 21 inches at the shoulder. On account of the depth of chest required, the legs should be moderately long, a very short-legged dog is to be deprecated. Hindquarters should be particularly well-developed, stifles well angulated, and any suggestion of unsound stifles or cowhocks severely penalized.

Head and Skull: Head powerful and wedge-shaped with a broad, flat skull, muzzle of medium length, a tapering foreface not too sharply defined. Lips black. Hair short and smooth before the ears. Nose black for preference, but may be brown or flesh-coloured. Strong jaws.

Eyes: Almond shaped, medium to dark brown in colour, set well apart with alert and intelligent expression. Eyerims should be black and unbroken.

Ears: Thick, not too long and slightly rounded at the tips, set well apart and well covered inside with hair. The ears should be fully erect in the grown dog.

Mouth: Upper teeth just overlap the underteeth in a scissor bite.

Neck: Proudly arched.

Forequarters: Legs straight and muscular with good bone.

Body: Back medium in length, broad and very muscular. Chest broad and deep, ribs well sprung, giving plenty of heart and lung room.

Hindquarters: Very muscular, stifles well angulated; cow hocks or straight stifles very objectionable.

Feet: Long, flattish and slightly spread out. Soles well cushioned with hair.

142

Gait: Should move freely with a strong agile drive, showing power and elegance.

Tail: Long and profuse, carried over the back when alert, sometimes drooped when at rest.

Coat: The body should be well-covered with a thick, close, soft and short undercoat; with harsh hair growing through it, forming the outer coat, which should stand straight away from the body and be free from curl.

Colour: Pure white, white and biscuit; cream.

Weight and Size: Dogs, 20-22 inches at the shoulder.
                  Bitches: 18-20 inches at the shoulder.
                  Weight in proportion to size.

Faults: Big ears with little feathering. Drop ears. Narrow width between ears. Long foreface. Blue or very light eyes. A bull neck. A long body. A soft coat. A wavy coat. Absence of undercoat. Slack tail carriage. Should be carried well over the back, though it may drop when the dog is at rest. Absence of feathering. Round cat-like feet. Black or black spots. Severe unprovoked aggressiveness. Any sign of unsound movement.

(**Note:** Male animals should have two apparently normal testicles fully descended into the scrotum.)

The Americans, Canadians and Australians all originally adopted the English standard, with minor variations. As of today, however, only the Australians maintain the exact same standard as the English.

Revision of the American Standard

In 1945, there had been constant complaining about poor judging of Samoyeds throughout the United States. It was felt that the standard was inadequate. Many judges had expressed their thoughts that the standard was in parts unwieldy, and in other parts too flexible for uniform judging.

As the breed was increasing in numbers, and being exhibited in areas never before known, the parent club president, S. K. Ruick, appointed Mrs. Agnes Mason to be chairman of a Standard Committee, with purpose of revising the standard. The members were Helen Harris, Berta Ruick, Lucile Miller, Martha Humphriss and Louis Smirnow. Country-wide participation in local discussion groups aided the committee. The committee worked to form an illustrated standard, but the American Kennel Club advised that illustrations should be used as an aid rather than as part of the actual standard.

Comments, examples, measurements and photographs were exchanged across the country. In 1946, the size specifications were altered, with suggested heights for bitches raised from 18"-20" to 19"-21", and the dogs from 20"-22" to 21"-23½". This was done when over 50 champions were measured, and it was found that there were only four within the previously suggested heights.

In 1952, Mrs. Mason added the breeder-judges Robert Ward, Vera Lawrence, Joe E. Scott, C. H. Chamberlain, and Miles Vernon, and the breeders Gertrude Adams and B. P. Dawes to the Committee. Mrs. Mason, now president of the parent club, appointed Mrs. Adams to be Committee Chairman.

A re-opening of the issue of the height of bitches as suggested by the breed standard occurred in 1953. The problem was that the membership had voted by mail (133 yes to 25 no) to raise the height of bitches to 22" because there was a desire to have it theoretically possible to have some bitches and dogs of the same height. There is no overlapping in either the American or the English standard. Many breeders and judges believed that in natural growth, some are always the same size regardless of sex, quite like other breeds and animals.

Work toward the new standard continued. The committee prescribed percentages to be used in the new standard in an attempt to avoid indefinite phrases such as *moderately long,* or *medium,* or *shorter than.* Precise angles and degrees for measurement came from hundreds of measurements taken of actual dogs, and of many photographs of past celebrated dogs. The actual number of degrees used to set the lay-back of shoulders and angle of the stifle, for example, were based upon the average of many measurements.

A great deal of opposition was encountered by the committee in setting a description of the head. Many believed that if percentages were used, or if the muzzle were defined as big, medium or short, we might be "keying" to one particular strain or individual. The description of the muzzle in ratio to the skull was finally adopted, as it allows for variance in size as well as slight variances to fit the balance of the dog being judged. A description of the style and expression of the head creates perhaps the greatest divergence of opinion among breeders in all breeds. Each is much attached to his or her own "linebreeding," which stamps the slight variance in heads. No matter what, however, the head must conform to the characteristics of the breed, and with the overall balance of the dog.

The committee, after reading comments from all sections of the country, decided to drop the weight suggestions of the old standard. Weight is a variable, based upon condition and health, and since the standard explores soundness and movement in such detail, it was felt that correct substance should be recognizable to the breeder or judge.

Disqualifications were held to a minimum by desire of both the Standard Committee of the Samoyed Club, and of the American Kennel Club. It was felt that a fault that would properly disqualify an animal should be quite objective, quite disabling, quite permanent, and quite foreign to the breed.

Great variance in size is not foreign to any breed, although objectionable to many breeders. It was decided to state in the standard that penalties should be assessed to the extent to which the dog appears to be over or under-size, according to suggested heights.

The greatest dissent came over disposition. This has always been the greatest asset of the breed. Even the earliest accounts of the explorers

144

mentioned how they could detect the Bjelkiers from the other dogs in the dark because they would be poking and nuzzling for attention and affection. They would be the dogs first upon the sleeping bags, seeking human companionship. The dogs were able to run in groups. These qualities endeared the breed to the early breeders, and there are many who still prize this trait above all others in the breed. However, to disqualify permanently for misbehavior in the ring has a note of finality about it that is hard to accept, based as it is on a brief moment's determination. Really, it is up to the breeder to eliminate this fault in training, and in choosing the sire and dam of a litter. A severe penalty is assessed in the ring for such behavior, and should prevent such animals from winning and thus being desired as breeding stock.

The new standard was approved by the American Kennel Club in February, 1957. It had thus required eleven years of work and research and writing to reach an agreement within the parent club for this revision.

One further change was made in 1963. The point scale to assess a value for each area of the standard met with great resistance by both the club members and the American Kennel Club. It was felt by some members that this created a system whereby some would ignore the whole dog because it was found to be lacking in one area. In other words, the point scale promotes "fault judging" rather than assessing the whole value of the dog upon his good qualities and nearness to the standard. After much discussion, upon the recommendation of the Standard Committee, confirmed by a vote of the membership of the Samoyed Club of America, and with the approval of the Board of Directors of the American Kennel Club, the entire point scale was dropped in 1963.

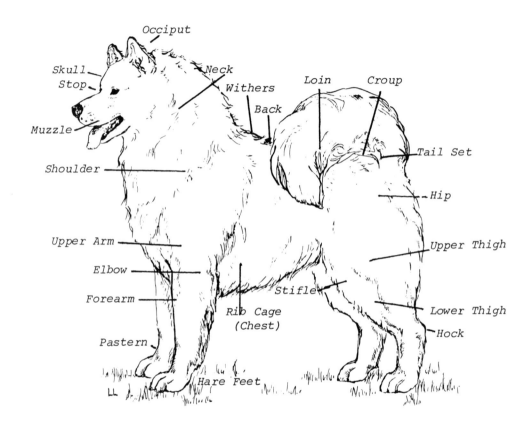

PARTS OF THE DOG

6

Official AKC Standard for the Samoyed

As submitted by the Samoyed Club of America, and approved by the American Kennel Club, April 9, 1963.

GENERAL CONFORMATION

(a) **General appearance.** The Samoyed, being essentially a working dog, should present a picture of beauty, alertness and strength, with agility, dignity and grace. As his work lies in cold climates, his coat should be heavy and weather resistant, well-groomed, and of good quality rather than quantity. The male carries more of a "ruff" than the female. He should not be long in back as a weak back would make him practically useless for his legitimate work, but at the same time, a close-coupled body would also place him at a great disadvantage as a draft dog. Breeders should aim for the happy medium, a body not long but muscular, allowing liberty, with a deep chest and well-sprung ribs, strong neck, straight front and especially strong loins. Males should be masculine in appearance and deportment without unwarranted aggressiveness; bitches feminine without weakness of structure or apparent softness of temperament. Bitches may be slightly longer in back than males. They should both give the appearance of being capable of great endurance but be free from coarseness. Because of the depth of chest required, the legs should be moderately long. A very short-legged dog is to be deprecated. Hindquarters should be particularly well-developed, stifles well-bent and any suggestion of unsound stifles or cowhocks severely penalized.

General appearance should include movement and general conformation, indicating balance and good substance.

(b) Substance. Substance is that sufficiency of bone and muscle which rounds out a balance with the frame. The bone is heavier than would be expected in a dog of this size but not so massive as to prevent the speed and agility most desirable in a Samoyed. In all builds, bone should be in proportion to body size. The Samoyed should never be so heavy as to appear clumsy nor so light as to appear racy. The weight should be in proportion to the height.

(c) Height. Males, 21 to 23½ inches; Females, 19 to 21 inches at the withers. An oversized or undersized Samoyed is to be penalized according to the extent of the deviation.

(d) Coat. (Texture and Condition). The Samoyed is a double-coated dog. The body should be well-covered with an undercoat of soft, short, thick close wool with longer and harsh hair growing through it to form the outer coat, which stands straight out from the body and should be free from curl. The coat should form a ruff around the neck and shoulders, framing the head (more on males than on females). Quality of coat should be weather resistant and considered more than quantity. A droopy coat is undesirable. The coat should glisten with a silver sheen. The female does not usually carry as long a coat as most males and it is softer in texture.

(e) Color. Samoyeds should be pure white, white and biscuit, cream, or all biscuit. Any other colors disqualify.

MOVEMENT

(a) Gait. The Samoyed should trot, not pace. He should move with a quick agile stride that is well-timed. The gait should be free, balanced and vigorous, with good reach in the forequarters and good driving power in the hindquarters. When trotting, there should be a strong rear action drive. Moving at a slow walk or trot, they will not single track, but as speed increases, the legs gradually angle inward until the pads are finally falling on a line directly under the longitudinal center of the body. As the pad marks converge the forelegs and hind legs are carried straight forward in traveling, the stifles not turned in nor out. The back should remain strong, firm and level. A choppy or stilted gait should be penalized.

(b) Rear End. Upper thighs should be well-developed. Stifles well-bent—approximately 45 degrees to the ground. Hocks should be well-developed, sharply defined and set at approximately 30 percent of hip height. The hind legs should be parallel when viewed from the rear in a natural stance, strong, well-developed, turning neither in nor out. Straight stifles are objectionable. Double-jointedness or cowhocks are a fault. Cowhocks should only be determined if the dog has had an opportunity to move properly.

(c) Front End. Legs should be parallel and straight to the pasterns. The pasterns should be strong, sturdy and straight, but flexible with some spring for proper let-down of feet. Because of depth of chest, legs should be

148

moderately long. Length of leg from the ground to the elbow should be approximately 55 percent of the total height at the withers—a very short-legged dog is to be deprecated.

Shoulders should be long and sloping, with a layback of 45 degrees and be firmly set. Out at the shoulders or out at the elbows should be penalized. The withers separation should be approximately 1-1½ inches.

(d) **Feet.** Large, long, flattish—a hare foot, slightly spread but not splayed; toes arched; pads thick and tough, with protective growth of hair between the toes. Feet should turn neither in nor out in a natural stance but may turn in slightly in the act of pulling. Turning out, pigeon-toed, round or cat-footed or splayed are faults. Feathers on feet are not too essential but are more profuse on females than on males.

HEAD

(a) **Conformation.** Skull is wedge-shaped, broad, slightly crowned, not round or apple-headed, and should form an equilateral triangle on lines between the inner base of the ears and the center point of the stop.

Muzzle—Muzzle of medium length and medium width, neither coarse nor snipy; should taper toward the nose and be in proportion to the size of the dog and the width of the skull. The muzzle must have depth.

Stop—Not too abrupt, nevertheless well defined.

Lips—Should be black for preference and slightly curved up at the corners of the mouth, giving the "Samoyed smile." Lip lines should not have the appearance of being coarse nor should the flews drop predominately at corners of the mouth.

Ears—Strong and thick, erect, triangular and slightly rounded at the tips; should not be large or pointed, nor should they be small and "bear-eared." Ears should conform to head size and the size of the dog; they should be set well apart but be within the border of the outer edge of the head; they should be mobile and well covered inside with hair; hair full and stand-off before the ears. Length of ear should be the same measurement as the distance from inner base of ear to outer corner of eye.

Eyes—Should be dark for preference; should be placed well apart and deep-set; almond shaped with lower lid slanting toward an imaginary point approximating the base of ears. Dark eye rims for preference. Round or protruding eyes penalized. Blue eyes disqualifying.

Nose—Black for preference but brown, liver, or Dudley nose not penalized. Color of nose sometimes changes with age and weather.

Jaws and teeth—Strong, well-set teeth, snugly overlapping with scissors bite. Undershot or overshot should be penalized.

(b) **Expression.** The expression, referred to as "Samoyed expression," is very important and is indicated by sparkle of the eyes, animation and lighting up of the face when alert or intent on anything. Expression is made up of a combination of eyes, ears and mouth. The ears should be erect when alert; the mouth should be slightly curved up at the corners to form the "Samoyed smile."

TORSO

(a) Neck. Strong, well-muscled, carried proudly erect, set on sloping shoulders to carry head with dignity when at attention. Neck should blend into shoulders with a graceful arch.

(b) Chest. Should be deep, with ribs well-sprung out from the spine and flattened at the sides to allow proper movement of the shoulders and freedom for the front legs. Should not be barrel-chested. Perfect depth of chest approximates the point of elbows, and the deepest part of the chest should be back of the forelegs—near the ninth rib. Heart and lung room are secured more by body depth than width.

(c) Loin and Back. The withers forms the highest part of the back. Loins strong and slightly arched. The back should be straight to the loin, medium in length, very muscular, and neither long nor short-coupled. The dog should be "just off square"—the length being approximately 5 percent more than the height. Females allowed to be slightly longer than males. The belly should be well-shaped and tightly muscled and with the rear of the thorax, should swing up in a pleasing curve (tuck-up). Croup must be full, slightly sloping, and must continue imperceptibly to the tail root.

TAIL

The tail should be moderately long with the tail bone terminating approximately at the hock when down. It should be profusely covered with long hair and carried forward over the back or side when alert, but sometimes dropped when at rest. It should not be high or low set and should be mobile and loose—not tight over the back. A double hook is a fault. A judge should see the tail over the back once when judging.

DISPOSITION

Intelligent, gentle, loyal, adaptable, alert, full of action, eager to serve, friendly but conservative, not distrustful or shy, not overly aggressive. Unprovoked aggressiveness to be severely penalized.

DISQUALIFICATIONS:

Any color other than pure white, cream, biscuit, or white and biscuit. Blue eyes.

7

Commentary on the Current AKC Standard

"General appearance" is an attempt to picture the dog as he evolved in his native habitat—a dog for hunting, herding and hauling—and the natural attributes which made him survive in that severe, barren, and cold climate. The Samoyed must be strongly built and *agile.*

The coat possesses density and quality to withstand not only weather and cold, but the formation of ice which would prevent movement and survival. The spiky stand-off guard hair keeps the snow and ice away from the undercoat. The white coloration, which is most natural to Northern Arctic animals, is for the conservation of warmth. Studies have shown that the make-up and color of the fur from Arctic animals prevents the conduction of heat from the body. Inexperienced people feel that such a thick coat must entail a lot of suffering in hot weather. Wrong! Mother Nature automatically substitutes a lighter overcoat every spring; a body covering like this is just as good an insulator to keep heat out in summer as to ward off cold in winter. It has been proved beyond a shadow of a doubt that the Samoyed, Arctic dog though he is, can withstand hot weather. You may see him in Africa, Puerto Rico, Southern United States, South America, and Japan.

The head described is the **typical wedge** of the wolf, the bear, the fox, the ermine, and the seal, which gives the powerful jaws and the ability of the teeth to rip and tear which a hunter must have. The eyes, through centuries of squinting in the bright Arctic sunlight, have the slightly slanting Mongolian look so necessary to survival. Note that the ponies taken on the Polar expeditions all suffered from snow blindness and became quite helpless.

The ears are extremely functional and movable to avoid freezing, and very heavily haired inside and out for protection. Do you know that there are no long-eared animals in the Arctic Regions? Long-eared dogs in cold weather have a tendency to form blood blisters in their ears, with subsequent freezing and gangrene.

"Expression" is the sum total of the expression created by the set of the eyes, the tilt of the ears, the size of the mouth, and the upward curve of the lip line. A Samoyed must have tight, close flews. The right expression has an intelligent, penetrating look, with a devilish and quizzical attitude which says to you, "Well what do we do now?" The Samoyed faces the world cheerfully, confidently, with a frank candor that is unmistakable. He returns your gaze squarely, honestly, and without trace of calculation. He has nothing to conceal.

The centuries-long association with humans, living in the huts and 'chooms,'' of the Samoyed people has created a disposition and expression unmatched by any other breed. The primitive harshness one might expect in both man and dog is subordinated to kindliness and friendship.

The dense undercoat is a vital part of the Samoyed make-up; but it is quite wrong to blame the lack of an undercoat for the lack of a stand-off outercoat. True, the perfect coat is both the under and outer coats, but when the outer coat is of a proper texture, it stands up without any aid from the undercoat even during the period of heavy shedding. It is a matter of texture, not length. The outercoat must be harsh to enable it to stand up. When you pat or dab the open palm of your hand flat on the guard hair, it should bend under pressure and spring back to the upright position immediately upon release. The hair should appear to protect the animal, like the spears of the porcupine, from the weather, dirt and snow, and wetness. The profuse coat does not lay down unless it is the improper texture. A flat lying coat is just about as poor a coat as a Samoyed can have. This type of coat is useless for the life which the Samoyed is born to lead and for the work it is supposed to do.

The proper coat on the Samoyed is the type which shakes free of water upon coming out of the lake, which does not permit snow and ice to pack into it and freeze, and which shakes free of dirt and mud when the dog dries and rolls in straw or grass. Quality of texture and type of coat are more important than quantity.

All details of body and leg structure listed in general appearance are for that all-purpose animal, **the hunter, the herder, the hauler.** These details give us a nimble yet sturdy dog that will not give up in the snow or long chases of game.

ACCEPTABLE HEAD
Broad flat forehead, stop well-defined, dark almond-shaped eye, thick ears, strong jaw with depth of muzzle, animation and a smile.

FAULTY HEAD
Apple-domed or peaked skull, large round eye, narrow skull, thin ears, weak jaw, sloppy flews, drop at corner of mouth.

153

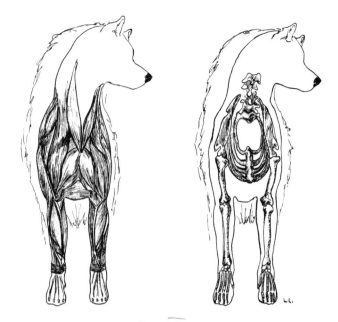

Correct front.

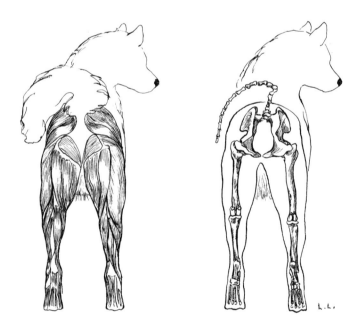

Correct rear.

154

The "3 H" Dog—Hunter, Herder, Hauler

The concept of **substance** is misunderstood in Samoyeds when individual dogs are praised for possessing massive bone. Substance goes with soundness and, in its broadest sense, indicates that the dog shall be so constructed as to be capable of doing his native job well. The Samoyed is only a fast sled dog when he is first a fast herder. Too many articles lead one to believe that the Samoyed is a massively boned dog. This great emphasis upon "good" and "heavy" bone emerged because of the fine-boned and weedy-type specimens exhibited in the early 1900s. Many of those owners obtained the idea that the bone on the Samoyed would be like that of an Eskimko or a Chow. Once Mrs. Kilburn-Scott said, "If a dog possesses unusual bone, he is write-off type." In working dogs, if you have a dog with too heavy bone, it is a dog that lacks speed, agility and grace to do his work as a herder, hunter, or sled dog.

Picture the Samoyed people hunting wild reindeer in Siberia. They build a corral with large wings of fences to guide the herds into the corral traps. Men and dogs spread out in a huge fan-like net and drive the reindeer into the trap. The reindeer are quite fast and nimble. The men and dogs are chasing them most of the day, and sometimes for several days. Think of the nimbleness and endurance that is required to run in the ice and snow. This certainly is no occupation for a Newfoundland or a Chow Chow.

Personally, from working dogs in teams, we know that the exceptionally heavy-boned dogs have actually passed out after several hours of intense work; likewise smaller dogs have given up and have been brought home on the sled. One would know better if one follows the accounts of the explorers and the dogs which survived their journeys best. Not the largest and not the smallest, but his 59 to 69 pound dogs were the last to be in harness. Strangely enough, in the sport of Greyhound racing at the tracks, rarely do you find a dog over 70 pounds or under 55 pounds. **It is not because larger and smaller do not exist, but because there is an optimum size for strength and speed.**

If our ideal Samoyed is to be graceful as well as beautiful, it must have sufficient body length to permit graceful movement. A compact body does not lend itself to good action, and using either males or females of this kind for breeding is to accentuate a fault of cobbiness.

"Torso" includes the neck, chest, loin, and back. We should begin with the neck and agree that, as we are describing neither a racer nor a draft animal, the neck should be moderately long. An animal, when he runs, uses the length of the neck to balance himself while at the gallop; therefore, a racing animal has an extremely long neck, while the draft animal has a short neck to consolidate strength at slower speeds. The Samoyed shall therefore have a proudly arched, moderately long neck, set for speed but not racy.

The definition of **chest** has caused much difficulty among owners,

The Samoyed bitch should be feminine without weakness of structure. Bitches may be slightly longer in back than males.

because the phrase "broad chest" has often appeared. Even in the new standard some misinterpretation occurs. One should not call the front of the dog his chest; this is his front or brisket. The chest rightly is at the lowest point between the front legs. The breadth is measured more by the spring in the rib cage. The barrel-chested effect is to be avoided to eliminate the comparison to purely draft animals. The approved standard is quite explicit and clear upon this point.

The **loin** and **back** are well described in the standard, but the important part they play in producing a proper topline could be expanded. The topline of the Samoyed is level except for the slight rise at the withers and slight slope at the croup. The full view of the topline may give the impression of quite a slope to the topline, but you will find that this is caused by the arch of the neck and the rounding out by the proper coat, which grows with a maned effect over the shoulders. There is a slight arch over the loin.

Description of the **tail** is excellent, but mention should be made of the disastrous effect upon the dogs in the Arctic which do not have the proper loose tail to protect themselves while sleeping. The explorers who docked their dogs found out that within three weeks their dogs had died of pneumonia. Tails too loose or too tightly curled are incorrect.

The description of **disposition** is fairly thorough in the standard. The unadvertised ability of the Samoyed to get along in groups in kennels and at shows benched without dividers was a standardized fact for over fifty years. No one thought much about this quality, it just happened. But unfor-

156

tunately, in some instances it does not happen now. We in America do not emphasize this strongly enough these days. It seems that which we most take for granted is the last to be missed.

Special features in the standard which must be observed while judging are: tail up and over the back at least once, moveable ears for protection, a topline which is neither too steep from front to rear, nor too high in the rear. The gait in action, never clumsy, must be a graceful, natural trot that indicates an eagerness to move. In other words, does he *want* to move?

One of the greatest values of the standard is that it provides a measure for evaluating your dog. Never evaluate your dog against another dog. The approved standard has been developed by many breeders of long experience, and approved by AKC. They based their observations upon the standards originally set down by men who knew the dogs under working conditions and the observations set down by explorers.

The Samoyed male dog should be masculine in appearance and deportment, without unwarranted aggressiveness and free from coarseness. Not square.

The Consideration of Size

Are the dogs larger or smaller now than they were in the past? Neither, for Fridjof Nansen listed his males as averaging 59 lbs. in working condition and his bitches at 50 lbs. Records show that Antarctic Buck was the tallest dog of the breed in 1909, and most of the descendants spring from him. He was reported by some at 21½ inches, and some at 22" measured at the shoulder, not at the withers. (In America, we measure at the withers—the highest point of the shoulder.) In 1925, the English Ch. Snow Crest was reported at 23 inches and 70 lbs. In 1930, English Champion Kara Sea was measured at 22.6 inches and 65 lbs. The English import Ch. Tobolsk measured at 23 inches and over 65 lbs. in 1922. At the same time, the English import Ch. Donerna's Barin was reported to be 22½ inches and 65 lbs. In 1948, Irish import Ch. Snowland Stara, the first champion in the British Isles after World War II, was 23½ inches and 68 lbs. In 1954, the imported Ch. Raff of Kobe was 23 inches tall and weighed over 90 lbs. before he was placed on a strict diet by the Powells of Alpine, Texas.

In the 1940s and 1950s, there were a few males at 21 inches and a fewer number at 24 and 25 inches. Catharine Quereaux, in America, stated:

> It is up to us as members and individuals who wish to keep the Samoyed a medium sized working dog type to know our standard and to impress it on our judges, and to impress upon them that a dog should win only in the degree in which it conforms to the standard. That variance in size is as much a defect as variance in other respects. *Smallness is a greater sin than largeness. For in the smaller dog, defects are more easily concealed than in the larger dog.* Anyone can measure from the floor to their own knee and knowing that measurement can thereby gauge size. Size must be considered in judging the breed or all that has been fought for in the breed will be lost.
>
> Further, we must impress upon our judges that the requirement of good bone does not mean massive bone. "Piano legs" as they are familiarly called have no place in our breed; the natural work of the Samoyed as sledgedog and reindeer shepherd must be considered. The Samoyed today is largely a pet, but must be judged for its fitness as a workdog, for the massive boned dog would do little in sled work, and the massive bone would be a great detriment in reindeer herding where fleetness is a requisite.

Miss Thomson-Glover wrote in 1930,

> With regard to breeding, owners are far from blameless; some have foolishly made a fetish of white coats and black points and let the more important points go hang. Others have inter-bred with no adequate reason beyond that it is more convenient, or cheaper. Now at long last, the novices of some years ago, are themselves bemoaning the shortage of fine bitches.
>
> Size is an unimportant factor compared with type and soundness. If an exhibit has balance, powerful easy movement, deep chest, well-sprung ribs, good front and hindquarters, coupled with a beautiful head, off-standing and weather resistant coat, and good feet, an inch more or less hardly counts. The

AVERAGE SAMOYED MEASUREMENTS

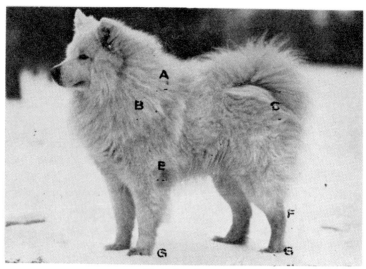

Ch. Dobrynia
Owned by the Very Rev. Msgr. Robert F. Keegan

The Sam is a herding, hauling, hunting work dog. He needs a heart-shaped body, with well-sprung ribs. Lowest point of chest approximates elbow. The measurements here are averages from the detailed measurements of more than 50 champions of the breed. Even the known details of the great champion of over 50 years ago, Ch. Kara Sea, are included. Showing his similarity to dogs of today, Kara Sea's length of leg from elbow to ground (E-G) was 55% of his height at the withers (22.6").

Height at Withers (A-C)	19"	20"	21"	22"	23"	24"
Length (B-C)— Shoulder point to hip point	20.25	21.50	22.50	23.	24.25	25.
Height at rear	19.25	19.75	20.75	22.	22.50	23.50
Barrel or circumference	24.50	26.	26.75	28.	28.50	29.
Pastern or ankle	3.50	3.75	4.	4.25	4.62	5.25
Depth of chest	8.50	9.	9.25	9.50	10.25	10.75
Length of ear	3.10	3.25	3.375	3.50	3.87	4.
Distance between eyes	1.87	2.	2.	2.12	2.25	2.25
Length of head (occiput to tip of nose)	8.	8.12	8.37	8.50	9.	9.50
Length of muzzle	3.25	3.37	3.50	3.87	3.90	4.125
Hock to ground (F-G)	5.75	6.	6.25	6.50	6.75	7.
Leg Length (E-G) (elbow to ground)	10.45	11.	11.55	12.10	12.65	13.20

Short coat, or new phase of coat growth.

Faulty coat—droopy, not standing off, poor quality.

owner of a small dog with type but perhaps a narrow chest, too light bone, indifferent shoulders and pasterns and softish coat, is apt to complain of great clumsy creatures above the standard and quite wrongly utterly ignoring their being far nearer the standard in essentials than their own exhibits. Owners of big dogs are prone to view the wins of small fry with surprised contempt, even if their own are leggy, plain, and shelly in body. Whatever comes nearest the standard at all points, whether big or small or medium, is the one who should win.

These opinions, no matter how varied, return us to the matter at hand. How do our present-day Samoyeds measure up to the Standard? All breeders have experienced what happens when we lose sight of the original purpose of the breed and over-emphasize something else. When size goes beyond nature's standard or the animal is bred smaller, many difficulties arise. Proportion of boning, soundness, disposition, and the like are affected. As a result, the dog can no longer do the job intended by nature.

Large Sams may be quick and agile. Small Sams may be clumsy and slow. Or, the reverse may be true. The key to correctness is AGILITY.

This is a Sammy smile! As modeled by Ch. Blue Sky's Breaking Away, bred and owned by Dr. P.J. and Elizabeth Lockman Hooyman.

8

Judging the Samoyed

The Arctic Breeds—
Differences and Similarities

(This excerpt is adapted from an article written by the authors, which appeared in Kennel Review, *October 1981. It is included here by special permission.)*

Both alphabetically and three dimensionally, we put the *Samoyed* exactly between the *Alaskan Malamute* and the *Siberian Husky*. All are distinctly individual Arctic breeds. Everyone has some pet peeve and ours is to have either judges or exhibitors subjectively or objectively classify the Samoyed as a fluffy, non-working or Fancy Dog. The Samoyed should be able to perform his legitimate work even if he does not have to work anymore. Function dictates form and so we should be able to assess the differences among these three Arctics as their functions are not the same and neither are their forms or gaits.

Yes indeed, the Samoyed is the medium (although the Siberian Husky talks medium and moderate a dozen times in its standard). The Samoyed is a bit larger than the Siberian Husky but smaller than the Alaskan Malamute. The Samoyed bone is less than required for a good Malamute but heavier than that required for a good Siberian. Samoyed bone should *never be so bulky* as to make a coarse, non-agile Samoyed. The Standard says "The Samoyed should never be so heavy as to appear clumsy, nor so light as to appear racy." *A SAMOYED IS AGILE:* a hunting, herding, hauling work dog or companion. He should never be a watered-down freighting Malamute nor a beefed-up racing Siberian.

His color is not just white. The color of Samoyeds varies in all shades of white to buff, often with deeper shading of lemon or buff; especially around his ears.

Regarding proportion, the Samoyed is similar to the other two breeds under consideration. He must have 55% leg height as measured from ground to elbow, or elbow to ground, depending upon the way your artist's eye views proper proportion of leg height to overall height of the dog at the withers. *Every Samoyed standard* (American, English, New Zealand, Australian and Canadian) states: *Because of the depth of chest required, the legs should be moderately long, a very short legged dog is to be deprecated."*

The Samoyed is *not square*, he is "Off-Square." The function of this form is to allow balance of running power enabling maximum reach in the forequarters with corresponding driving rear power. To quote the standards again: *"A short coupled loin would make him practically useless for his legitimate work, but at the same time a close-coupled body would also place him at a great disadvantage as a draft dog. Bitches may be slightly longer in back than males."*

It is the Samoyed proportion of 55% (elbow to ground) for leg as compared to the remaining 45% (elbow to top of withers) with the correct 45° shoulder layback that gives the shape of the Samoyed, built for endurance and snow conditions.

There is *no disqualification, either under or over, as to size* (as there is in the case of the Siberian Husky) but rather a recommendation in the U.S.A. of 21–23½ inches for dogs and 19 to 21 inches for bitches, measured at the withers, with deviations to be penalized according to the extent of the deviation. Note that Foreign Standards differ: the Swedish-Norwegian-Finnish is 22–24″ males and 19–22″ bitches. The English-Canadian-Australian is 20–22″ males and 18–20″ for bitches. When judging the breed in any country or any state, we find the Samoyeds are really all the same with the same varieties of sizes, shapes, heads, coats, and gaits.

The Samoyed head is his stamp of distinction and sets him apart from every other breed. The "lighting up of the face with the *smile*" is a total picture created from the thick well-set ears, the curved mouth and lip-line and the dark brown eyes. Combined with the typical outgoing temperament and stable personality, all that produces the typical expression of the breed.

The *temperament* denotes the style of the pack animal and here is a likeness rather than a difference in the Northern breeds. The Arctic breeds must get along with an established pecking order of the group in order to work together. As these three breeds are natural dogs as opposed to man-made breeds such as the Doberman and German Shepherd Dogs, they do possess likenesses as well as differences. All three have weather-resistant coats, double coats which include the soft downy undercoat and outer coat standing off from the body which is designed to repel snow and water.

The texture of the Samoyed coat is of greater importance than the quantity of hair. Pressing the palm of the hand against the vertical hair, the coat should feel spiky to the touch. Any indentation made in the hair should bounce up like a spring recovering. Buff color in exhibits should be used in the breeding program to preserve this proper quality of coat texture and therefore we achieve the creamy white to buff to silver white colors.

Samoyed pasterns should be mentioned as being different from the other two. In the Malamute, pasterns are more upright as are the Siberian's (who do also mention flexibility). However, the pastern of the Samoyed approaches a 15° angle on its way to being as flexible as the German Shepherd Dog, stated as 25°. This flexibility enhances the quick motions of the herding type activity. Some Samoyeds may be criticized as being "down in the pastern" when in reality it is not the bone angles but the leg-feathering which is a deceiving illusion. A thorough judge will fold back all of the leg feathering on Samoyeds, Collies and Shelties to ascertain the proper angulation of the pasterns.

The Samoyed's snow shoe foot is different. It is a hare foot, longish, strong, *not splayed*, with hair between the toes. His foot type could mean either salvation or demise on the trail, in the wild or in the show ring!

With all the differences among these Arctic Breeds, there are also fundamental likenesses. None of these breeds should ever be barrel chested. Their work requires great endurance; therefore, for maximum lung and heart performance, these vital organs must be encased in the heart-shaped rib cage described in the standard; rather than any round-shaped, 'water-melon' body. Depth of chest reaching to the elbow is vital.

While all three breeds carry their tails over their back, each does it in a different manner. Actually all Northern animals either carry their tails over their backs or in a high plume or else they have no tail or very short tails; also all northern animals have shorter, thicker ears than moderate climate animals. Examples are: the Fox, Ermine, Arctic Rabbit, Polar Bear, Mink, Linx, Siberian Husky, Samoyed and Alaskan Malamute. They all have eyes that are protected from snow-blindness by shape and design.

The Samoyed carries his tail over his back and it must touch and drape either side he prefers. One should be able to slide a hand between the tail and back at the root, when judging, to insure that it is not a 'snap-tail' which would indicate a flat croup and straight stifles. The Siberian carries his tail in a 'flag' without touching his back while moving or standing. Malamutes should carry their tails as a waving plume. So much depends upon structure for any of the breeds from tail set to tail carriage, i.e., low tail set with much angulation; high tail set or snap tail with straight stifles and flat croups, with no reach, extension or drive.

The Samoyeds' loose tail with the profuse feathering can be observed to be over his nose and face while curled-up and sleeping. History books quote that this is the way he filters the harsh Arctic cold and thus breathes air rather than frost (or possibly big-city pollution). His tail tells you his mood of the moment as it wags gently or vigorously while talking.

The ears have great mobility for all three breeds. Up when alert, down and folded well into their ruffs when running, working or sleeping. All of this from their native land where large, thin, immobile ears would be damaged by freezing temperatures. The Samoyed's triangular ears are set

165

closer together than the Malamute's, but not as high as the Siberian's. Their size should match the wedge of the head. The length of the ear when folded toward the muzzle should approximate the distance to the inner corner of the eye. Puppy ears may seem large but remember the adult coat and ruff will round out the wedge.

None of the Arctic breeds should have a *round eye!* Sammies have a kind of isosceles triangular-shaped eye, set in a slight slant (quite like the eye of a good Collie). (Note: all dogs have round eyes, it is merely the shape of the eye-rim that is distinctive to each breed. Very few standards mention this fact but the Shetland Sheepdog and Great Dane standards do.)

Northern breed eyes should not be sunken or protruding and never too close. Remember they are designed to live with bright snow and ice glare. Standards call for dark eyes which does not mean black. Dark brown eyes give more expression. Blue eyes disqualify only the Samoyed, not Siberians or Malamutes.

One great difference in the three breeds is the preparation for the dog show. All have double coats, but the Samoyed's coat is both longer and without markings. It must be thoroughly combed prior to a bath. For its denseness, it must be blown dry after the bath, followed by brushing and a complete comb-out. All of this special show preparation should be done at least two or three days before the event, in order for the coat to revert to its proper texture. Proper nutrition and sufficient brushing weekly should care for the Arctic coats. Of the three Arctics, Samoyed coats have no doggie odor. As judges, we expect to have any exhibit presented clean and well-groomed, and hope they each meet their standard.

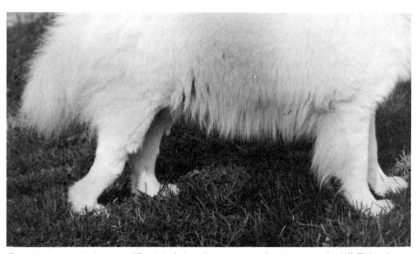

Samoyed standard states "Double-jointedness or cowhocks are a fault." This photo illustrates double-jointedness.

(Author's Note: In supplement to our own observations we here present observations on judging by some respected authorities.)

Judging Samoyeds

by Derek G. Rayne—distinguished all-rounder

As a judge of all working breeds for over 40 years, I have seen many changes in all of these breeds.

In evaluating any working breed, type and soundness do not always go hand in hand. A lovely head often rests on poor shoulders! The most common fault in many working breeds is poor shoulder placement. In short coated breeds poor shoulder placement is visible to the ringside. In coated breeds, such as Samoyeds, a judge may have to use his hands or wait till the dogs are moved in a circle when the lack of reach will be noted.

We have more good Samoyeds than we had 40 years ago, almost every section of the country has dogs of quality. Unfortunately, with the increased popularity of many breeds, a judge has to go over a lot of mediocre dogs; the percentage of good dogs does not increase with the size of entry.

In 1978 I had the honor of being one of the judges at the Samoyed National Specialty Show in Portland, Oregon. During that weekend, I became aware of two things that should be of concern to the Samoyed breeders. Some are too large and some are too small. Correct size and uniformity is very important to a breed. The second item of concern I observed was the loss of the true "Sammy" expression. Many dogs had light eyes with a hard expression and others had non-typical heads.

Some years ago, I wrote that if a dog is looking over a fence and only the head is silhouetted against the sky, the viewer should be able to distinguish a Siberian Husky from a Malamute or an Elkhound from a Keeshond, without seeing the rest of the dog. Of course, this holds equally true for a Samoyed. The head is the character of the breed, and should never be sacrificed for soundness or showmanship.

167

FAULT FINDERS:

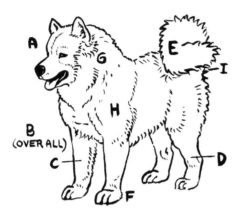

A: COARSE, BULKY HEAD

B: ENTIRELY TOO SHORT & COBBY

C: EXCESSIVE BONE

D: HOCKS TOO LOW SET (ALSO PASTERN 'KNEE')

E: TIGHT CURLED, DOUBLE CURLED OR HOOKED TAIL

F: FEET TOO LARGE AND ROUND

G: BULL NECK (SHORT, FLESHY)

H: LOADED SHOULDER

I: TAIL SET TOO HIGH

A = SHALLOW CHEST

B = SLAB (FLAT & NARROW) SIDES

C = ROACH BACK

D = GAY (FLAG) TAIL

E = COWHOCKS

F = WEAK LOIN "WASP WAIST"

G = OVERANGULATED

H = "SICKLE HOCKS" (CANNOT STRAIGHTEN LEG)

I = TOO RANGY

J = TAIL SET TOO LOW

K = HOCK SET TOO HIGH ("LONG HOCK") MORE THAN 1/3 HIP HEIGHT

168

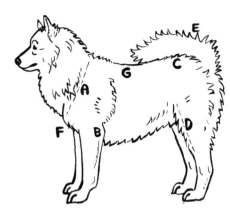

A = UPRIGHT (STRAIGHT) SHOULDER

B = INADEQUATE LETDOWN OF ELBOW

C = HIGH REAR, LEVEL CROUP

D = STRAIGHT STIFLE

E = "SNAP" OR "SQUIRREL" TAIL

F = HOLLOW FRONT (LACK OF FILL IN BRISKET)

G = SWAYBACK

A: EWE NECK

B: FLAT, THIN SPLAYED FOOT

C: LONG WEAK BACK

D: STEEP CROUP

E: RING TAIL

F: LIGHT BONE

E: TAIL TOO SHORT

FAULTY

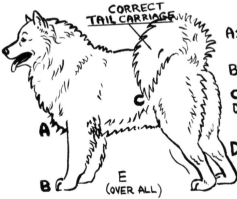

CORRECT TAIL CARRIAGE

A: "PIGEON BREAST" (PROTRUDING & FLESHY)

B: SMALL HIGH "CAT FOOT"

C: SLACK LOIN

D: DOUBLE-JOINTED HOCK; LOOSE HOCK

E: TOO SHORT LEGGED

E (OVER ALL)

The Samoyed is a Working Dog

by Mrs. Agnes Mason

Mrs. Mason was, until her death in 1970, an honorary life member of the Samoyed Club of America, Past President and Past Honorary President of the parent club, and honorary member of the Samoyed Club of Los Angeles. Her impact upon the popularity of the breed is exceeded only by her influence upon the quality of the breed. After nine years of Samoyed breeding, she forecast as clearly as if it were 29 years. In 1944 she wrote as follows:

First and foremost, it is my opinion that in order to determine the standard we should decide if it is the desire of the majority of Samoyed owners to keep our breed in the Working Dog class. If they continue to place in the Working Dog class as they have in recent years they will soon find their place at the top as Best Dog in Show. This will publicize the breed more than anything else could, and a breed judge should always place Best of Breed the dog that has the best chance in the Group. Judge Julius DuPon of California told us at one of our meetings that this was his consideration. If every judge regardless of his knowledge of the breed kept this in mind, I believe we would have more sincere and better judging.

A working dog is one of the most interesting of breeds and this last war had made the public more work-dog conscious. A 35- or 45-pound Samoyed hasn't the chance in the Working Group that a larger one has, regardless of type. I believe to arrive at a larger standard, we should be influenced to some extent by Nansen's experience on his expedition when he advises that the medium-sized Samoyed endured the longest. As near as I can figure this would be about 60 pounds. Personally, I like the 60- or 65-pound male standard and advocate our enlarging the standard to 45 to 60 pounds for females, and 50 to 65 or 70 pounds for males. We find that in our dog teams the females work as well as, if not better than, males. This gives plenty of leeway for a judge to consider type. Any Samoyed over this weight could be penalized accordingly, yet if he were outstanding he could still win.

Naturally, frame should conform to weight. I think an overweight Samoyed is as much out of condition as one too thin. We have both in our kennel. However, the largest percentage are in condition as we like them for sled work. A Samoyed so large that his heavy bone makes him clumsy rather than agile and graceful is not a good sled dog, nor good at herding. Neither should they be bred cobby merely for show purposes.

A Samoyed with long hair should not be given the advantage over a shorter coat merely because of length of coat. Different judges have told me they did not care for the long Pomeranian coat. We naturally breed for good coat, but I think a sound Samoyed with shorter coat of good quality should be considered over a less sound one with a longer coat that might help his percentage on general appearance. We have had judges who judge on general appearance only, never going over the dogs for soundness, or gaiting them for leg action. I remember when we purchased Dascha from Mr. Pinkham he said, "A Sammy should never lose his waistline." At the time I did not understand just what he referred to. Of course, a deep-chested Samoyed in condition for work would have a waistline. Too long a coat on the back covers the beauty of the contour of our breed.

I do not think the short-legged Sammy is as attractive as the medium-size, or rather the larger present standard of today. Our present standard states they should not be short-legged, but a height of 19 inches could not be anything else if the chest is deep. Body and legs in my estimation should be given preference over head and tail carriage, and coat over black points. One judge said, "I like a black nose but a Samoyed does not work with his nose; gait is more important."

The Importance of Preserving Samoyed Type

by Mrs Edna Travinek—Working Group Judge

A strikingly handsome dog. An appealing and feminine bitch. Both possess the ideals of type, soundness, balance and style.

Essentially an Arctic dog noted for its functional versatility, the Samoyed has, over the years, managed to retain its basic type—established by the pioneer breeders years ago.

Perhaps the Sam's lesser popularity with the public has proven to be an advantage in preserving the overall type—especially when we consider the obvious breakdown that has taken place in other functional breeds through mass production and/or lack of constructive study of suitable bloodlines.

A change in Samoyed type that I have noticed is a tendency toward cupped tight feet. This is correct for the Great Pyrenees, but not for the Sam, who is supposed to have the hare foot, or as some might choose to call it, "snowshoe" feet.

The Samoyed standard requires well-bent stifles. There is a tendency toward straight stifles, if not the actual occurence of straight stifles. Although excessive grooming can also give the illusion of straightness. Thus it becomes important for the judge to get one's fingers beneath the carefully treated and brushed hair to determine correctness of stifles. And, we are aware of the shoulder problems confronting dog breeders today to some degree, including Sams.

By its standard the Sam is classified as a herding/sledding dog. Therefore the functional Sam is a moving Sam which should be equipped with a 90-degree angulation, both fore and aft. Such a structure will provide a good reach in front and a strong drive in the rear—suggesting a smooth, well-oiled machine capable of covering much ground.

We cannot change the skeleton, but the gait can be improved by roadwork with a car or bike and the Sam on a line for those who lack space at home. A daily trot at a set speed will condition the dog and do wonders for slack muscles which hold the framework in place. Start slowly with a quarter of a mile and build up to a few miles. The entire dog will benefit, physically and mentally, including his trademark—the Sammy smile.

Two Excerpts from a 1930 critique

by Miss J.V. Thomson-Glover

A born showman looks about him, proudly interested in everything within range. I do not care to see Samoyeds standing about, or tailing around like a flock of sheep. People think a dog shows well if it stands motionless, with its eyes glued to whatever the handler has in his hands. . . .

An eye entirely foreign is creeping into the breed, and perhaps novices do not realize how much beauty and Samoyed character is thus lost.

Hear, hear!

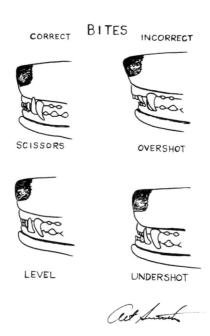

Samoyed Heads

Mrs. Ivy Kilburn-Morris is among the most respected figures in the breed. She has indeed grown up with the breed, identifying with it over eight decades. She has long been concerned with Samoyed heads, and writes:

"I find many of these changed and not of the original type, resembling more the Chow or Keeshond. In some cases the true Samoyed expression is entirely lost. The fault lies in the structure of the foreface: the skull above the eyes is too broad, the stop rather too pronounced, the muzzle too short and the mouth too wide and 'lippy.' Sometimes the eyes are too large and prominent, more round than almond-shaped, or badly spaced. These changes give a hard expression, foreign to the breed.

"There is also another type of incorrect head, where the eyes are inclined to be too close together, and there is not sufficient stop. . . . No matter how good a dog may be in other respects, if its head is not correct, it is not a typical specimen."

The judge is employed to find the *best* dogs—not the smallest, not the largest—the *best* dogs!

Richard Beauchamp, editor-publisher of *Kennel Review*, in writing to breeders of the Bichon Frise, made comments that are equally applicable for breeders of the Samoyed:

"When size is significantly reduced in this or any breed for that matter, one does not reduce all body parts proportionately. I have found that as size decreases, the upper arm shortens and the shoulder straightens. The straightening of the shoulder, of course, gives the individual a longer back and a shorter neck. Reduction of length in the upper arm creates less front angulation in the rear quarters. It goes without saying that this seriously restricts the easy reach and drive which is the hallmark of the Bichon." (Or the Samoyed).

"The judge who arbitrarily decides he is 'for' or 'against' the dog which falls toward either end of the ideal at the expense of the well-made dog is not serving the best interests of the breed, and is in fact simply gratifying his own personal preferences, which is not what good judging is about!"

The authors reiterate that the drag of the Samoyed breed is shortness of leg, and it should be penalized to the extent of the deviation. Ideally, the elbow should approximate 55% of its height at the withers. This lack of quality of proportion, and lack of characteristic anatomy for the Samoyed, if combined with poor coat quality, will give an off-type Sam.

An additional caution—Avoid both large coarse mouths that show sloppy flews and ugly faces! We so plead.

Correct movement. Single tracking.

Correct movement, from the side.

174

9

Ideal Samoyed Movement

by Karl Michael Smith (Ice Way Samoyeds)

AN OUTSTANDING MOVING DOG is an exciting dog. His beauty and grace in the ring and in the field, his powerful driving rear, working in harmony with his fully extending front, thrill the knowledgeable exhibitor and spectator alike. The pride and satisfaction in owning such an animal transcends winning any prize or award. A Samoyed is a working dog and cannot be an outstanding specimen of his breed unless he is an outstanding moving dog.

The trot is the gait at which most judges will move a dog when evaluating its movement. The trot is a two-time gait: the left front and right rear moving together, followed by the right front and left rear. To insure perpetual support the front foot moves slightly in advance of the back foot.

The trot is well suited for traveling on rough ground, and over long distances at a moderate speed. It is the mode of travel used by dogs in seeking out wild game. It is also an excellent gait for assessing movement in its relation to structure—it shows the strong and weak points in a dog's moving parts more readily than any other gait.

A dog with correct structure, when moving at a brisk trot, will display a maximum amount of drive in the rear assembly. This thrust generated by the rear assembly is propelled through the loin, back and withers to the front assembly. If the shoulders are correctly placed the shock passes through them with a minimum effort, being absorbed by the muscles.

The forward motion generated by the rear assembly will shift the equilibrium of the dog forward. The shoulder should open to the fullest extent possible to compensate for this shift. This can be best accomplished by a shoulder that is set at 45 degrees. The front leg should have good length in the upper arm allowing the front leg to reach out in a long stride close to the ground, thus counteracting the instability created by the drive of the rear. The neck and head will be thrust forward moving the center of gravity forward, resulting in acceleration and speed.

To better understand the effect that structure has on a dog's movement we can divide the dog into three sections: the front assembly; the topline and body; and the rear assembly. Under actual conditions the sections must work together in complete harmony.

Front Assembly

The front assembly consists of the scapula or shoulder blade. The shoulder is long and sloping and set at 45 degrees to the ground. The humerus or upper arm forms a right angle with the shoulder blade and is approximately the same length. The forearm joins the humerus at the elbow joint and is set at an angle of approximately 135 degrees. The pasterns are joined to the forearm at the pastern joint; they have a moderate 10-15 degree slope.

The front assembly has many functions. It supports about 60% of the weight of the dog. It provides a portion of the propelling force, particularly on turns. The front assembly absorbs the shock delivered forward by the rear assembly and it helps the dog maintain balance. A correct front assembly allows the dog to single track, offsetting lateral displacement or the moving from side to side.

The shoulder blade is the key to a good front. A sloping 45-degree shoulder allows for a longer and wider blade than does the more vertical or 60-degree straight shoulder. Muscle action is increased by the longer length of the blade; the greater width of the blade provides for larger muscles increasing muscle strength. The 45-degree blade lies alongside the thoracic frame. It moves in a longer arc than the more vertical 60-degree blade. It supplies more lift, and its movement is applied parallel to the line of locomotion.

A dog cannot reach past the angle of his shoulder. A 45-degree blade gives maximum reach. While the 60-degree blade gives a more vertical forward motion, going up and down as much as forward, the 45-degree blade allows for a longer reaching, ground covering stride—allowing the pad to hit the ground as momentum expends itself, minimizing stress on the front assembly.

The humerus or upper arm is approximately the same length as the shoulder blade. It is set at about 90 degrees to the blade, letting it extend further back on the body allowing for the longest possible arm without increasing the height of the dog. The longer upper arm has a greater arc of travel, allowing for a longer stride. The longer arm increases the length of the tricep muscles and those activating the forearm. The arm's ability to absorb shock, generate power, and its ability to lift are all enhanced by its greater length.

When moving, a dog strikes the ground with the heel of his paw; the shock goes directly to the bones of the pastern. The pastern must therefore have a slight bend and not be rigid. Sloping pasterns will differ from broken down pasterns.

176

RELATIONSHIP OF BONE STRUCTURE TO THE OUTLINE OF BODY AND COAT

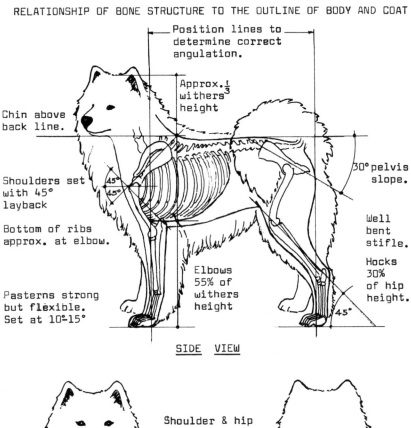

Position lines to determine correct angulation.

Approx. $\frac{1}{3}$ withers height

Chin above back line.

Shoulders set with 45° layback

Bottom of ribs approx. at elbow.

Pasterns strong but flexible. Set at 10°-15°

Elbows 55% of withers height

30° pelvis slope.

Well bent stifle.

Hocks 30% of hip height.

SIDE VIEW

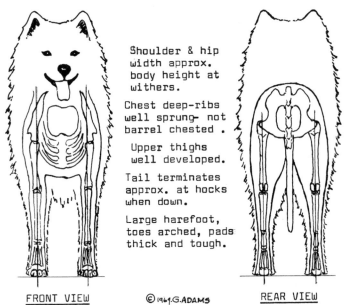

Shoulder & hip width approx. body height at withers.

Chest deep-ribs well sprung- not barrel chested.

Upper thighs well developed.

Tail terminates approx. at hocks when down.

Large harefoot, toes arched, pads thick and tough.

FRONT VIEW

© 1969. G. ADAMS

REAR VIEW

The sloping pastern will absorb the shock of the striking pads, keep the front from knuckling over and increase the front's ability to lift. Dogs with large shoulder blades set at 45 degrees and a long upper arm set at 90 degrees will require a reasonable slope to their pastern.

Topline and Body

The top line consists of the head and neck, the back, which is divided into the withers, the mid-back, the loin and croup, and the tail. The body consists of the chest, the rib section and the abdomen.

The head and neck together shift the center of gravity from side to side on turns. When running, the dog extends its head and neck forward; this creates instability by moving more weight forward and creates speed. If a dog wants to stop, the head and neck go up throwing the center of gravity toward the rear of the dog.

The neck is an integral part of the front assembly. All the muscles that draw the leg forward, directly or indirectly depend on the neck for support. The cervical ligament is the basic strength to the forward movement of the leg. The neck muscle, like all muscles, contracts 2/3 of the length of its fleshy part. To increase the movement of a part, you increase the actual length of the fleshy part of the muscle; to increase strength, you increase the area of the muscle.

The ewe or concave neck is caused by a weakness of the neck muscle and gives poor support in moving the leg forward. The bull or short neck shortens the length and therefore the movement of the muscles that control forward leg movement.

The withers lie behind the neck on the vertebral column. The first seven vertebrae are involved in shoulder action. They are different from the vertebrae composing the rest of the spinal column; they are longer and are pointed upward and toward the rear of the dog. They support the neck ligament and the muscles coming from the shoulder blade.

The mid-back consists of 6 vertebrae. The spinal column should be straight and form a line parallel to the ground while the dog is standing. The back should be level but not the back line, because the loin must have an arch.

The area of the loin consists of 7 vertebrae. The vertebrae are inclined forward to give better support to the rearing muscles. The power generated by the back legs is passed through the loins and spinal column to the front assembly. The loins also help in handling the shock of the forehand landing. The loin does not receive support from any bones, but is set with an arch like a bridge for strength. The slope of the croup and the tail set are good indicators as to the slope of the pelvis.

The chest and rib section are very important in the makeup of a good moving dog. To provide for a good single tracking front, we trade width of

Balanced trot—medium speed.

FAULTY GAITS.

Too wide.   Too close.   Cow-hocked.

chest for depth. The first four or five ribs should not be as "well sprung" as the rest. They should be more flat-sided to give more freedom to shoulder blade action. The deep narrower body is a more efficiently built body for work than the round barrel-chested body. It provides more heart and lung room and helps combat lateral displacement while moving. Heart and lung capacity is influenced more by the length of the rib than its mid-curve. Body depth should be measured through the 9th rib to give a true idea of heart room. Tuck-up must confine itself to the abdominal section.

The abdomen lies behind the rib section. The standard calls for a tuck-up. During locomotion this allows the large muscles from the pelvis to the base of the ribs to operate in a straighter line, than would otherwise be possible.

Rear Assembly

The rear assembly is comprised of the pelvis. The pelvis is set at about 30 degrees to the horizontal. The femur or thigh joins the pelvis at the hip socket forming a right angle. The femur is about the same length as the pelvis. The stifle joint connects the lower leg to the thigh and is set at approximately 90 degrees. The hock joint joins the lower leg to the hock and forms an angle of about 120 degrees. The hock is set at a right angle to the rear pad.

The rear assembly lends support to the dog, but its main function is to generate power. The power delivered by the hind leg is in proportion to the difference in the leg's extended and contracted length during stride. This calls for a well-bent stifle, approximately 45 degrees to the ground to deliver sufficient drive. When sufficient drive is achieved the leg is carried forward to where momentum is exhausted. At this time the leg receives the shock of ground contact. Power is delivered from the time the leg becomes vertical until the pad is airborne.

The rear assembly is designed primarily for propulsion. *While the front fights to maintain stability, the rear constantly creates instability.* It is this process by which movement or locomotion is achieved. It is important that the stifle be well bent; this lengthens the femur bone and its corresponding thigh muscles. It also provides for longer muscles to the hock joint.

Just as we want the longer thigh for speed and power, we want the shorter hock for endurance. "Hocks close to the ground," reduce the load on the Achilles' tendon, and by their shortness allow for a longer thigh.

The back leg is carried forward by muscles coming from the pelvis and attaching to the upper and lower thighs. The leg is drawn back by the strongest group of muscles in the rear assembly. The muscles come down from the pelvis and croup and wrap around the top of the lower thigh. This wrapping allows the muscle to draw the stifle joint back and also to straighten it. The muscles of the loin and back also enter into the action.

These muscles draw back the hind leg and are called "rearing muscles."

A well angulated stifle is one of the best ways to assure strong "rearing muscles." This will lengthen the muscles giving more muscle action and also provides for more muscle area with a corresponding gain in muscle strength.

Balance

Balance depends not only on head size to neck length, on the ratio of neck length to back and leg length, on depth of chest to length of leg and overall body length to height, but the angulation of the front assembly must be in symmetry with the rear.

In viewing the dog on the side, balance is not achieved if the front shoulder and upper arm are well set, but the rear assembly lacks angulation. The dog will have more reach than drive. Balance is also not achieved if the rear is well angulated, but the front assembly is set more vertical. This dog will have more drive than reach. This condition accounts for many gaiting faults.

In viewing the stationary dog from the front, the front pad is set directly under the muscular support of the shoulder blade, the rear heel pad is set directly under the pelvis joint. When the dog starts to move at a slow speed this position does not change, but as speed increases the pads converge toward a center line beneath the dog, commencing a single tracking action. The dog begins with static balance and moves into various positions of kinetic balance.

In concluding, I must acknowledge, with regret, that some of the top winning Samoyeds in the country do not have the correct angulation called for in the standard. For various reasons they win despite this inadequacy. Doing their share of winning, the breeders and owners of these dogs do not find it necessary to breed for more angulation. But most people, once they have been fortunate enough to own and show a dog with correct shoulder layback and a corresponding well-angulated stifle, will never again settle for less.

References:

THE DOG IN ACTION, McDowell Lyon, Howell Book House Inc., N.Y.

DOGS A HOBBY OR A PROFESSION, V. 11, C. Gardiner & E.S. Gibson, Canine Information Center of Professional Breeding Services Inc., N.Y.

DOG ANATOMY ILLUSTRATED, Robert F. Way V.M.D., MS, Dreenan Press Ltd., N.Y.

THE NEW DOGSTEPS, Rachel Page Elliott, Howell Book House Inc., N.Y.

SAMOYED, ILLUSTRATED STANDARD, Gertrude Adams, Samoyed Club of America Inc.

Ch. Snowfire's Bo Peep, Top Brood Bitch (SCA Award) for 1979 and 1980. By Shondy of Snowridge ex Ch. Kobe's Katusha of Encino. Owners, Dr. Merrill and Rowena Evans, Seelah Kennels, Iowa.

Ch. Archangel of the North Starr, at 7 years. Dam of 15 AKC champions and 10 foreign champions. Owners: Dr. and Mrs. R.J. Hritzo, North Starr Samoyeds, Ohio.

Ch. Samkist's Classy Chassis, dam of 7 champions by Am. & Can. Ch. Moonlighter's Ima Bark Star. Bred and owned by Sharon Kremsreiter.

182

10

Breeding the Samoyed

In WRITING this book, we have come to our own conclusions on breeding Samoyeds. While we do not wish to disparage the reading of books on genetics, or to discourage the acquiring and using of knowledge of line-breeding and inbreeding, we recommend outcrossing as a frequent program *for the novice to follow*—especially outcrossing based upon the physical attributes of the parents and grandparents. Many of the top winners in this book were so bred.

Some breeders interpret the standard according to their human likes. They line-breed to "stamp" a particular feature, and glory in the comment that "Oh, that's a So and So *line* or *kennel*. You can tell by looking at it." But by creating a dominance for a particular look, they may also double the "bad genes" as well as those they have selected as "good". This would be particularly true in the case of hip dysplasia, straight stifles or double hocks.

In breeding, a knowledge is needed of the strengths and weaknesses of the grandparents, as well as of the parents, to know how to evaluate the choice of a mate. For instance, to improve a too-broad or too-narrow front one does not select a mate with the opposite fault, thinking thus to come out with an "instant mixture". Consider the dominance of the stud and the brood bitch by *studying the get*. In this consideration, heads are the most diversified feature, but Sams should always have a Samoyed expression.

Please do not gather from this that we are opposed to line-breeding. Actually, we line-breed most of the time, and occasionally may in-breed as well, but we are prepared for the good and the bad. However, we do not believe that the novice is ready for the sometime results of a brother-sister or a father-daughter breeding. If a beginner desires to line-breed, we suggest that he first consider a grandfather to granddaughter breeding, or vice-versa. Remember, this is the way the breed was probably bred in its natural state, and the poor ones fell by the wayside. Without line-breeding in the beginning, we would not have a Samoyed breed. Oftimes what we consider to be an outcrossing is in fact an unknown or unrecognized line-breeding.

But most important, we have been warned through the years by Louis Smirnow, Helen Harris and Agnes Mason and others, that *we should always breed to the standard of the breed.* That means, breed for: *Type,* a dog that is in appearance everything we look for in a true Samoyed; *Soundness,* a dog free of anatomical weaknesses of hips, legs and angles, one that gaits properly; *Temperament or Disposition:* a dog absolutely dependable, stable and happy; and *Style:* a dog with that indefinable something that sets the good Samoyed apart, the outstanding specimen that exudes *elegance, quality* and *ring presence*—with or without a good handler.

Before you breed, we would suggest these requirements:

1. You have a bitch that is above average stock, sound in body and temperament.
2. The plan for her breeding has been studied and carefully made on paper after thorough study of compatible bloodlines. That the bitch and the prospective sire will offset each other's possible weaknesses.
3. That both are X-rayed normal.
4. That your aim is to produce puppies better than either the father or the mother.
5. That your bitch has been wormed about one month before her season.
6. That her booster shots are up to date, as the puppies receive immunity from their dam's milk *only* if their dam has immunity.
7. That she has had a complete health check by your veterinarian.
8. That she is between one and two years of age before being bred for the first time.
9. That both dog and bitch be tested for brucellosis (an important cause of reproductive failure).

While most Samoyeds whelp normally, and do not require that a veterinarian be in attendance, it is a wise and comforting precaution to have one ready "on call." It is recommended that arrangements with him will have been made for that extraordinary emergency.

In this book we have confined ourselves to veterinary observations specifically of interest to Samoyeds, born either out of our experience or those of respected breeders. For a more detailed veterinary guidance in cooperation with your veterinarian, we suggest that our readers consult *Dog Owners' Home Veterinary Handbook* by Delbert G. Carlson, D.V.M. and James M. Giffin, M.D., or the AKC's official *The Complete Dog Book,* 17th Edition—both published by Howell Book House, Inc., New York City.

Ch. Kim's Ladybug (1967-1977), dam of 10 champions including Group winners. Owned by Audrey Lycan, Winter Way Samoyeds, Alabama.

Am. & Can. Ch. Frostar's Tanara (1958-1971), dam of 6 champions. Top Producing Dam, 1969. Tanara was foundation dam of the Laskeys' Suruka Orr Kennels.

Am. & Can. Ch. Kuei of Suruka Orr, C.D., the Samoyed Assn. of the Midwest's Top Brood Bitch for 1975. Dam of Am. & Can. Ch. Kipperic Kandu of Suruka Orr, C.D., winner of 3 BIS. Owners, Mel and Miriam Laskey.

185

Explorer's Royal Choice Lady, shown by her breeder-owner-handler, Birgit Hillerby, Sweden, winning Best in Show Junior at the Malmo International show in Stockholm. Lady is by Int. & Danish Ch. Sir Jonah of Banff (owned by Kirsten Jorgenson, Aalborg, Denmark) ex Birgit's Ch. Explorer Lady Jane. Because of the quarantine laws in Sweden, Lady is from the litter produced by artificial insemination with Jonah's frozen semen from Denmark to the dam in Sweden.

Photo, Andreas
(Carl A. Andreasson), Sweden.

Birgit Hillerby showing Nor. Ch. Explorer's Lady Jane to BOB in Sweden, at 7 years of age. Judge was Mrs. Yvonne Sydenham-Clarke, breeder-judge from Australia. Lady Jane is out of the dam Ch. Shatazah of Antares, who Birgit imported from Joe and Joanne Marineau of California.

186

Frozen Semen—*Handle With Care*
by Mike Smith

In the early summer of 1981, Ice Way Kennels became involved in the shipping of frozen semen. We were contacted by Tina Colborne of Ron Mar Kennels in Canada. She had an interest in breeding to our Ch. Ice Way's Ice Breaker, but felt that the distance involved would make shipping difficult. She was interested in having frozen semen shipped to her in Canada; at that time, a litter could be registered in Canada using frozen semen, although there were as yet no provisions for registration available in the United States. The canister that was to be used for shipping the semen was rented from a horse ranch on the East Coast and shipped to us by bus. After a considerable amount of inquiry we were able to locate an establishment that worked in association with the American Kennel Club in the development of freezing canine semen.

Life Forces, Incorporated is a company whose primary purpose is to collect, freeze and store semen from dogs. The program was established by Dr. Stephen Seager at the University of Oregon Medical School in 1967. It is now located at Texas A&M in College Station, Texas. At the time we contacted Life Forces Inc., 47 dog breeds had semen frozen and collected at the facility. Breaker would become the first Samoyed to partake in this procedure.

Some advantages of frozen semen are: ease and reduced cost of transport, a reduction in the spread of disease, and the ability to breed to older or deceased studs. In general, it would extend the breeding potential of outstanding stud dogs.

The most significant disadvantage in making a stud dog's semen available after the dog's breeding life is over, is the reluctance of many breeders to go with a young stud dog. Less knowledgeable breeders might be inclined to breed to an older dog because it has produced a large number of champions rather than to a younger dog—even though the younger, but less famous, dog would be a better breeding for that particular bitch. A knowledgeable breeder will breed to a stud dog because of the qualities he produces, not his number of champions. Over-zealous stud dog owners would be trying to get one more champion out of "Old Fred" long after their efforts should have turned to one of their younger stud dogs.

Some of the principles employed in the freezing and storage of canine semen might be of general interest to the stud dog owner. The semen is ejaculated in three factions. The first faction is clear fluid; the second faction, rich in sperm, is the faction used in the freezing process; and the third faction is a prostate gland secretion. After the semen is manually extracted from the male—a teaser bitch is very helpful in the procedure—the ejaculate is examined for color, viscosity, ph, percent and progressive motility of the sperm, amount of sperm per cc, and total sperm count. The semen is then stored in the dog's individual container and frozen with liquid nitrogen at approximately –320 degrees Fahrenheit.

The best age for a dog to have his semen collected is usually between 2 to 5 years. He will generally have a higher sperm count and it will be of better quality at this age span. Life Forces Inc. estimates that 2 to 6 bitches can be inseminated with one ejaculate and that about 5 to 10 ejaculates can be collected over a period of two weeks. At this rate, in a two-week period, it would be feasible to store enough semen to inseminate fifty or more bitches.

Life Forces Inc. is now concentrating its efforts on storing the semen of older dogs for future use. At this time there are not many veterinarians trained in inseminating the bitch with thawed semen. However, new centers are slated to open soon in California, the East Coast, and upper Mid-West. This should make it easier to have a bitch inseminated than it is at present. **Breeders interested in using frozen semen should contact the American Kennel Club.** Additional regulations, that apply to the registration of litters produced through artificial insemination using frozen semen, now supplement the pamphlet *Regulations for Record Keeping and Identification of Dogs*.

Feeding the Bitch
Before and After Whelping

When a bitch becomes pregnant, it is not necessary to change her diet. In fact, it is better to keep the bitch on the same diet as long as it is nutritionally complete and well balanced. However, there are several feeding changes that the bitch goes through. About four weeks after mating, the bitch should be allowed to eat all she wants. This is necessary because her daily food intake will increase approximately 20% over normal quantity. Most of the additional weight she takes on during this period will be deposited in the embryo, reproductive fluids and membranes. As the bitch begins to get heavier with puppies, she should have her meal divided up into two or three smaller meals so she will be more comfortable after eating.

A second change in a bitch's food consumption occurs just after whelping. During this time her food intake will again increase as milk production increases. By the third or fourth week she will be consuming about twice her normal amount of food. The third feeding change will occur as her puppies begin eating solid food and stop nursing. The bitch will naturally eat less as her milk production decreases. However, during this time it is a good idea to further restrict her food intake to help decrease milk secretion. This will help her through the weaning period.

Whelping and Puppy Care
by Joyce Cain (Samtara Kennels)

Development of traits and characteristics begins in newborn puppies the moment they are born. Keeping the puppy clean the first months of life forms a pattern of cleanliness. This does not imply frequent bathing, but does suggest a sparkling white puppy without the necessity of a bath.

The dam should be as clean as a top show competitor when the puppies first arrive. Although her last bath should be at least three weeks prior to whelping, special care may be taken by bathing her feet and allowing her to sleep or rest on clean rugs. If necessary, she should be exercised on a leash.

When the time for whelping approaches (any time from the 58th day to 63rd day or so), line the whelping box with clean rough material for better footing for both dam and puppies. Newspapers are not recommended for Samoyeds as the ink rubs off on the white coats.

Begin your paper work. Record her temperature daily from the 57th day on. Normal is between 100 and 101 degrees. About three days before actual whelping, her temperature will drop to 99 degrees and "hold." Now watch temperature twice a day. When it drops to 97 degrees, and the water breaks, you may expect her first pup within hours.

During the whelping and the time when the dam has a heavy discharge, an absorbent disposable pad with a plastic lining may be placed under her. After each puppy is born in its membraneous sack filled with fluid and as soon as the dam has severed the cord from the whelp's abdomen, the pad can be rolled up with the placenta and discarded. The dam will be busy cleaning her whelp and will hardly notice. She may be allowed to eat one or two afterbirths, which is normal, but disposal of the others is recommended. Most important is to count them and account for every one.

Some breeders prefer to remove the newly born puppies to another warm box during each successive whelping, thus keeping them clean and dry and out of danger of being smothered by the dam. Between whelpings they should be returned to her if possible. Always keep the puppy box in a place where she can see her babies.

The fewer people around the better. Please, no strangers.

The whelping may take any time from two hours to twelve hours with pups arriving at any interval of time from five minutes to two hours.

Do not delay if any of the following danger signals develop:

Call your veterinarian:

1. If the bitch is straining, squatting, has a pup only partially expelled or has hard labor for more than an hour without any delivery.
2. After whelping is finished, if bitch begins heavy panting, or trembling, is restless and has a worried expression, or if mucous membranes are pale. Though conscious, she may become paralyzed

189

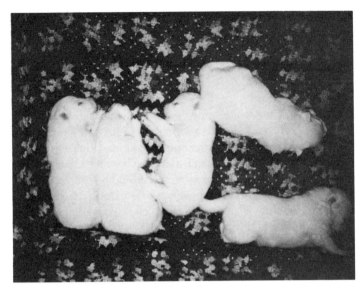

Puppies from a Samtara Kennels litter, pictured at two weeks old—sacked out.

At seven weeks old—adventurous. Some ears are beginning to come up.

and unable to stand. Immediate care is needed and your veterinarian will give an injection of calcium gluconate. This eclampsia is a condition occasionally encountered by the bitch at whelping. It usually occurs twenty-four to thirty hours or even four or five days after whelping.

When the puppies have been whelped and fed, the dam will need to be let out for elimination. Before she returns to her pups, bathe her skirts and dry them thoroughly. It will encourage her to keep herself clean. This is also an excellent time to change the bedding in the whelping box.

Puppies will start nursing usually when whelping is completed. Give the bitch warm milk and broth to aid her milk flow. The first two days are critical in newborn puppies. They must be kept warm and they must nurse. A puppy should have a round full stomach and be contented. The dam must clean and lick her pups, especially in the abdominal region. This action stimulates peristalsis, setting proper elimination. If the bitch fails to do this, you must gently rub the abdomen from the head to the tail with thumb or fingers, rhythmically, so the puppy will urinate and pass its fecal matter.

A post-whelping checkup should be made at the veterinarian's as soon as possible.

Your paper work consists of recording time or arrival of each pup and its sex and weight, and accounting for the afterbirths. Record the bitch's temperature twice daily for two weeks so you may see the doctor if her temperature increases above 102 degrees.

At three days, cut the dewclaws, if any, on both front and hind legs. Take litter to the veterinarian for this or do it yourself as follows:

Use sterilized curved sharp scissors to cut the gristle—nub, and paint with ferrous sub-sulfate, i.e.—Monsell's powder. Have someone take the dam for a walk during this minor surgery, so she will not be upset. It is not difficult but be sure to get the whole piece as deep as necessary so they won't grow back.

Puppies are bathed by the dam during the first weeks of their lives; therefore, the breeder's only concern is keeping the dam and the whelping box clean.

Feeding Puppies

When feeding puppies, hold the pan so that they do not step into it. Try an orange juice squeezer dish to discourage stepping in dish. Allow the dam to remain close by and allow her to clean up any puppy that has gotten dirty while eating. When they have finished, remove the pan immediately. If the dam starts washing their faces to clean them, they soon will learn to wash one another.

Offer the puppies water frequently but do not leave it where they will walk in it or spill it. If they do get wet, towel them dry. The puppy who loads himself with water will not eat his ration of feed and will make more puddles than you can wipe. He must have water but he need not fill up on it.

Some dams will refuse to remove the excreta from the bed, others will continue after the supplemental feeding has started, and a rare few keep the whelping box clean through the eighth week. Once again, newspaper is not recommended. Training the puppy on paper condones elimination indoors and helps them to acquire a habit which must be broken later.

Take each puppy outdoors before feeding when they have awakened from a nap and again after a meal. The reasoning to all this added work of carrying one at a time is teaching the puppy discipline. You get his complete attention and training is simplified. The younger the puppy the more frequently he will have to relieve himself. Mistakes will happen, and if they do, clean them up at once. Clean bedding when needed will discourage mistakes and by the fifth week each puppy will beg to be first.

Wait until the pups have had their first serum shot before showing them off to friends and neighborhood children.

The puppies' eyes will start to open at seven to fourteen days from birth. The lids part first at the inner corner and extend to the outside.

Cut sharp puppy toe nails every five to seven days while they are nursing.

When there are too many puppies for the mother to care for, or weak puppies, supplement feedings should be given.

Yolk of 1 egg
½ cup evaporated milk
½ cup boiled water
1 teaspoon white Karo
1 drop of a baby vitamin

If puppies do not seem to tolerate milk, a milk substitute may be used.

Puppies can be fed once a day, beginning at 3 weeks of age. Hamburger mixed with a high protein cereal and 2 parts boiled water is a good first meal. At 5 weeks of age, feed a mixture consisting of two scrambled eggs, one can of chicken or beef (such as *Kal Kan*) and one cup of small meal of kibble (such as *Purina Puppy Chow*). If meal is large, it can be put in a blender or pour hot water over and let stand until softened. The mothers are still kept with the puppies at this age, but removed at feeding and several hours at a time. As the puppies approach 6 and 7 weeks of age, they are eating two meals a day. Feed just enough so they will clean up each meal. Put mother back with the puppies at night.

At 7 weeks, the puppies are weaned from the mother. At this time, alternate a morning feeding of cottage cheese mix (2 parts cottage cheese with 1 part meal) and the egg mixtures every other day. The evening meal continues to be *Kal Kan* meat, meal, vitamins and water mixture. This schedule of feeding continues until pups are 6 months of age, then go to grown dog's feeding and one meal a day.

Overfeeding

Lon D. Lewis, D.V.M. warns against overfeeding puppies, which could lead to: hip dysplasia, osteochronditis, enlarged joints, dropped hocks, daisy feet, crooked legs, wobblers' syndrome or lameness. Overfeeding a puppy may predispose it to a variety of skeletal problems later in life, not to mention obesity and possibly a shortened life span. For these reasons, dogs should not be allowed to eat free choice until they have reached 80-90% of adult size. However, if your Samoyed wolfs his food down, it would be best to regulate his intake at each meal.

Samovar's Thorin Wendigo checks first edition of *The Complete Samoyed* with his owner, Mrs. Patti Burr, Canada.

Television star Betty White and author Dolly Ward at taping of "Pet Set" show with 6-weeks old litter by Almost Christmas Chatter ex Boutique.

11

Selecting a Puppy

THE selection of the puppy is of paramount interest to both the breeder and the buyer.

The prospective buyer should:

1. Read about the Samoyed.
2. Write to reputable breeders asking for explicit information on their stock and evaluated potential. Show superintendents and judges are sources for leads to reputable breeders.
3. Visit all possible kennels. A breeder does not necessarily own a large kennel.
4. Attend sanctioned matches, shows, and specialty shows.
5. Look at as many Samoyeds of all ages as possible.
6. Talk to their owners.

If you are in a well-populated area, you may be able to pick out your own puppy from the litter. This may be fortunate or not, depending on how well you have studied the breed.

If you are in an area in which there are no Samoyeds being bred or shown, you will have to depend on a sort of mail order business between you and the breeder. This may be fortunate or not, depending on how "good" the breeder is. BEWARE. There are many breeders who wish only to make a sale and may not know much more than you about how to evaluate puppies.

If you want a pet Samoyed, you should study the breed first. Selection of your pet is as important as selection of a show dog. You may end up with both, though you "do not plan to show." We think the ideal purchase is a pet who may be shown, or the show dog who may be your pet. They are always in this dual role anyway. Most people would not deliberately buy a Samoyed with an eye to "campaigning" this breed at shows all over the country unless it were their pet.

The initial investment in a puppy or half grown (6 months-2 years) Samoyed is the smallest fee, compared with the care, time, and monetary and emotional costs you spend on your pet-show dog. It "costs" no more to raise your show dog than to raise your pet. The costs involved in entering the show game may be written off as "entertainment," as there is no better family sport than the dog game. It may intrigue both the child and the gray haired grandparents in the family. That is togetherness.

The puppy is most frequently chosen at the age of eight weeks; but don't disregard the advantages of selecting a half-grown Samoyed. Starting with the head, notice the placement (not too close) and shape (almond) of the eye as well as the degree of darkness. Check the circumference of the muzzle, especially for depth and breadth on either side of the nose button. You do not wish a snipy muzzle when he grows up. Ears may not be up yet, but check the thickness and strength of cartilage to determine whether the ears will "come up," as well as their placement on the head. Ears should not be too large or be set too low, as this will detract from the expression.

Grasp the knobby knees to judge the bone. If the knobs are missing, the puppy may lack bone and size. Knobs are more observable at about three to four months.

Hold the puppy securely around the chest and observe the legs hanging down. Do they hang straight in both the front and rear? If they toe out while gaiting, the puppy may walk or stand improperly. Watch him move about. Does he walk and trot with some spring and rhythm of gait? Do his feet point straight ahead? Does the rear drive match the front drive, or is one too strong for the other?

Tail set is quite obvious, so see that it is not too low or too high. Measure the spring of the rib cavity with your hands. If you feel a barrel shape, don't choose that darling one. If you feel a heart shape, it's probably A-okay. All coats look fluffy—you'd better check the sire and dam—and better yet the grandparents—to predict the type and amount of coat.

Study the pictures again—imagine the dog without any coat. Proportion of length of neck and squareness of the whole puppy standing is a matter of how the parts combine to make the whole picture. Legs should not be short. We have included pictures that show puppies at different ages and what they grew to look like as adults. *Notice disposition. Never* choose the shy one, the wetter, the withdrawn pup.

Even the best "picker" can be disappointed, but evaluation of the ancestors and the puppy "on the spot" is the best you can do. In addition to the puppy's inherited potential, tender loving care, nutrition, exercise, and some *luck* combine to give you the "pick of the litter."

And, of course, be sure that your puppy has had his protection shots—parvo vaccination, distemper, lepto.

Some items to expect from the breeder to take home with you besides your new puppy:

196

"I belong on the furniture." Ch. Kalmarli's Adrian of Nola, at 4 months. Owners, Bill and Dean Stanfield.

Four-months old litter enjoys a funny story. By Ch. Samkist Super Bonanza ex Ch. Devonshire's Liberty Belle. Breeder-owners: Paul and Betty Powell.

1. His registration paper. A common error in terminology is the interchange of the words "papers" and "pedigree." The registration *papers* are issued by the AKC from the litter number previously recorded by the breeder with the AKC. With a bill of sale, it is evidence of ownership.
2. The pedigree is provided as a courtesy by the breeder to give you a document which lists the sire and dam, the grandparents, great grandparents—as far as a six generation pedigree usually. This is his family tree!

   If an older dog or a puppy that is already named by the breeder changes ownership, you will need to send his papers to the AKC with a fee for transfer to the name of the new owner.
3. A reputable breeder will give you a record of the puppy's shots and dates of worming.
4. Also, he will provide a menu list of his current diet and even a supply of kibble to carry him over in his new surroundings, thus avoiding changes of diet as well as environment.

You should provide a small chain collar, a leash, and a #400 crate (the size of which is designed to be large enough for comfort when he is grown).

The following chart, showing an average increase in weight of puppies through their first eight weeks, is based on statistics compiled by the authors over a 25-year span:

Age	Average Weight
At birth	14 oz. to 18 oz.
One week	1½ lbs. to 2 lbs.
Two weeks	2 lbs. to 3 lbs.
Three weeks	3 lbs. to 4 lbs.
Four weeks	4 lbs. to 5 lbs.
Five weeks	5 lbs. to 8 lbs.
Six weeks	7¾ lbs. to 8¾ lbs.
Seven weeks	9 lbs. to 12 lbs.
Eight weeks	11 lbs. to 14 lbs.

The darkening of the black points, such as eyes, nose and lips varies greatly with the bloodlines, but generally will follow this pattern:

1. Rarely a few spotted noses at birth.
2. On the fourth day, a few eye-rims will begin darkening.
3. On the fifth day, at least half of the litter will have black eye-rims and noses will appear smoky.
4. At one week, all eye-rims appear dark and all noses are spotted with black. Now dark spots are showing on lips.
5. By the ninth day all eyes appear darker and ready to open, but will probably not open until the 13th or 14th day.

Ch. Ice Way's Bialou Mishka, at 9 weeks.

At the age of eight weeks, the following characteristics should be established enough to determine what they will be in the adult dog:

1. Shape and set of eyes, color
2. Biscuit shadings
3. Size of ears and placement
4. Set and carriage of tail
5. Disposition (outgoing to timid)
6. Bone—large knuckles for proper size
7. Gait

Ch. Sherica's Ethereal Candida with 5-day old puppies. Owners, Dave and Marguerite Seibert.

6 weeks old.

12

On Raising Puppies

by Susan North

THE breeder's responsibility for raising puppies on a sound psychological foundation is just as great as his responsibility for raising puppies that are free from parasites and innoculated against distemper. Emotional health is actually more precarious: a worm infestation can be treated, but a puppy that has not received socialization before the age of three months will be permanently crippled emotionally and can never realize his potential in forming a responsive relationship with a human being.

Based upon the research of Drs. Scott and Fuller at Jackson Laboratory (I highly recommend their book, *Genetics and The Social Behavior of the Dog*) and the practical application of their conclusions at Guide Dogs for The Blind as described in Clarence Pfaffenberger's most interesting book, *The New Knowledge of Dog Behavior*, it is now possible for breeders to give their puppies the best possible head start by some simple training and experience at a very early age.

When you breed a litter, you are bringing lives into this world and must, I believe, accept the responsibility for them. Your pet puppies have just as much right to the time and attention as that show prospect that you think is going to all that winning for you. If you don't have time for the pet puppies, you really don't have time for the litter! Breeders too often assess their litters, picking out the show prospects and then ignoring the pets who are sold as quickly as possible with a minimum investment of time and money. Nothing could be more foolish or detrimental to the breed as a whole. The real public relations job in dogs is done by these pet puppies who in their daily lives contact many, many people, leaving an impression for better or for worse. By investing a modicum of time you can build a firm emotional base for each and every one of your puppies and help to assure dispositions that will be a credit to you in or out of the ring.

Now how does one go about preparing these puppies—and just what kind of temperament are we really after? I think one could find some difference of opinion among breeders as to just what ideal temperament was—just as breeders differ in their ideas about head proportion and sound movement.

I personally feel that the one hundred percent extrovert that sells himself so well to puppy buyers and judges alike is not completely desirable. A totally fearless dog, a dog without caution or reserve who is indiscriminately friendly with every passing stranger, a dog without nerves or sensitivity may be the handler's delight, but frankly he is not my idea of an intelligent animal. It is possible, I think, to have a dog that shows himself off proudly, a dog that is polite, manageable and sensible, but still a dog that has his dignity and maintains his natural cautions about new people and new situations.

If you have a dog that is self-confident and secure and that knows he can trust you, you can ask him to do certain things. You can ask him to stand still in the ring while some stranger goes over him from top to bottom—and this dog will do it because he has learned to trust your judgment, not because he is necessarily delighted with attentions from a total stranger.

Friendship with an intelligent and aware animal must be earned. So I permit some reserve in my dogs; I welcome some selectivity in their friendships—and this is because I have great respect for each of my puppies as individuals and feel they are entitled to develop their own unique

202

personalities. The training program that I follow with my puppies is not designed to turn out robots or totally uniform dispositions.

The idea, rather, is to take some time to explore with each puppy his own personality, to cultivate his particular potential at that so very critical early time when it is possible to do so very much.

Begin to prepare this ideal emotional climate with your bitch in whelp. She is all important—and if she is the right type of bitch (and the others should NOT be bred), then she can give you a great deal of assistance with these puppies. She should be loved; she must be happy; she should have extra, tender attentions as well as extra calcium. She must be made to feel very, very special—and when it is time for her to whelp, you MUST be there for this is a joint venture.

You begin with the puppies at birth, not waiting until that almost magical twenty-first day when the puppies first find the world opening up to all their senses. Touch, taste, and smell are somewhat operational at birth although most neo-natal behavior is a matter of reflex response. The newborn puppy is certainly concerned, however, with food and warmth— and so I supplement all my puppies with a bottle even when this is not indicated by the size of the litter or the condition of the bitch—feeling that by this bottle feeding you begin a regular, pleasurable human contact.

The tactile sensitivity of the tiny puppy is quite developed, and I like to

Hoof 'n Paw Pacha with her companion Jacques Umphrey.

The right outfit for washing? Kros Paws Tannhauser, owned by Elva and Fred Libby, Florida, holds still for a cleaning.

Am. & Can. Ch. Ice Way's Bialow Mishka, winner 1979 SCLA Tournament. One of the Top Twenty, 1980. His owners, Doug and Pat Gillis write: "Mishka's accomplishments are all the more interesting in that he is one of the few Samoyeds that has contracted valley fever (a deadly disease) and lived to win again in the ring."

handle my puppies constantly, beginning immediately to turn them gently on their backs. To lie on one's back is to be utterly defenseless and by making this a routine exercise is pleasurable from the beginning, you start the bond that will become absolute trust. One can spot at this time the puppies that resist—and these will invariably be the same puppies who will have an initial freeze reaction to a new situation, the puppies with an additional emotional vulnerability that will need a bit more work along the way.

Do not, however, confuse sensitivity with shyness and instability. A sensitive and aware intelligence, a curiosity and a certain wariness are necessary for survival. A dog totally without caution or insensitive to his surroundings is not equipped to care for himself in any kind of living situation. The path from the crate to the exercise pen three times a day is NOT a living situation—and NO dog should be so impoverished as to think it is!

Up to the fourth week the routine is just daily contact and handling. Raw meat is first fed from the fingers—and what a treat that is, again supporting the concept in that tiny head about pleasurable human contact. As the babies begin to eat out of a pan, I accustom them to my "puppy call"—I prefer a clucking noise with lots of "puppies, come"—and within a few days this call brings them instantly and eagerly to their feet and you've gotten still another lesson across.

At four weeks I take the babies one by one and put them in a strange place. I leave them in the position they automatically assume—usually a sit—and move two feet away, coaxing with my puppy call. Up to this time the puppies have known only the place in which they were born and it is very interesting to see their reactions to totally new surroundings. Some puppies will vocalize immediately and constantly and, in my experience, these are the puppies that will continue to have a great deal to say throughout their lives. Some puppies back up rapidly in an escape reaction. Others, the more dependent types, come directly to the one familiar object: my shoes—and refuse to budge, while others pick themselves up and march off in a show of great independence.

I NEVER allow any of the puppies to become fearful. For the first time in their lives they are consciously faced with a totally new problem, and the experience that I want them to have is NOT fear but rather that of conquering their first anxiety and being reassured by human contact.

Even the simple training that I do with my puppies involves problem-solving behavior on their part; from a number of responses that they could make, they learn to select the one which most quickly brings them praise. **At four weeks** I start with light puppy collars and brief times in a crate—always in groups of two or more as isolation at this stage is very frightening. Between six and twelve weeks the real training begins. This training period

Ten Samoyed bitches perform in the Circus Vargus act. *Photo, courtesy Betty Ross.*

The all-champion Grey Ghost team, owned by Wayne and Janet Heffington, Saline, Michigan, may be seen at the Jaycee's Happiness Fair giving rides to the emotionally and mentally handicapped children, or at Christmas parades bringing Santa to town. In 1974, they began with "Grey" pulling a little red wagon for son Jon in the local Pet Parade. By 1976, it was a team of three, and in 1977 the all-champion Grey Ghost team was pulling a snowmobile sled on wheels. Janet writes: "All the team came home matted with cotton-candy, orange pop, sloppy kisses and tired, but they are always eager to go back. (God truly blessed this breed!) To hear an autistical child squeal in delight, to hear the astonishment of his counselor, was our greatest reward. A Sam is a friend, a joy, a people!"

206

establishes for the puppy a time when he is removed from the dominance of his mother and the interaction with his brothers and sisters and is taken off to be your very special dog, the center of your attention. I snap a light lead on the collar, under the chin, and the puppies usually trot right along. You never run into the resistance that you encounter if you put off lead training until three or four months. You support the puppy with your clucking noise or whatever sound you prefer—and because that sound has always meant "On your feet and good things coming," the puppy will be happy and willing to follow you. Once in a while you run into someone that is not going to cooperate and sits down solidly, refusing to budge. LET HIM SIT—he'll soon be bored with that! And when he moves, go right along with him. Soon enough he'll be going along with you.

Introduce the sit, the stand, the stay—always briefly and without force. When the puppy is headed for me anyway, I introduce the "Come"—again no forcing, no dragging, no corrections—just suggestions about what the puppy was about to do anyway! At this point you will get the feeling that this baby is training you.

Now if all this sounds like I'm suggesting you make a lot of spoiled little darlings who get praised for doing exactly what they wanted to do anyway, let me correct that impression. I do indeed believe in discipline. An undisciplined dog is not a secure dog because he does not know what you want and constantly has to face your displeasure. Moreover, an undisciplined dog is a danger to himself. There are several stern corrections that I do impress upon these baby minds and there is no nonsense about it.

One of the most critical of these lessons is that regarding electric cords. I lay an inviting length of cord on the living room rug and bring the puppies in one by one. Invariably they go for the cord, and when they do, POW—a loud NO and a good shaking by the back of the neck. (This shaking by the back of the neck is instant canine communication for "Don't try that again.") I make this lesson a harsh one, knowing it must be effective once and for all. I also allow puppies to almost dash out the door on their own impulse—and quickly and firmly close the door right on them, holding them there for a few struggling seconds—and the babies generally wait for an invitation from then on.

We also give a lesson in cars—the puppies are allowed to wander in front of a car whose motor is running, and when the puppy gets to the critical spot, a loud blast on the horn is usually enough to convince him to avoid the front ends of cars whose motors are running.

If I had a swimming pool, I would also include a lesson on how to swim and how to find the steps; as it is, I can only warn new owners that this is their responsibility.

The word NO is completely eliminated from *teaching*. If the puppy is wiggling and refusing to stand, just keep repeating the Stand command, telling the puppy *what* you want, NOT telling him that he's not doing what

Ch. Hoof 'n Paws White Cloud (Am. & Mex. Ch. Hoof 'n Paws White Knight ex Ice Way's Sunshine Mardee). Best Bred by Exhibitor at 1980 SCA National Specialty. Breeder-owner: Mardee Ward. Co-owner: Dave Abila.

Left: Whitney Pezzoli, a son of Am. & Mex. Ch. The Hoof 'N Paw White Knight. Right, Whitney Susitna (Ch. Kiskas Karaholme Cherokee ex Dushanbe's Special Blend). Owner, Victor Pezzoli.

Ch. Kiska's Sabrina Snow Daisy. Wh. 2/14/73, by Ch. Kiskas Karaholme Cherokee ex Sabrina of Snow Basin. Breeder: F.D. Harrison. Owners: Don and Del Wells. Daisy's wins included BOB at Mission Circuit show under Gerald Mitchell, breeder-judge from England.

you want. The NO is reserved for specific crimes like chewing on the couch, puddles on the rug, or biting ankles. The gnawing and biting that reaches a peak in the seven or eight week old puppy can be stopped quickly by returning the pressure on the jaw when the puppy takes your hand in his mouth. Immediately the puppy will only be interested in spitting you out, and if you hang on for another few seconds, he'll be so delighted to get you finally out of his mouth, that he will not be apt to chew on you again.

Once the puppy is going well on the lead, he is exposed to different kinds of terrain, flapping canvas, lawn mowers, and bicycles. He learns to go OVER small obstacles, go around others; he goes under ladders, in and out of doors, and up and down stairs. Inside the house he meets the vacuum cleaner, noisy pots and pans, electric trains, and assorted household confusions.

By this time he is lying happily and quietly on his back for a tummy rub, and it is a simple matter to teach him to lie on the grooming table with which he is already familiar from his regular brushings. He has had his mouth examined constantly and been given his calcium pills regularly so that medication need never be a problem.

In the sixth week I teach the "Carry"—and it doesn't matter to me what object the puppy likes to walk around with—a ball, a glove, a stick— anything that delights a particular puppy enough to make him hold his head proudly and trot around on the lead showing off. You are building neck and head carriage control in the best possible way with this exercise and laying the groundwork for the retrieve which is the next lesson.

The retrieve is a most important exercise psychologically. It involves the puppy going away from you, off on his own towards an object he likes, and then returning with his treasure to share it and please you. Some puppies make an immediate and instinctive retrieve. The puppies that at four weeks reacted to the new surroundings by clutching your shoes will now be the puppies that love you so much they can't bear to leave you long enough to run after the ball. But they will learn—make the task as simple as possible. Run with them and pick the ball up and give it to them and praise them profusely for carrying it around. By the ninth or tenth week you will see a dramatic grasp of this exercise and should have a whole litter of willing retrievers.

Like any pack oriented animal, like man and like monkeys, dogs learn by example and imitation. In your kennel you probably have older dogs whose behavior is exemplary in one way or another; use these aunts and uncles to help you educate the babies. An older steady dog on a grooming table will quickly teach a youngster about "sitting out" and you reenforce the example by the already familiar "Stay" command. Take the puppy in the car with a calm rider so the puppy learns to sit quietly and will wait patiently while you go into the store.

I also accustom the puppies to going around with me off leash. At this age they are still very dependent and will naturally follow. If the first freedom off leash doesn't occur until they are older, you will run into the smart alecs that run off to be chased and you've allowed an unnecessary bad habit to begin.

At ten weeks I separate the puppies into single crates for a nap every day, giving each an incredibly succulent round bone, trying to make the isolation as pleasant as possible. By three months all the puppies are happily sleeping alone at night in crates and naturally housebroken.

I keep mothers with puppies much longer than the general practice because I feel a good mother is such a good influence. Of course by six weeks, mothers do not care to be with their babies ALL the time, nor is it good for the puppies; but I do arrange it so that mothers and children spend some time together every day.

As for coat, I sacrifice it—on both mothers and puppies. Coat can always be grown, but puppyhood is a matter of weeks, at the most months, and this should be a time for playing and running and exercise emotionally and mentally as well as physically. The show puppy that is isolated at three months for the sake of coat is cheated out of a very important part of his life and you can't ever make it up to him. The business of showing comes soon enough, and I won't have my puppies robbed of their childhood just to make them into hairy child stars.

As the interaction between the puppies themselves increases, the order of dominance in the litter will become apparent. I try to minimize the dominance. I keep more toys available than there are puppies. Dry food is available at all times and when the meat meals are served, I feed singly or in amiable groups of two. If fighting does occur, I shake both puppies by the scruff of the neck and insist on immediate friendly contact. I am not interested in terrier spirit and I do not want the fighting pattern to begin.

If one puppy is noticeably subordinate to all the others and becoming timid, I remove him before he comes to view defeat as inevitable. Often an older, outgoing puppy won't compete with him but take care of him instead and pass on some of his already established confidence. It is most important to avoid any sense of failure. One of the most interesting discoveries made at Jackson Laboratory was that once a puppy has learned to fail, he becomes reluctant to try even a simple problem. Success seems to breed success, and what you want to accomplish is to convince the puppy that he is self-reliant and can handle the world around him.

My approach to all this is admittedly unscientific. I have no test cases; I don't withhold socialization from a control puppy to prove a point. These are not dogs in a laboratory, these are my babies—and I want the very best for every one of them. With every new litter I find different things that are helpful, a refinement of technique here and there, a new lesson that has come to mind.

It is not possible, of course, to foresee or simulate most of the new situations that your puppies will encounter in their new homes. But what you can do is give them a framework of reference: they will know they have encountered new situations in the past and been able to cope with them. You will have built their self-confidence to a point that they can adjust and take things in their stride. Because you protected them from failure during those sensitive weeks, they will not be imprisoned by doubt and anxiety but instead eager to tackle new things with confidence and assurance.

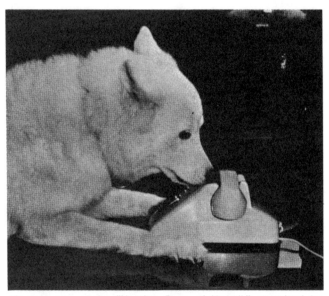

Kauanu, one of the "Hearing Dogs of Hawaii," organized by Samoyed owner and AKC Obedience judge, Ted Awaya. Hearing dogs are specially trained to help deaf people. They respond to sounds—the ringing of a telephone, doorbell or knock, alarm clocks, or smoke alarms—by alerting their masters, and indicating where the sound is coming from. Ted reports that it takes from four to six months to properly train a dog and its potential owner to the process. The first dog trained by Ted for this was, of course, a Samoyed.

A compact kennel. Gaylis Samoyeds (owners, Mel and Helen Lindell) in Oklahoma. Starctic Kachina (coming out doggy door), her son Nikita Sobaka of Gaylis, Kiskas and Tundra.

Crates are cozy. Ch. Moonlighter's Me Hallmark Too shares lebensraum with young buddy, Kevin Brighton.

13

Special Care
for Samoyeds

START from his puppyhood with daily observations. Look at his eyes. Open his mouth to look down his throat. Examine his teeth. This is training for both master and dog.

Periodically take his temperature with a rectal thermometer. Grease the bulb end with vaseline before inserting it gently and hold about 2 minutes. Normal is about 101°.

If you are with the dog daily, you are more able to observe abnormalities of appetite, energy, dull eyes, a funny cough, or indications that could be the forerunner of serious problems and may require a visit to his friend, your veterinarian.

With sound nutrition and adherence to cleanliness and definitely your attention, your Samoyed will thrive. Keep the dog clean through grooming and care and through careful attention to the cleanliness of his living quarters.

Some General Hints

We are not the first to recommend that you depend on your veterinarian for proper diagnosis and treatment of your Samoyed. But there are a few helpful hints about home care that, with common sense, might save you a trip to your Samoyed's doctor; even your veterinarian would appreciate it. First, take the temperature, and with any rise or fall call your veterinarian. Otherwise—

For upset stomachs: Charcoal biscuits—and keep the milk of magnesia handy.

For simple diarrhea: Use cooked rice instead of kibble.

For eye care: Boric acid solution and an opthalmic ointment.

For cuts or wounds: Hydrogen peroxide followed by Panalog spray (Pfizer). To stimulate hair growth and prevent scars apply vitamin E daily.

For ear trouble: Treat with Furacin powder after cleaning with alcohol on cotton swabs (gently). Others recommend Panalog Ointment, which is fine for any skin irritation.

For nerves from thunderstorms: An aspirin, and some love.

For an ounce of prevention: On returning home from a show, it is a good practice to wipe off feet with Lysol or Chlorox solution.

For a fussy eater: Cooked chicken and rice are a good combination to help put on weight.

For baths: Stuff ears with cotton and put a drop of mineral oil in each eye to prevent irritation from soap.

Provide proper shelter and ventilation. From the Oahu Samoyed Fanciers' *Bulletin* (Amy Sakata, Editor) comes a warning that is as true anywhere in the world as it is in Hawaii:

Do not leave your Samoyed inside your car for any length of time. (This is especially important in the summer, but is a rule that can well apply all year round.) Even though you roll the windows down 6 inches or so, it is not enough. Try sitting in a car yourself with the windows down 6 inches, and notice how hot it becomes. Too many dogs have died as a result of prolonged unattended stays inside a hot car.

When you are traveling, and are not able to give your dog his usual drinking water, to prevent diarrhea from drinking strange water simply add one teaspoon of lemon juice to a pan of water, or purchase distilled water.

A suggestion for summer travel: Fill a plastic milk jug half full of water, and freeze it. Cut holes in the sides and place it in a pan. As it melts, the dogs will have cool water.

Liver bait while traveling: Handlers keep their bait for a long time on long trips. Boil beef liver, cut it up in strips and bury the strips in salt in a container with a lid. Refrigerate. For use—take what you wish out, and wash off the salt.

Drop Ears

Ears usually come up, but if you are impatient and want to help, wait until after their teething, about four months. *Barbara Hayward* of San Antonio suggests the following method, recommended by her veterinarian: Buy Kire-felt at your druggist. A brand name is Dr. Scholl. Cut it to the desired shape of the ear. Peel the plastic off the adhesive back and tape it into the insides of the ear or ears. Then tape the entire ear around with adhesive tape and leave it on for five to ten days. It's important that the ear be held absolutely erect. Repeat the "bandaging" if necessary until the muscle is strengthened so the pup will hold it up by himself.

If the drop ear is prevalent in the whole litter or in several litters of the same stock, one had better look to a change of bloodlines to eliminate this serious fault, for although the standard does not say a drop ear is a disqualification, it does say the ears shall be erect. Ears should be erect before the dog is shown. It is not a universal problem, but breeders must be aware and eliminate the fault by selection of stock throwing no soft or drop ears.

Crates

A crate is a prerequisite to safety. In the car your dog is comfortable and windows may be opened wider for he won't be jumping out to follow you. A crate is indispensable for the Samoyed bathed, groomed, and ready for the show. It is HIS place, and he likes it. It does help to keep him clean. If his crate is left on the floor with the door ajar, you will find your dog will walk in to lie down for a catnap. We prefer wire crates to solid metal ones.

Deworming

Recommended times for having stools checked by the vet: Four weeks, eight weeks, twelve weeks, six months, and one year. A twice yearly check for the adult Samoyed is adequate under normal conditions. Either have your veterinarian worm your dog or use *only* the medication he prescribes for the type of worms and the dosage he prescribes.

Immunization

Veterinarians vary on this subject, but suffice it to say your Samoyed must have shots for Distemper, Hepatitis, Leptospirosis, Parainfluenza, Rabies and since 1978, Parvovirus, at the proper times your vet advises.

Pat Gibo's Samoyed (Hawaii) with friend.

215

Samoyed Nutrition
by Eileen Whitlock-Kelble

(Mrs. Kelble, a professor in Home Economics at the University of Tulsa, has been a breeder and owner of Samoyeds for many years.)

In both the Arctic and the Antarctic, especially where the terrain is variable, unknown, or treacherous, the dog-drawn sledge still provides a valuable means of transport. Although these lands support a varied wild life, it is often necessary to travel long distances with no resources other than those that can be depoted or carried.

Fresh meat in the form of white whale, walrus, seal, or bear have always formed the basis of the northern dog's diet. Perry stressed that the dog's food was meat and meat alone. Croft suggested six pounds of fresh meat, with extra blubber if necessary, as the ideal daily diet during cold conditions. Lindsay emphasized the importance of feeding fresh meat before starting on long sledge journeys.

Dried fish, especially cod or halibut, has been widely used. Mawson estimated that two pounds of dried fish represented six pounds of fresh fish (which he felt was an adequate daily ration). Thomas recommended two or three pounds of dried fish with two pound cubes of blubber, though he felt that a full diet of seal meat is preferable.

Pemmican as a sledging ration is prepared both locally and commercially. It contains 66% protein and 33% fat and its preparation consists of lean beef, dried and pounded, mixed with fat. Although it is considered one of the best rations available, all authorities agree that it should be supplemented with fresh meat as frequently as possible. A diet of 100% pemmican usually results in persistent diarrhea.

On the trail the usual practice is to live off the land except for depoted rations. Fresh meat under those conditions can become a precarious luxury. Many explorers who have relied on game found themselves and their dogs in very short supply. Nansen, who used Samoyeds, was reduced to feeding dog to dog until he was forced to consume the remaining dogs himself.

Some authorities, however, maintain that no matter what he is fed, the husky dog appears to thrive. Some of the early explorers gave little thought to the problems of feeding their sledge animals which resulted directly in the failure of several of the expeditions. Scott, for example, who also used Samoyeds, admittedly was not an expert on the subject of dog handling. Food for the dogs on his Discovery expedition was a ration of 1½ pounds of deteriorating stock fish daily. For the later Terra Nova expedition the ration was $^2/_3$ pound biscuit. When the dogs became "quarrelsome and fickle" he finally realized that they were underfed. After much soul searching, he decided to feed dog to dog. According to his reports, the "dogs never pulled their own weight and left each member of the party with an unconquerable aversion to the employment of the dogs in this ruthless fashion."

216

When Amundsen compared the unhappy experience of Scott's expeditions to his own, he determined that it was the master who had not understood the dogs. On his own expedition he provided seal meat and dried fish in addition to the pemmican, and all this was supplemented with fresh dog meat. Twenty-one of the fifty-two dogs returned from his expedition "bursting with health and putting on flesh."

Subsequent expeditions included those of Mawson, Shackleton, and Byrd, the British Grahamland Expedition, the Norwegian, British, and Swedish Expedition, and the Commonwealth Transantarctic Expedition, all stressed the importance of supplanting the diet with fresh seal meat and blubber whenever possible.

More detailed works on the nutritional requirements of sledge dogs began with the building of a permanent population of Antarctic sledge dogs in 1945. It is now estimated that adult working sledge dogs require between 3,000 and 8,000 kilocalories per day, dependent largely on the extent of their activity. Seal meat, although it is composed almost entirely of protein (33%) and fat (66%), still appears to be the ideal diet for sledge dogs.

However, in the United States today the typical Samoyed is not a sledge animal. His role is that of family caretaker, companion, and member of the family. Therefore, his needs are not identical to those of the working sledge animal.

Comparatively few direct investigations of nutritional requirements of dogs under normal household conditions have been made. However, it is felt that for certain breeds of dogs the requirements are known with some precision because dogs have often been used in experiments designed to study the nutritional needs of man.

Most good quality dry type dog foods sold today meet the requirements for vitamins or exceed them. Since experimental animals have been reared on these diets through several generations with no ill effects, it would seem that most good quality commercial dry type foods are totally adequate to maintain optimal growth, reproduction performance, and resistance to the usual environmental stresses.

Most commercial dog foods are manufactured from a wide variety of ingredients. The average commercial dry type dog food is palatable to the Samoyed over extended periods and is adequate nutritionally. If the owner feels that supplementation is necessary, the addition of 100% meat and most by-products or fat is recommended. This supplementation does not necessarily add to the nutritive value of the food but it may improve palatability for some Samoyeds.

The fat content of most dry type dog foods is kept low by the manufacturer to increase the shelf life of the product. Therefore many Samoyed breeders add fat to the food in the form of bacon drippings or other meat drippings, particularly during periods of cold weather or heavy work. Too much fat can result in reduced food intake and therefore decreased intake of necessary nutrients. Vegetable oils as a supplement are not recommended as animal fats are more palatable to the dog and are more readily usable by him.

Beef, chicken, turkey, veal, lamb, and their by-products are excellent supplements. Horse meat may give chronic intestinal upsets to some Samoyeds or may result in persistent allergic reactions. Cooked liver in large quantities will cause diarrhea, as will pasteurized, homogenized cows milk. If eggs are added to the dog's diet, they should be cooked. The avidin in the uncooked egg white combines with the biotin in the dog's other foods, thus making the biotin unavailable and creating a biotin deficiency over a period of time. The dog's biotin requirement is much higher than man's.

Feeding the Samoyed is always a topic of much discussion. Probably as many methods exist as there are breeders. The Samoyed coat and boning seem to be the subject of many special diets designed specifically to grow coat or induce heavier boning. It is well to remember that genetics will determine the potential for your Samoyed. Feeding can only determine how near to the full potential he will reach. Food cannot improve any dog beyond his genetic capacity. The use of supplements in excess of the dog's needs and tolerance can actually be dangerous by upsetting the delicate metabolic balance of the dog's body. Some nutrients such as Vitamins A and D and the trace elements become toxic at high dosage levels. Therefore it is recommended that *diet supplementation be approached with caution.*

Another fallacy that is so popular with novice owners is that the dog is a carnivore, a meat eating animal. This does not refer to muscle meat alone such as hamburgers, steaks, and roasts. The dog in the wild, as the sledge animal in the Arctic and Antarctic, consumes the entire carcass, thus insuring himself of a well-balanced diet which cannot be obtained from muscle meat alone. Any dog fed only on hamburgers, steaks, or chops will not thrive.

Canned commercial dog foods usually vary quite widely in composition and nutritive value. Some are 100% meat and meat by-products while others contain very high percentages of cereals and water. Their content may be identical to dry type dog food with only water added.

Table scraps or food fed from the table will not harm the Samoyed. However, they may create a feeding problem when the Samoyed decides that human food is more to his liking than dog food. Also, table foods can add excessive amounts of carbohydrate to the diet, which may upset the balance of the body.

Vitamins and other supplements are recommended only during periods of rapid growth, during pregnancy and lactation, and during illness upon the advice of a veterinarian. At all times give only the recommended dosage. If more than one supplement is given at a time, do not duplicate a given nutrient.

Some Samoyeds easily become problem eaters. For their own sake it is important to deal quickly and at times harshly with them. First make sure that the failure to eat a certain food is not due to illness. Then offer your

218

Samoyed only the food you want him to eat. Offer nothing else until he eats. He may refuse to eat for a few days but this will not hurt him. Dogs live in the wild for days without eating. Occasionally you will find a certain food your Sam simply does not like, but this is rare. Most Sams who have not been allowed to become problem eaters will eat most anything.

Skin Allergies in the Samoyed
by Judy Bennett

Unlike people, dogs exhibit most allergies through skin eruptions, even inhalent allergies. One of the first signs visible to the owner may be a wet spot in the coat where the Sam has been chewing and scratching to relieve the itch. Upon closer inspection, a red irritated patch of skin may be noted. If left unattended, this irritated area will begin to "weep" and infection will begin to cover the surface of the skin. Combined with the dog's continuous attention to it, the area will soon be a flaming mass of oozing infected skin which will spread at an alarming rate.

Like many conditions, an ounce of prevention is worth a pound of cure. Once an animal is suspected of being allergic, he should be sensitivity-tested by a qualified veterinary dermatologist to determine just what allergens are involved. A course of antigen injections may be prescribed and custom mixed to the individual. By far the most common allergen and the most stubborn to treat is to fleas. Compared to the expense of treating hot spots, not to mention the associated discomfort, allergy treatment is a bargain. It should be stressed that it may not always be a cure; however, it should lessen the severity of the dog's reaction.

If the problem is caught early, topical treatment can also be very effective. One type of product used very successfully in my kennel is a spray calamine lotion which contains an antihistamine with eucalyptus and menthol. The cooling effect of this spray helps relieve the burning and the calamine controls the itching. Better yet, the dog also does not care for the chalky taste and gives the area a chance to dry up and heal. It should be noted that veterinarians recommend cleansing of the area before any treatment. I have found this contrary to my ultimate goal, that of drying the area so that healing may begin. In this situation, coat need not be removed because the spray goes through the hair to coat the skin. If such an aerosol product cannot be found, a similar liquid product may be sprayed through any disposable pump type bottle such as the one hair spray or deodorant might come in.

Breeders should be aware that while specific allergies are not inherited traits, the tendency to have allergies *is* hereditary. Animals that are constantly exhibiting the described symptoms and found to have sensitive skin, should not be candidates for a breeding program. It is through the efforts of breeders like ourselves that the healthy future of the breed will be insured.

Samovar's Thorin Wendigo shows off his foot pads.

"Romeo," owned by Diane Chenault.

Typical Samoyed disposition. Ch. Samkist Super Bonanza demonstrates warmth for a totally unknown boy at a rest area on a trip by his owners, Paul and Betty Powell.

220

Summer Care

Regarding special care of Samoyeds during the hot summer months, Dr. Ivens, veterinarian and Samoyed breeder of the 1950s, wrote: "In my opinion it is not essential to change the diet to any extent; a good, well balanced diet should do in hot as well as cold weather. However, the addition of any of the sour milk products to the daily schedule is sometimes wise. Sour milk, buttermilk, or cottage cheese will do; the most effective is acidophilus milk, which has merely a greater concentration of the active organisms than the former have. Tomato juice, about one half cup per day, is also good. Merely mix it in with other foods. In the average dog, a diet of straight meat is sometimes conducive to moist eczema in hot weather. One might also use a variety of basic meats, such as lamb, or fish, in place of the more widely used beef or horsemeat. With the occurrence of eczema, any dietary change may bring improvement."

Provide fresh water regularly. Ice cubes or blocks of ice water can be added.

If puppies are in distress, fill plastic gallon milk jugs with ice cold water, and place them in the whelping box or puppy pen. Watch the puppies snuggle up to get cool.

Keep the coats groomed regularly.

NEVER CLIP A SAMOYED! By clipping, one exposes the sensitive skin to the elements, and can do great harm. Your Samoyed's coat acts as insulation against both hot and cold climates.

For skin treatments, home style: Use bactine for moist eczema or cuts or most abrasions. Use Vitamin E oil to help on "hot spots" or after hair is surgically removed for some reasons, and you are helping it to grow back.

Hip Dysplasia

Dr. Joan Turkus Sheets, M.D. (who owned the Best in Show Samoyed, Ch. Sam O'Khan's Chingis Khan) wrote on hip dysplasia for the first edition: "There is a significant incidence of hip dysplasia in the Samoyed, as in other large breeds, and as breeders it behooves us to be aware of this hereditary disease whose incidence may be decreased by selection.

"Hip dysplasia is a hereditary malformation of the hip joint in which the normal relationship of the ball (femoral head) and socket (acetabulum) is disturbed. There is a poor fit between the two, and the joint is "loose." As a result of this joint instability, degenerative joint disease (osteoarthritis) usually develops.

"The diagnosis of hip dysplasia can only be made radiographically, not on the basis of physical examination or gait. Affected animals may move quite well, particularly those with mild degrees of dysplasia. The hip joints are normal in all puppies at birth; the abnormalities appear with subsequent growth and development. A final diagnosis of normality cannot be made until skeletal maturity at approximately two years of age. It is most unfortunate that the diagnosis of hip dysplasia cannot be made earlier.

"No line is completely clear, and probably all Samoyeds are genetic carriers. Some lines do better than others; these are the ones whose breeders have been conscientiously X-raying and selecting dogs for a number of generations. At the present time, the breeding of a normal sire and dam still yields up to a 35% incidence of dysplasia in the offspring. (One normal parent and one near-normal: 41%. One normal parent and one dysplastic: 55-60%. Both parents dysplastic: 85-90%). Genetics is a game of chance."

Authors' Note: In 1977, we visited the State Veterinarian College near Stockholm, Sweden, which has a great research program on Hip Dysplasia, as they were among the first to diagnose it 30 years ago. We were told that they are convinced that there are four factors: heredity, environment, nutrition, trauma or early injury that predisposes a dog to H.D.

Pups should receive a good, nutritious diet, yet not be permitted to get fat and roly-poly. They should romp and play and go for walks on lead, but a forced exercise program (e.g. roadwork) should be avoided until development has stabilized at about 6 months. Puppies need good footing, so keep them off slippery surfaces and trim nails and pad hair. All this just makes good common sense.

Samoyed breeders are still being encouraged to X-ray their breeding stock and may submit the films to the Orthopedic Foundation for Animals (O.F.A.) for examination and certification. (Consult your veterinarian on this and on O.F.A. procedures.) Some dogs who are usually "serviceably sound" can live out comfortable lives as pets.

It takes an objective and philosophical viewpoint to be a breeder, and we must take particular care to keep the hip dysplasia problem in proper perspective. One cannot breed for clear hips alone and throw away breed type, conformation, and temperament. Wouldn't that be ridiculous? Nor are normal hip joints the only aspect of soundness to consider in a breeding program. There are certainly dogs certified by O.F.A. that have poor rear ends or who are poor specimens of the breed otherwise.

I applaud the efforts of our pioneer breeders who attacked the problem with the assistance of their local veterinarians—they have paved the way. If we pool our resources, we will, with O.F.A.'s help, solve the hip dysplasia problem faster and more efficiently.

An interesting footnote. Alan Katz, of the Minuteman Samoyed Club, tells us of Ashley, a Sam with hip dysplasia, whose love of running and being part of the team decided Alan to go ahead with his veterinarian's recommended surgery on the pectinal muscle. The operation was successful and allowed Ashley to continue on the team. (Lucky, too, because surgery does not guarantee success.)

Care of the Aged Dog
by Rosemary Williamson

Authors' Note: While on a judging visit to New Zealand, we stopped for tea at George and Rosemary Williamson's Patterdale Farm (Auckland, N.Z.) and visited their spotless Quarantine Kennel. It was a highlight, for we met their grand Border Terrier "Winston"—18 years and 4 months old. He was the Head Man of all Terriers and Quarantine boarders at the kennel—where both old and young experience such tender loving care. We asked Rosemary for these helpful observations because, as she says, "Whatever the breed, old age will form the same pattern."

"Winston" was named for Winston Churchill. He looked so much like him, and he was and still is just as determined and as bold a character.

"Winston" entered the show ring at the age of 10 years, and was greatly admired by many overseas judges. Even at 16 years, his body was wonderfully preserved and firm, and he came home with many Best Veteran sashes.

I mention all this because old age can start as young as 10 years old. The term deterioration is probably better. Fortunately, this is a slow process, and one becomes quite used to the situation and adjusted to having to really care for an old dog in the house. If you have really *loved* the dog in its young days, and it has done well for you and has given you years of pleasure, you will find that you will do all you can for it in its last few years, months or days. I must emphasize that patience and understanding is very necessary, especially with a dog like "Winston" at his age.

Each month the Vet suggests we review the situation to see if there has been any further deterioration. The main reason for this is that we must never have a dog that suffers from pain or is just thoroughly miserable.

Dogs in old age must be fed twice a day, a small meal in the morning and a small meal in the evening, instead of one large main meal. They love their food like all old folks!

Diet plays a large part in keeping the old dog healthy. Raw grated cabbage, raw grated carrot, raw meat with fat, bone broth gravy and kibble with wheatgerm, and regular vitamin pills is a good meal for a dog of 12 weeks up to even 18 years old.

Regular worming and grooming and flea spraying is essential. Regular visits into the garden for the aged dog are essential. It is rather like having a baby, as you have to think for them. In this way carpets will not be soiled.

The aged dog sleeps for many hours. Make sure the room is draught-proof. If the windows are open, close the door and always have a wool rug to cover the dog with, while sleeping, for warmth. Immediately they waken up, put them outside. A coat for the winter is well worth having to keep the back warm, as the aged dog feels the cold.

Quite often, the aged dog will go deaf or partially blind. As long as he can see enough to get around and hear enough to be called, he will be happy.

Naturally he will be much slower with everything, this is where patience on your part will be practised!

All of a sudden he is more dependent on you and wants to follow you everywhere. This is where you have to learn to be conscious of a dog behind you when you turn around, otherwise you can do yourself harm by falling flat on your nose over him! Or you go into a bedroom and he has followed you into the room, and he will come out only when he is ready, after he has sniffed at this or that or the other thing! Unlike a young dog who does this and in seconds has beaten you out of the room, the old dog takes his time to do exactly the same thing! So you have to have patience and to realize he is doing just the same thing as the younger dog, but taking so much longer.

Touch plays a great part in old age. With "Winston" being a small dog, he is lifted down the steps into the garden but he manages to come up by himself. If you catch at them quickly or suddenly it will startle them if they are partially deaf. It is better to touch them gently first and then lift them up and gently place them on the ground, because generally their legs are not as strong and it puts them off balance.

It is amazing when a bitch is in heat how an aged dog can lose many years off his life and play the part of a virile young dog! Particularly with "Winston." At his great age, he is first in the queue for the girls! So he thinks. Instead of walking every which way, his legs suddenly acquire extra strength and he has been known to run, at great speed, if he thinks that the bitch on heat is in the offing for him. I am sure that it is these sparks of interest that keep him going.

I have found that all the other dogs have a great respect for him. I know for sure that he is top dog and that all the others realize he is to be regarded as a very respected veteran and a very popular one, too.

Physiotherapy is a good thing for the aged dog with weak back legs. It is very helpful to have heat and massage. I am very fortunate to have a physiotherapist who will use his wonderful hands on dogs, cats and even cows. A slipped disc can be manipulated back by a physiotherapist, so therefore the dog doesn't have to suffer unnecessary pain.

There is one development that puzzled me, and that I discussed with my Vet. A short time ago "Winston" appeared to be unsettled on the occasional day. He would bark to go out, then bark to come in, and bark to come into the kitchen, and then promptly bark to go out again. I seemed to be going round in circles, opening and shutting various doors so many times!! We came to the conclusion that he was just having an "off" day and that this does happen. They are not ill but rather more unsettled than usual. Fortunately we haven't had illness all the way along. It is a good idea to keep checking ears, eyes and teeth at regular intervals.

To end, I will recall an incident which happened while I was away at a show! I have quite a few Border Terrier bitches and they all come in heat

224

Ch. White Star IV (1966-1980). By Ch. Sho-Off's Czar of Whitecliff ex Ch. Tsonoqua of Snow Ridge. Star was still winning BOBs and BOSs when she was 10 years old. Owners: Wilna Coulter and Jo Geletich.

together. The bitches were at one side of the house in a large grass run and George went into the pen to repair a small hole in the fence closely followed by "Winston", who was his constant shadow. George knew he was there but didn't fear a thing with "Winston", who was aged 15 years at the time, because of his weakness in his back legs. Happily repairing the fence, George glanced round to see "Winston" & "Birkie" tied! How?? Nobody will ever know! "Winston", being the character he is, just acquired the extra strength.

Nine weeks later I learned from George what had happened—a beautiful very rare blue and tan Border Terrier dog puppy, which we kept ourselves. The puppy was named "Calypso", Greek for Hidden Secret! Aptly named, and shown with great success. "Calypso" has sired lovely puppies and has a wonderful temperament and a great character like his sire. Determination was in the fore here with "Winston".

Old age can be a great success if you personally are prepared to make it so. It is up to you, the owner of an old dog, to either see it through right to the end or terminate it. There is no other choice. But you know what my choice has been!

Ch. Scheherazade, C.D. (at 9½ years of age), pictured winning breed at Flagstaff KC 1980 under Mrs. Irene Bivins. Whelped 12/23/70, by Igor of the Tundra ex Amy of the Tundra. Breeders, John and Mary Ann Butler. Owner, Marguerite Baird, Arizona.

14

Grooming

by Mardee Ward

SAMOYEDS have no doggy odor, it's true, but they must be groomed for health and beauty on a regular basis. They do not need a bath to be clean. Dry baths are possible using only brushing and mixture of cornstarch and baby powder or commercial powdered preparations which are rubbed through the coat and brushed out again. Some owners bathe their pets once a year for the Christmas season. The "show Samoyed" is bathed for shows and the treatment rivals any Poodle parlor.

Equipment needed: Grooming table; a long pin brush set in rubber; a slicker brush (Warner); a nylon brush; coarse and fine tooth combs; pet nail clippers or electric nail grinders; scissors and thinning shears; a "chalk" box; and some spray bottles.

Daily grooming is the ideal—but that is not often achieved, so we'll settle for two or three times a week as a realistic goal. This may not mean you do a complete all over brushing. It would be better to do an area thoroughly (with brushing followed by combing from the skin out) than to skim the complete surface.

Brushing and Combing

The purpose of frequent brushing and combing is to maintain cleanliness and remove the loose and dead hair; to prevent matting and knotting of the silky hair, especially behind the ears; and to tone the skin and stimulate new hair growth.

The method: First, decide where you are going to begin. Divide the dog into sections, i.e. the forequarters, the hindquarters, the sides, back, neck, stomach, head and tail. I find it much easier to have the dog lie down while being groomed. Then as you work and take periodic breaks, you can remember where you left off. I prefer to begin in the shorter hair, the legs or

226

stomach and work into the longer hair. So with your left hand, part the coat as you move up the leg briskly brushing down small sections from the skin out. The Warner slicker brush and fine comb work best on the shorter hairs of the dog. When you reach the longer hairs, the pin brush and coarse comb work better. Be sure to concentrate on the problem areas. The elbows and hocks need special attention as does the stomach and inside the legs. When brushing around the sensitive parts of the male and female use the nylon hair brush and you may need an assistant when working in this area.

Particular attention should be paid to the heavy ruff under his neck. It helps to train him to hang his head over the table, enabling you to get at the thick hair from his chin down the neck and front. Be especially gentle on the tail. He does not like this part and will try to turn to keep you from getting at it. Using the pin brush or nylon brush, start at the base of the tail and brush out away from the tail bone. Establish a part and work up the tail, when you reach the end go back to the base and start again. Repeat until you have gone around the tail completely. Never brush or comb the tail hairs straight down the tail bone as the hairs do not grow that way and your dog will protest.

Finally, after he has been brushed and combed by sections, use the pin brush vigorously, brushing the body coat toward the head, the stomach down and the pants and tail out. Remember that brushing is always followed by combing. Exhibitors who are most proficient in preparing the show Sam recommend a complete grooming before the bath.

The Bath

Equipment needed: A shampoo for white or silver hair (often blue); or Ivory soap or any biodegradable soap; mineral oil to put in eyes; cotton to plug ears; towels and wash cloth; a forced warm air dryer (human or special dog dryer); bathtub or large stall shower; and a spray attachment with a sturdy fastener for the outlet. On a hot day you may bathe him on a table in the yard if you are able to attach a hose to warm water.

There are two kinds of baths; a quick bath and a full wet bath.

The **quick bath** is used when you want a clean looking dog and his outer coat is dirty, but his skin is fairly clean. This method is often used on a show dog between full baths as too much bathing is not healthy or necessary. The quick bath uses minimal water, therefore the drying time is greatly reduced. First, in a small pan or bucket mix warm water and a little soap. Using a wash cloth, dip and ring out and rub all over the dog, getting just the outer portion of the coat damp. This picks up the surface dirt without saturating the undercoat. Repeat until dog has been completely wiped down.

Then, using a pan of clean warm water, rinse dog in same fashion as washing. Towel dry so dog is just damp, but not dripping wet. Take a mixture of cornstarch and baby powder (2:1 respectively) and start working into the coat, concentrating on the legs, stomach, ears and face, and rear. Be careful not to get too much in the body coat as it is more difficult to get out of the longer hair. Continue rubbing with the mixture until coat feels dry, then let dog shake (you should be outside for this part). Now you are ready to start brushing it out. A strong blow dryer is excellent at this stage as it helps separate the coat and blow the powder out while you brush with the pin brush. When you are finished, your dog will sparkle and smell good; it takes a third of the time a full bath will take.

The **full wet bath** is called for when you want that total and complete shine from the skin out. Prepare your dog for the bath after he has been brushed and combed prior to bath day. Put the cotton in his ears and a drop of mineral oil in each ear (to prevent soap irritation). Be sure the dog will have good footing in the tub or shower with a rubber mat, and have the water lukewarm before starting.

Washing: Completely wet your dog and begin soaping. A little soap goes a long way but be sure to use enough. Begin with the head and back and work your way down to the toes and the tail. Scrub, scrub, scrub, with your fingers, especially on the elbows, hocks, hips, feet, and ears. Squeeze the coat in your hands in a kneading fashion rather than circular movements as this can tangle the coat. One sudsing should be sufficient unless he is really dirty as the secret to a clean dog is in the rinsing.

Rinsing: Begin at the head and be careful not to get water down the ears. Squeeze the coat as the warm water runs over the hair as you work down the back to the shoulders, neck, chest, sides and legs. Always rinse the stomach and tail last as the soapy water goes there last. No creme rinse is necessary as the Samoyed coat has a harsh texture of its own which allows it to stand up rather than lay down.

Drying: Use your hands to squeeze and slick down the body and legs to remove the excess water from the coat. Remove Samoyed to area where he can shake himself well. Towel dry with many towels, rubbing briskly back and forth. The dog will normally shake often; if not, blow in his face and say "Shake." Place on grooming table for blower drying with WARM air. It takes from 36 to 48 hours to dry an adult Samoyed in full coat without a dryer, so if you must dry him naturally provide some clean, draft-free quarters, preferably in the house. The crate is indispensable at this time.

When thoroughly dry, comb as you did before the bath. It will be easier now. Before he steps out for his showing, whether it be a family reunion or a dog show, polish with the following: Comb with the fine tooth comb on the thick furred head and face and chin. Brush with pin or nylon brush up and out on the ruff, chest, shoulders, and leg feathering; brush down and out on the belly fringes, thighs, pants, and inside legs. Fluff the tail by holding tip and brush out from the base and working up to tip.

228

Trimming

The English, Australians, and New Zealanders abhor trimming. They favor the profuse featherings around the hocks and feet.

Americans perfected the art and demand for extensive grooming, sometimes to the detriment of a given breed. If you choose to trim, *do it so that it looks natural and uncut.*

Hocks and Feet: Do not overtrim, just neaten the foot and hock.

Whiskers: A personal preference whether to trim or not. Same with scissor trimming the edge of the lip line. This may improve the smile and show more contrast. (Because whiskers are living sensors, Mom prefers that whiskers be left alone, not cut.)

Cut nails: Use clippers or grinders. Long nails will cause arched toes to become splayed and spoil otherwise good feet.

The body coat should never be scissored or clipped unless called for due to medical reasons. The Samoyed is a natural breed of dog and his coat affords a natural protection for his benefit.

If you choose to take your Samoyed to a grooming shop, make sure they know how a Sammy should be groomed and caution them not to overtrim, if at all.

After all these instructions, we might add that nothing takes the place of consistency in care, good health, and daily brushing. Excuse us while we groom a couple of Samoyeds.

Getting ready.

Liz Dickson showing WD Prince Caliph and Tony Chavez showing WB Belaya Peppermint Patti at 1975 San Diego Samoyed Club Specialty. In background, judge Anastasia MacBain and superintendent Maggi Simmons (with hat).

Am. & Can. Ch. Tasha of Sacha's Knight ("Teka"), going BOB at Westminster 1982 under judge Kathleen Kanzler. Owned by Mardee Ward (handling) and Dolly Ward. "Teka" was the No. 1 Samoyed bitch for 1980, 1981 and 1982. Winner of SCLA Tournament, 1982, under three judges simultaneously scoring their choices. BISS Houston Specialty, 1978 and San Diego Specialty, 1984.

230

15

Show Handling

by Mardee Ward

Y OU CAN START TRAINING your Samoyed for the show ring as early as eight weeks of age. However, since he must be at least six months before participating in A.K.C. licensed Sanctioned Matches and Shows, you'll have plenty of time to prepare yourself for your first show. Use this time to check out some of the following:

1. Write the American Kennel Club, 51 Madison Avenue, New York, New York 10010 for the free booklet "Rules Applying to Registration and Dog Shows." Read it thoroughly at least once and then study particular sections. Keep it for reference. Amendments appear in the A.K.C.'s official magazine, *Pure-Bred Dogs/AK Gazette.*

2. Study the Breed Standard. This will enable you to evaluate your dog. Learn not only about your dog's virtues, but also the faults according to the Standard. Each dog does have faults. Knowing these will be of value to you in the show ring so you may avoid calling attention to the faults by poor handling.

3. Attend Sanctioned Matches and dog shows as a spectator;observe handlers and ask questions. We repeat, *ask questions!*

4. Inquire about Handling Classes in your area and attend. These classes will give your dog exposure to noise, other dogs, strange surroundings, and people. You will learn the basic principles of show handling.

5. Enter your dog in Match shows for practice. Classes will be the same but there is no "winners class" as there is in a point show. Point shows award points to the Winners Dog and Winners Bitch toward championships.

Conditioning

Both you and your Samoyed need to be in condition for the show ring. You and your dog are a team, and must practice together so as to present a picture of harmony. Since you must run when the dog gaits or trots, practice running with your dog so that it looks smooth and natural.

To achieve this team effort, hours, days and months are spent running or gaiting with your dog. Since dog shows are held in a variety of places and on different surfaces, you should practice accordingly. Practice on the sidewalk, in the street, at the park, in a parking lot, and inside a building if at all possible.

Conditioning implies that a dog exhibit good muscle tone, healthy coat and skin, healthy teeth and gums, in essence, a true picture of vitality.

Training for the Show Ring

The training of a puppy is the same whether he is to be only a family pet or an illustrious show dog. Five to ten minutes, 2-3 times a day is an ideal time allotment for working a young puppy on the leash. Train with a "choke" chain collar so the puppy doesn't learn to pull you around. Short little jerks with a vocal command to "heel" will encourage him to respond. The dog is worked on your left side with the leash in you left hand.

The older dog—6 months and up—has a longer attention span and should be worked 15-30 minutes daily. Show work consists of: Posing with all four legs square ("show stance"); Examination, being touched all over; and Gaiting, or trotting. Practice with the proper show equipment—a thin choke chain collar and a show lead. Be firm, but make it FUN! Coordinate your hand and voice commands and be consistent. The sequence you use in stacking your dog in a show stance should be the same every time, i.e. tell dog to "stand," then set left front leg, then right front leg, then left rear, and finally right rear leg. With the leash in your left hand, bait or alert your dog with your right hand.

Once your dog or puppy is standing, have another person "examine" him so he gets used to having strangers' hands go over him, especially to have his teeth looked at to see how the bite comes together. The males will need to let people touch their testicles as they are checked in the show ring by the judge. In developing a vocabulary with your dog, use clear, one syllable words whenever possible. For example, "Stand," "Stay," "Heel," "Gait," or "Trot," "Good Boy," "Good Girl," "Bait" or "Cookie." Remember, when communicating with your dog your tone of voice is of great importance. At the end of a training period, be sure to praise your dog both physically and verbally.

232

Club Matches and Shows

Some people are joiners and some are not. What you do depends on what kind of a person you are fundamentally. Even if you have never liked social clubs or church groups particularly, you might try a dog club. You can get a liberal education there. All of man's human relationships found in any group may be found there. You have to deal with people if you are in a club. It is no place for a hermit! There are few hermits, if any, who go to dog shows or join clubs even if they own a dog.

Would you believe that dog clubs are not just for dogs? Well, it is true and those who say "This is a dog club, let's keep the people out" are unrealistic. Constitutions, which are the rules of the game, are read and debated by people, not their dogs, even though the club is formed because of the interest in the breed or all breeds.

All activities relating to purebred dogs are supervised by the American Kennel Club. Know their rules and regulations and abide by them. A copy of the rules may be obtained by writing to the Secretary, American Kennel Club, 51 Madison Ave., New York, N.Y. 10010.

Specialty clubs are formed for the breed on the local scene. Parent clubs are formed for the breed on the national scope. Parent clubs work with the AKC for the protection of the breed, guarding the standard and the activities influencing the breed.

All breed clubs are formed to hold AKC sanctioned events, which include one or two dog shows a year, usually on the same weekend of each year. This is when the breeders bring out the best they have planned and produced in their breed. This is when the novice dog owner attends his first show unless his Specialty club has been actively holding fun matches and sanctioned matches for his breed alone. This is when the club people put forth their best efforts to "put on a really big show." This is when the social activities may be combined with the competitive sport.

Samoyed people are beginning to become a part of this broader aspect of the dog game. Usually "Sammy people" stay within their own group, hardly casting an eye to any splendors of another breed not of their choice. While this may be considered meritorious and faithful, it is a type of tunnel vision we are glad to see waning as more Sammy people begin to join all breed clubs and look at breeds other than Samoyeds at a show or event. We do not fear that Samoyed people will choose any other breed because of "integration."

Do not hesitate to locate your local groups formed for education about dogs in general and your breed in particular. There is as much of a hobby to be had in clubs and their work as there is in enjoying your Samoyed.

Matches are of several kinds. Fun matches are for fun and are practices for the more formal matches called sanctioned matches.

Sanctioned matches are held to give: puppies and young dogs training in a ring situation; the owner-handlers practice in managing their dogs; club members practice in the various facets of putting on the show; apprenticing judges and stewards an opportunity to put their book learning into the live laboratory of actually judging the dogs and dealing with the people who are learning everything from handling to good sportsmanship. Seek out such advertised events and attend them, first as a spectator and then as a participant. There is a growing trend to assess more weight to the importance of matches. We believe America is developing the dog sport to the level of the English, Australians and New Zealanders, who provide Open shows (our matches without points) and Championship shows (our point shows, awarding points toward championships).

The sport of dog shows has so many parts to it, you will never learn them all to perfection. But just think—you can try for a lifetime. Shows give you a destination for travel and something to do when you get there. Condition your Samoyed, love your Samoyed, train and show your Samoyed, and take him to shows and it can make a whole life for you and your family. The most wonderful people in the world have become our friends through the "dog game" activities, which are all-inclusive.

For your guidance in obtaining information on shows and matches in your area, we include a listing of the secretaries of the parent club and the eleven licensed local clubs. In addition there are about a dozen other local clubs around the United States in the formation process.

SAMOYED CLUB OF AMERICA
Mrs. Kathryn Molineaux
19707 Bear Creek Road, Boulder Creek, CA 95006

The Samoyed Club of San Diego
Margaret Simmons, 4420 Lowell St., La Mesa, CA 92041

The Samoyed Club of Los Angeles
Mrs. Dolly Ward, 5841 Fitzpatric Road, Hidden Hills, CA 91302

The Samoyed Club of Washington State
Marilyn Lewis, 4141 SW County Line Rd., Port Orchard, WA 98366

The Potomac Valley Samoyed Club
Patti Rasmussen, P.O. Box 33, Lincoln, VA 22078

The Greater Milwaukee Samoyed Fanciers
Mrs. Jeanne Nonhof, Rte. 1, Box 176, Waldo, WI 53093

The Samoyed Club of Houston
Anne Peil, 4512 Langtry Lane, Houston, TX 77041

The Northern California Samoyed Fanciers
LaVera Morgan, 2820 Erin Ct., Richmond, CA 94806

Metropolitan Atlanta Samoyed Club
Ginger R. Aldrich, 3296 Holly Mill Ct., Marietta GA 30062

Ch. Czar Samusz of Karshan, C.D., BOB at 10 years of age at SCLA Specialty 1981. Also Veteran Class winner. The year before, Czar was the Highest Scoring Dog in Trial at the Los Angeles Specialty. Wh. 8/16/72, by Tuffy of White Frost ex Czarina of Kashan. Owned by Terry Bednarczyk and handled by Rich Clement.

Ch. Weathervane's First Million (Ch. Polar Star's Tiger ex Am. & Can. Ch.Karatyll's Tia of Weathervane), winning BOS at SCA Specialty 1975. Co-owned by Marge Million Clark (left) and Jean Scovin (right).

Ch. Kauzja's Kwintus Fabrikus (Ch. Kauzja's Silver Baron ex Ch. Kauzja Cheefa-tu) BOB at SCLA Specialty 1982 over entry of 113. Multi-Group winner. Breeder-owners: Walt and Jan Kauzlarich. Handler, Cheryl Cates.

235

The Chicagoland Samoyed Club
Arlene Hefler, 482 Charlotte, Crystal Lake, IL 60014

The Minuteman Samoyed Club
Carol Cook, 182 Georgetown Rd., Boxford, MA 01921

Samoyed Assn. of Minneapolis-St. Paul
Kathy Wiley, 7909 Stevens Ave., South Bloomington, MN 55420

A Few Do's and Don'ts at the Dog Show:

1. Before the judging of your breed, observe the judging of the breeds ahead of you by the judge who will be judging your breed. Note his ring procedure and you will know what is expected of you and your dog when your dog is judged.
2. Before entering the ring, be sure your armband obtained from the ring steward is on your left arm so the number is clearly visible to the judge.
3. As you enter the ring, have your dog under control on your left side and looking alert. The first impression the judge gets of your exhibit is important.
4. Remember you and your dog are working as a unit to bring out the best in the dog. ALL attention is to be on the dog, not on you, the handler. You will detract from your dog if you bend over him or allow too long leads to drape over him. By standing too closely to his side or allowing him to lean on you, you do not present him well. Hold the bait unobtrusively.
5. When gaiting, moving your dog at a trot, keep him at an arm's length on a *loose lead*.
6. Be sure to follow the judge's instructions. If you do not understand them or do not hear the judge, just ask him to repeat or clarify.
7. Last but not least, if you must correct your dog's behavior in the ring, do so inconspicuously.

Keep one eye on your dog and one eye on the judge. The finer points of handling come with experience. However, it's possible that you may never quite get the hang of it—in which case you should hire a professional handler.

236

Ch. Northwind's Black Magic, winner of Award of Merit at 1979 SCA Specialty. Dam of Am. & Can. Ch. Northwind's Robin Hood. Breeder-owners: Jack and Helen Feinberg.

Ch. Statussam's Troublemaker, by Ch. Kondako's Rising Sun ex Tasha of Sunflower, bred and owned by Dr. Mary Ellen and Joseph Torrez. Trouble, winner of 40 BOBs and 20 Group placings including several Firsts, won the 1985 SCLA Tournament. Handler, Cheryl Cates.

237

Ch. Samoyland's Vojak, U.D. (1945-1952), the first Samoyed on the West Coast to win dual championship (Obedience and conformation). Trained by his owner, AKC-licensed professional handler, Tom Witcher of San Francisco, Vojak performed on TV and in benefit programs for handicapped children, service organizations, etc.

Companion dogs are companionable outside of the ring, too. Am. & Can. Ch. Kombo's Silver Prince, C.D., by Am. & Can. Ch. Tod-Acres Fang ex Can. Ch. Snow Ridge's Sonya. Bred and owned by Mr. and Mrs. Louis Weltzin, of Canada.

238

Dress for the Ring

Dog showing is an active sport. If you are handling, dress appropriately. Men should wear a suit or slacks with a sports jacket.

Women may wear slacks; however, a nice A-line skirt with pockets (for bait) and blouse are dressier.

Be careful not to wear too full a skirt or dress as it can interfere with the dog gaiting.

Be sure to wear comfortable running shoes. Heels, sandals or clog-type shoes are dangerous for showing dogs.

Colors of clothes should complement your dog, so stay away from white or light colored apparel and shoes.

The dog show goes on regardless of the weather. Plan your showing wardrobe to include rain jackets, coats and all-weather footgear. You must still be able to move and run.

Some 'Don'ts':

1. Avoid wearing dangling jewelry that may distract your dog, or get caught in his coat or lead.
2. Avoid having money or jingly things in your pocket as they are distracting to other exhibitors, the judge, and to your own dog.
3. Avoid wearing sunglasses in the ring. Eye contact with the judge and your dog is lost. Both are very important.

Junior Showmanship

Many children go along for the ride while their parents engage in the sport of dogs, whether it be conformation showing or obedience or sledding. Many children will exhibit an interest in participating when they are ready. Some parents will push their children into dog activities. No matter how they arrive, the children may benefit in manifold ways.

Junior showmanship is divided by age groups and sometimes by sex. The beginning age group is for 10 to 13 year olds and the older group is from 13 to 17 year olds. The beginning junior handler starts in the Novice class. After he or she has won three first places the junior then goes into the Open class.

Sportsmanship. If it is manifested in a good light by the parents, it will be learned in that light by the youth. If the reverse is true, it is unfortunate. This is the pattern of learning, though it may have its exceptions. Therefore, the adults in the dog game must teach the younger set the right way. That can be a challenge.

The junior handlers learn to win and lose gracefully, we hope. They learn the proper care of canine life and how to communicate with their animal. Instead of getting into trouble because they have nothing to relate to, nothing to be superior to, nothing to love, they may be found grooming and training their "show dog."

239

One of the more prestigious competitions for juniors is that held at the Westminster Kennel Club show in New York City each February. The rules for entry are based on previous wins, and competition is very keen. Kathy Hritzo, 16 years old at the time, won the Junior Showmanship competition handling her Samoyed at the 100th Anniversary Westminster in 1976.

Professional Handlers

There may be a need for a professional handler. Not all people are able to handle animals, or have the time or inclination. We are all individuals of different leanings and capabilities.

The Professional Handlers Association has high standards of ethics, and they are what they are titled—"professional" in this field. However, not all professional handlers are members of the PHA. Names and addresses of handlers may be obtained from superintendents of dog shows, or through advertisements in the catalogs or magazines.

In selecting a handler, you will want to talk to him (or her), to "size him up" for yourself, to see him handle dogs, and to see his kennels or facilities. Fine, reputable handlers will welcome such an investigation.

At left, Mardee Ward handling Helen King's Ch. Tilka's Tinka to a win in 1960. At right, 21 years later, Mardee handling Ch. Tasha of Sacha's Knight to win of the Houston Specialty.

240

Ch. Snowline's Joli Shashan, C.D.X., first winner (in 1969) of the annual trophy for the outstanding Obedience Samoyed, donated by the Juliet T. Goodrich Trust Fund, and awarded by the Samoyed Club of America. Pictured here in the "long sit" at an Obedience trial, Shashan was by Ch. Joli White Knight ex Ch. Lady Sasha of Kazan, C.D. Breeders: Nancy and Laurel Alexander. Owners: Mr. and Mrs. Thomas Mayfield, Calif.

Ch. Joza of Mar-Vin-Lou, with Mrs. Virginia Belikoff of Indiana, visit a kindergarten to give a demonstration in Obedience training.

O.T. Ch. Barron's White Lightnin', the first Obedience Trial Champion Samoyed in AKC history. Top Obedience Samoyed (SCA), 1979, '80, and '83. A multiple High in Trial winner. Wh. 12/15/76, he is owned by Barb and Dan Cole, Missouri.

Am. & Can. Ch. Nordika's Polar Barron, C.D., Obedience titlist and one of the Top Twenty in the show ring. Wh. 2/10/78, "Kappy" is by Ch. Snowacres Nordika ex Ch. Princess Tovara of Snowacres. A Merit Award recipient at the 1980 Specialty, his record includes a Best in Specialty and multi-Group wins. Owners, Barbara and Dan Cole.

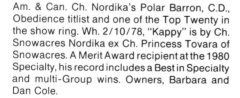

242

16

Obedience Training for the Samoyed

by Don and Dell Wells

Don Wells, an AKC Obedience judge, is an Obedience trainer for two Obedience clubs in El Monte, California, and a member of the Southwest Obedience Club of Los Angeles, California Handlers Advanced Obedience School, Samoyed Club of America, Golden Retriever Club of Los Angeles, and the Golden Retriever Club of America. A delegate to the Southern California Dog Obedience Council, he has finished Samoyeds to championship as well as to Obedience degrees. His wife Dell is "feeder and conditioner" of their team operation. Don and Dell are active members of Rio Hondo K.C.

UNTIL as recently as ten years ago, a Samoyed was considered virtually untrainable, as far as top competition was concerned. Even today, many of the best long-time trainers consider our beautiful "big white dogs" an Obedience casualty.

This became a challenge to me, because I found the Samoyed to be above average in intelligence and affection, and to possess a loyalty to their masters that would be difficult to surpass.

In my opinion, some training techniques used in the past were abusive and overly harsh, physically forcing an action without first letting the dog understand what was being asked of him. I then vowed never to use excessive force on either my own or my clients' dogs.

As trainer/handlers we must first know and understand exactly what we want our dogs to do, and then should devise a way to show them step-by-step what we want. A Samoyed, being an intelligent and willful

Am. & Can. Ch. Dajmozek, Am. & Can. U.D.T., the first Samoyed to earn both Canadian and American Utility Dog Tracking titles. The third Samoyed to earn the Tracking title in the U.S. and the first for Canada. Owned by John and Deborah Orr. Debbie and "Seke" were a team to be remembered. Debbie, a guiding light in SCA activities, was the tragic victim of an accident involving a drunken driver.

Blanca Belleza of Cypress, C.D.X., P.C.X., loved, trained and handled by Don and Dell Wells. Now in retirement, in her prime she carried a 198.5 average (out of a possible 200). Winner of two SCA Specialty trials, she was always "in the ribbons" in the Delaney and Shuman System ratings.

244

animal, will not usually be forced into any action he does not understand. While he won't break down in spirit, he will actively resist. On the other hand, if he is shown true affection and understanding, and given praise for correct action, he will cooperate fully.

If you are to Obedience train a Samoyed, you must first earn (and I mean EARN) his respect through daily—even hourly—contact, genuine care and affection, fairness in corrections and consistency in your actions and expectations.

Understanding and praise are what dog obedience is based upon. Your dog wants, with all his heart, to please you. So show him how, then PRAISE, PRAISE, PRAISE and watch him sparkle!

Obedience groundwork begins long before you physically take your Samoyed out to the training grounds or training class. A wise trainer will first spend considerable time observing his dog to learn what he likes and dislikes, and how he responds to differing tones of voice or to hand corrections. No one should know your dog better than you do. Observe how he reacts to various situations. Do you know which way he turns when retrieving a ball? Is he left-handed or right-handed? Does he panic easily, or is he "super-cool"? What makes him happy or sad? Only when you've studied your dog are you ready to start serious Obedience training.

Many owners of Samoyeds, as well as of other breeds, are firm believers in basic Obedience for all dogs, whether they are kept as pets or entered in competition. Only the degree of accuracy demanded need differ.

Look for an Obedience class taught by a competent and humane trainer. Then you, as owner/master, will understand how to teach, and your dog in turn will learn to understand you and please you.

You must be the leader, and your dog the "pack-member" to obtain a really good Obedience Samoyed. This leadership must never be relinquished—even for a moment. I stress again that you do not need to use force (such as hitting or kicking) to maintain this leadership. Once the status is established, your Samoyed will recognize it more than you will.

This leadership status should be established as early as possible and maintained throughout your dog's life. You will find this rewarding even if you only want to teach your dog good manners, so that both of you are at ease in nearly every situation, and you can be proud of him.

It is quite easy to establish the leader-follower status with a puppy. However, as your dog gets older and matures, he will challenge your "right" to be leader, as he would in the wilds. This challenge can be quite mild in a shy or easy-going Samoyed and not become a problem. But with a dominant Samoyed, a physical challenge for authority may be made, and you—as master or pack-leader—must not back away, or your authority will be lost.

Some other beginning suggestions: Before starting a training session, try to allow your dog a few minutes to relieve himself, and to become

Members of the Northern California Samoyed Fanciers preparing for the Long Sit in Obedience at their 1981 Qualifying-A Match. Left to right: Barbara Horne Cole; Karen Tye; Christina Adkins with Com-Rades Autumn Prince Ai-Ki, the high scoring team in the trial; Art Adkins and Pat Enslen.

Trailblazer Star at Sunset, C.D. Breeder: Judy Mears. Owner: Mrs. George Lohmiller, Colorado. Star better be obedient; she shares companionship with Angora bunnies being raised at the Lohmiller home for color and spinning.

Ch. Karana's Diko Apollo, C.D.X. (Am. & Can. Ch. Oakwood Farm's Kari J'Go Diko ex Ch. Travois Penelope). Breeder-owners: Iris M. Clough and Johnnie M. Rogers, Colorado.

246

accustomed to the training field. And always try to end your training sessions with a "Well done!" exercise, so that you both may stop on a happy note.

Early in practice training it is well to pick a method to release your dog from a strict attention to your commands—i.e., a clap of the hands or anything that will let him know he may relax his concentration on you, a relaxation that lets him be a dog instead of your "shining star" until he is called to heel position again. In the beginning your dog's period of attention will be quite short, say 10 to 15 minutes, but as he learns, the sessions can be greatly extended. They should always be spaced with short rest periods so that you and your dog can collect your wits.

At start of the first lesson, teach your dog to sit by your side in the heel position. One method to get him to sit is to pull up on the leash and push down at the hip area, repeating the word "Sit". Once he sits, praise him lavishly. If he gets up during this praise period, correct immediately in a stern (mean) voice. Place him in a sit position, and praise him in a friendly, pleasant voice.

Pets and companion dogs are continually confused, especially when young and in the process of forming lifelong habits. Since a dog is basically a creature of habit, make every effort to avoid this confusion and maintain consistency. A prime example of unintentional confusion for your dog might be allowing him to get up on your furniture one time, and then chastising him for doing it the next time. You must be the controlling party. Your dog may not be able to distinguish between the two different sets of circumstances. When he is a puppy, a dog can be molded into whatever you want him to be by using simple Obedience techniques and an understanding of canine behavior. Decide what your dog will or will not be allowed to do, then enforce the established rules.

Another example of training and consistency is "Area or Room Training". By correcting a dog whenever he enters a room that he is not allowed into, then praising lavishly when he leaves upon your command, he will soon learn that room is "off-limits", and will not enter. After all, no one—not even your dog—will invite an unpleasant experience. A mean or angry tone of voice, as contrasted with a happy one, will surely show your dog the difference between right and wrong.

This same procedure—using a friendly or stern voice to convey "Right" or "Wrong" respectively to your dog—will work for any situation. It is not necessary to use a loud, screaming voice, since dogs hear well and respond to the tone of your voice, not the volume.

Sometimes a dog will learn one exercise very quickly and be very slow learning another, depending on his particular experience. Each exercise, no matter how simple, will have to be repeated many times. So always be patient, correct as necessary, and praise—even after you have physically moved him to the desired position. Remember, each small success deserves a large praise, which then leads to another success. *Two or three correct actions WITH PRAISE, and he will never forget that exercise!* You then reinforce his actions by repetition and praise, attaining greater accuracy as you continue day by day training.

I have trained Samoyeds (and other breeds) that have sorely tried my patience. It seems that at just about the time you feel your Samoyed is getting "solid" on a given exercise, he will find some new way to foul things up! That's our Sammys.

Let me cite an experience with one of our own Samoyeds, a fine performer who carried an average of 198.5 out of a possible 200. While training for the Novice recall (in which the dog comes and sits in front of the handler on command), she decided it would be great fun to run right past me. This girl did recalls at an absolute dead run and often was going so fast that to even begin to stop in front of me (let alone, sit) was impossible. We worked on the exercise for some time, with me jumping out of the way, getting run into, or being by-passed completely. (However, I would never take her enthusiasm away from her, as I want my dogs to be enthusiastic and fast.) Finally, we got the exercise done correctly and she realized what I wanted from her. From then on, we had perfect recalls nearly every time. The point I want to stress here—never dampen your Samoyed's enthusiasm. Instead, make every effort to capitalize on it!

It is well to note here and now that a Samoyed may try your patience to the point where you lose your temper. This happens to experienced as well as inexperienced trainers. When it does happen to you—and it will—if you are really trying to work up a good dog-handler relationship, recognize the situation for what it is and stop, sit down, get your dog next to you and "talk" to him. If you have established a good understanding with your dog, he will "talk back"—and tell you by his actions that he is really sorry. When you both have relaxed and made friends again, resume your training. Losing your temper can be a problem. Recognize this, and don't hestitate to take the time to think it out or else find a different way to show your dog what you want him to do.

In closing, keep these key points in mind:
1. PRAISE, PRAISE, PRAISE!
2. Take your Samoyed to a competent and humane trainer.
3. Visit the training classes first.
4. Do not let anyone give harsh corrections to your Samoyed.
5. Never, never starve your Samoyed of real affection or human contact.

Ginny Corcoran and "Robin" tracking in Colorado. Ginny wears gloves because the line is made of parachute cord.

Tracking harness—made of heavy cotton webbing with four sets of Velcro closures.

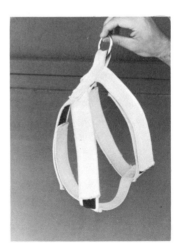

Colorado provides a scenic backdrop for dog sled activity. At top, team driven by Merle Mays. Below, at Dillon Lake, 1979, with driver Bob LeCour.

17

The Samoyed as a Working Dog

J UST as the Morgan horses that we ride for pleasure are known as the all-purpose horse, so are the Samoyeds admired as the all-purpose dog. Beverly Ward of New York writes:

> The Morgan was equally at home pulling the plow on weekdays, taking the family to church by buggy, giving the little children rides on Sunday afternoon, participating in the races of yesteryear and was still a beautiful, proud horse with spirit, under the saddle. A majestic, noble animal, with the dependability to adapt himself to any task.
>
> Our Samoyed can and will pull a cart or a sled. He will be a hunter; sometimes, unfortunately, it is the neighbor's cat. He will herd, again, perhaps the neighbor's cat. He will do himself proud in Obedience, in his more serious moments. He will guard, although he prefers you do his biting for him. He will step into the show ring with all the spirit and beauty that anyone could want. He will be your companion, give you his coat off his back to keep you warm and all the while he will never allow life to become dull. Given a chance, most Samoyeds will do all these things, some better in some things, but they all excel in the last category.

If the Samoyed has a definite place outside the home or show ring, it is as a multi-purpose sled dog somewhere between the Siberian Husky and the Alaskan Malamute. The Samoyed is just a bit larger than the Siberian and a bit smaller than the Malamute. The Samoyed pulls just a bit more per day in freighting than the Siberian; and while smaller than the Alaskan Malamute and not his equal in heavy freighting, the Samoyed will travel faster and eat less. The ability to eat like a Siberian means less food need be carried. This is borne out by their use by the Canadian Forest Ranger and Park Service. Until about 1961, the Canadian Rangers used St. Bernards to haul heavy loads into their snow-bound stations. *The Complete Saint Bernard* has a picture with the Saints and refers to the Samoyeds being used as point and

Author Bob Ward driving a happy bunch: "Chatter," King, Witan, Raini and Skippy.

Hoof 'N Paw sled team, 1976—Mardee Ward driver. At lead, Ice Way's Sunshine Mardee. At left point, Starctic Tipsioux (now in Germany); right point, litter sister Starctic Kachina. At left wheel; Ch. Hoof 'N Paw White Knight; right wheel, litter brother Hoof 'N Paw Pistol Pete.

lead dogs to break trail. Improved trucks and track-laying vehicles now carry bigger loads into the stations in the summer and fall, and the Samoyed has thus become the team dog for medium loads and messenger work.

Sledding

Activities outside the show ring bring many pleasant moments with people, and the insight you can gain about your dogs may be even more rewarding. The second Samoyed who owned us was named Ch. Starchak C.D. We called him Chatter because of the way he talked in the morning. While Chatter was successful in the show ring, it really was in other fields that he was most enjoyed. As a lead dog, he acquired the knack of judging the length of his team. Before making a turn, he would seem to look back and gauge the width needed to swing the team around a corner or tree. We actually believe that he did not like the sudden jerk and abrupt halt that came with wrapping the sled against a tree. Whatever his reason, it was amazing to watch him. This talent did not come to him at an early age, but at about five years. When you consider that he was in harness and competition at the age of twelve as a lead dog, there were many years of learning for us. This ability is not unusual for lead dogs. Lloyd Van Sickle had several, as did Bob Richardson with Siberians.

Once bitten by the hobby bug of sledding, you become a romanticist. It helps to also become an athlete. You meet people and see places you never knew existed, and begin to know your dogs in a different light and understand the structure, length of leg and grit that make such teamwork possible.

Some people maintain that dogs do not think, but are creatures of habit. Consider this incident. During a mail run from Ashton, Idaho to West Yellowstone Ranger Station, a distance of 64 miles, Lloyd Van Sickle lost the trail in a blizzard. After many attempts to find the road in eight feet of snow, Lloyd told Rex, the lead dog of his all-Samoyed team, to "Go home." Several near disastrous turns and stops later, Rex took off through the forest. (These sudden stops really create tangles in the lines when one is driving a hook-up of 15 dogs.) Rex began threading his way through the National Forest, leading the team with only a slight pause and cocking of his head now and then as if listening, and the team and Lloyd eventually reached Ashton, Idaho. But they came into town from the South instead of the North as would be usual from Yellowstone. We went out with Lloyd several times to look at the path which Rex had followed into town, but it just didn't make much sense to us. Determined to find out what Rex knew that we didn't, we took him out on a leash and tried the same thing over again. Finally, when off the main traveled path and with repeated commands, "Go home," he finally cocked his head, listened, and took off at a trot in the still deep snow. Thankfully, as we were running behind in deep snow, he

Lloyd Bristol driving a Startinda team with Ch. Starchak's Witangemote at lead.

Author's team, pictured above, carried letter shown below in world championship race at Truckee, California in 1949. Each driver carried a similar envelope.

THE HUSKY AND MALEMUTE
They herald the growth of the Snowland
And progress is marked by their trail;
A railroad now goes where they brought out
The Truckee, Sacramento and Frisco mail.
He's first in the growth of the Northland
And without him this land would be lost,
For there's never a stream in this country
That the Husky and Malemute trail has not crossed.
—Pat O'Cotter.

DOG TEAM COVER

This Letter Carried by Dog Team
During World Championship Race at Truckee, California

BOB WARD
DOG SLED DERBY
TRUCKEE, CAL

stopped and cocked his head as if listening again. This time we listened. We heard the humming and crackling of tiny voices, and realized that the noise was coming from the Forestry Telephone lines laid through the trees, rather than on regular telephone poles. We were convinced that Rex associated the humming of the lines with people, and by following the sound of the telephone lines into town we duplicated the "new" trail which he created that day.

This same Rex and his kennelmates were removed from the show bench of the Golden Gate Kennel Club in 1949 for a rescue mission. They were taken to the Donner Pass Area of the High Sierras, where a plane had been forced down in a heavy snow storm. Lloyd Van Sickle hooked two teams together to drag the small plane down to where a tracklaying jeep could attach to it.

At the San Mateo Kennel Club show in 1952, at the Bay Meadows Race Track, there was a race between five teams of dogs taken off the show bench following the breed judging. We became so confident that we hooked up all five teams into a 25 dog hook-up. A great problem arose when we neglected to take into account the fact that some of the ganglines and tug ropes were made of nylon. The fact that nylon stretches when under stress created difficulties as the dogs are hooked both by the neck lines and the rear tug lines. When the lines stretched we had to quickly lengthen lines to give the dogs space to work. The load that we were attempting to pull was a full-sized Ford automobile. It seemed as though we would have had no problem in moving it if the man made lines had been as strong as the dogs.

A complete summation of the activities of Rex of White Way with his trainer and driver Lloyd Van Sickle further shows the versatility and endurance of a trained dog. The itemized list does not list the three exhibitions a day at the Sportsman's Show, nor the three-a-day with the team pulling a calliope through the grounds at the San Diego Exposition, or the fact that this calliope had been pulled with four ponies and that nine dogs handled it very well. In his "off-time" Lloyd actually hauled mail for the United States Post Office between Ashton, Idaho, and West Yellowstone.

Rex was a first generation breeding of English imports through his imported father, Ch. White Way of Kobe, and his dam, Ch. Herdsman's Faith, sired by imported Spark of the Arctic. Rex was bred by Agnes Mason, and his plaque is inscribed:

1948 Winner of Childrens Race; Leader of Freight Race; Lead on U.S. Mail team; Leader of exhibition at the California State Fair.
1949 Leader of winning team at the Truckee Races; Led rescue team to plane crash at Truckee, California, pulling out 3 downed planes; The Cedars rescue; Leader of team into Ever Valley snow removal rescue.
1950 Hollywood Sportsman's Show Exhibition; Nevada Day Parade, Carson City; March of Dimes Exhibit, San Francisco; Homecoming Parade University of California; Leader of runner-up team at the Truckee Races.

Picking up air mail in Idaho for fast delivery by dog team. Driver, Lloyd Van Sickle, trainer for White Way Samoyeds. At lead, Rex of White Way.

1951 Leader of Winning team at San Mateo Show and leader of 25-dog team pictured here.
1952 Removed from bench of Golden Gate Kennel Club Show to take doctors to snowbound train in the Sierra Mountains.
1953 Led a team of Targhee hounds to win the West Yellowstone Dog Derby; Broke the world record weight pulling contest with 1870 pounds. Worked as leader in team pulling 600 pound loads to repair Donner Lake piers in winter emergency; Movie work and guard duty for John Wayne on location for *Islands in the Sky* motion picture.
1956 Winner of several events at the Big Bear Valley Sled Races; won several show points and one major.
1957 Died in August.

The real mushing ability of the Samoyeds was demonstrated February 1948 in the All-American Dog Derby at Ashton, Idaho. Two of the drivers at the Idaho Derby were Bob Van Sickle and Lewis Price, who had been in the Sled Dog Section of the United States Army in World War II, under the command of Captain Major Godsol, the well-known all-breed dog show judge.

Six thousand spectators from thirty-three states cheered a team of five white beauties. Lou Price parachuted from an airplane over the starting line with the team and sled. The sled and team of Samoyeds came floating down from a 1400-foot altitude, and was then hooked up and driven in the race. This was a practical demonstration that airplanes can drop rescue crews in remote areas during winter.

During a sled dog team exhibition at the Harbor Cities Kennel Club in 1950, the "Sourdoughs" (a group of Alaskan veterans who get together to re-live the days of the Klondike) were having a convention in Long Beach, California. One, a small, wiry man approached the team with great interest and introduced himself as Leonhard Seppala. He was probably the greatest and best known of all sled dog drivers in the history of sledding. He organized the Race to Nome with the badly needed serum for a raging diphtheria epidemic, and a statute of his lead dog Balto, built with pennies collected by school children in America, stands in Central Park in New York

256

City. Seppala related that Balto really was not his regular lead dog. Togo was his favorite lead dog, and with him he had won so many races. Balto belonged to Leonhard Seppala, but was a freighting dog who usually ran at point which is behind the lead dog. The serum run was really made with a series of six teams and drivers which Seppala helped to set up, and many of his stable of 122 dogs were the ones used in the various teams. Used as the lead dog on the last relay with the serum, Balto thereby received the total credit. To us the most interesting fact of Seppala was his devotion to purebred dogs in his teams. He used Siberian Huskies, and had a preference for white ones when he could manage it.

Coincidentally, Seppala was in partnership with Mrs. Margaret Ricker with a kennel of Samoyeds and Siberians in New Hampshire in the 1920s. Mrs. Ricker married the son of Fridtjof Nansen, the man who first really brought the Samoyed dog to the notice of the explorers in the 1890s.

Leonhard Seppala continued his interest in Northern Dogs until his death in 1967. He officiated at Sled Dog Races in and near Mt. Rainier, Washington, where he lived. His Bow Lake Kennels were well-known to all Northern Dog owners.

Training a Sled Dog

To train your dog to harness, you first need a lead dog or "pilot." If you are to work only one dog he needs to be a lead dog. When the final goal is a complete team, you must have a good lead dog for safety and your own physical comfort. An accomplished leader will eliminate much running in the snow by the driver to straighten harnesses. A well trained leader requires fewer commands, and there is less confusion in crowded or noisy situations.

Start with a 15 or 20 foot training lead, and permit the dog to walk out in front of you. Use either the training harness as illustrated or the pulling harness of the Siwash type. Do not use a choke chain collar, but do use a leather or sold no-slip type. You do not want to confuse this training with show or obedience.

Make the work pleasant, for you want to develop a willing worker. Once your dog begins to start out on his own in front of you, encourage him with commands of "Hi, Hi," or "All right, All right." The command of "Mush" is largely one of fiction. It is not a sharp enough command— probably as it started with the French word "Marche" it was guttaral enough, but not as "Mush." Many drivers begin to add their own variations in commands, which is a great aid if one later participates in sled races with other teams. By using different words your team will not then respond to commands of other drivers.

Traditionally sled dogs have been trained by other sled dogs. Lead dogs have been trained by other lead dogs. Today that is not feasible for most owners. Because of the speed with which a dog moves, a bicycle is an

257

excellent aid to the training of a lead dog. Command "Hi" and whistle to start. At the beginning, it is a good idea to give a command whenever the dog begins to do something, for this will associate the action with the command. The one independent action which you must not permit is *stopping*. Always stop a dog or a team before they get tired and stop of their own will.

Assuming that you now have a dog which will lead while you are riding a bicycle, permit him to go ahead on the lead until he is pulling you. Maintain a steady pace by the use of the brake to create just enough pull to keep your tug line taut. Take advantage of every fork or turn in the road which you dog comes to, to begin the commands, "Gee" for right, and "Haw" for left. Many times you will have to jerk the dog to the right or left while giving the commands. Always give praise to him for success even if you had to do all of the turning. This system of jerking for right and left becomes valuable if you can settle for one jerk for right or "Gee" and two jerks for left or "Haw." This, along with the whistling to start, will be a help when you have many dogs and the leader cannot hear your commands. Do not rush your dog by placing other dogs behind him as soon as he begins to obey commands. Work the dog for several weeks by himself and then only add one or two dogs if he is strong enough to drag them around upon command.

To add the "Turn-a-bout," use the command "Gee" followed by another "Gee" when the dog has moved a few feet in the new direction. This creates a wide swinging turn which is necessary to avoid injuring or running over the dogs in the team with the sled as it spins. Some drivers do command "Gee, Come Here," or "Haw, Come Here," but this does create quite a sharp about turn and often trouble. An about turn at a high speed or running is also dangerous.

You will find that your dog prefers to stand when you halt for a rest. This is a good habit to foster. Tell him "Stand Stay." If your halt is a long one, the command "Down" is necessary, for later when you are working a team, run-a-way teams are avoided if the team is trained to "Down." Your lead dog must be particularly good at the "Stand Stay," for you shall expand this to the command, "Hold It," when you are harnessing up the team. When you tell him to "Hold It," pull on his tug line and make him stay in position.

The command to "Whoa" and the reining in are the same as those used to stop a horse. A series of short jerks to throw the dogs off balance becomes their signal when voice commands cannot be heard in the wind and snow.

Once you have trained a lead dog he becomes the trainer for all successive leaders. Your point dogs which run behind the leaders most often learn the commands in one season's work. When a point dog shows promise of leading, merely lengthen the tug line until he is running alongside the leader. Gradual lengthening of the line will place the novice lead dog out in front. Many drivers have been successful with a double lead dog hook-up.

Alan Katz, president of The Minuteman Samoyed Club, training on gig and sled. Alan knows that lead dog Ashley (5½ years) will bring him and the team in, even if Alan gets lost.

Kay Bailey and team of Wolf River Samoyeds of Waldo, Wisconsin.

While most dogs may be trained for simple work as lead dogs, remember that a great one is rare. Sex is no determiner. A lead dog must be able to resist temptations of chasing other animals or being distracted. He must be able to outrun the majority of the team. He must be trainable to commands. Above all, the lead dog must like to work and run.

Thus far we have been discussing the training of the lead dog, not really dog team driving. To drive a team we must know that, as in obedience work, the voice and manner of command is all important. A few suggestions which seem to help:

- Limit each command to one word and as few syllables as possible.
- Gather the team in readiness to start by calling the dogs' names sharply. Some drivers call "Hupp-Hupp" or "Now-Now." These must have a tone of eagerness or anticipation.
- Command "All right" or "Hi" to start the team forward.
- Reprimand an individual dog by calling his name sharply. Do not use a word that would reprimand the entire team.
- Stop the team with a long drawn out "Whoa."
- Animate your voice to each need. Remember that the dog responds to sounds and inflections rather than specific words. (Try your dog with his name spoken gruffly, then kindly.)

Major Rodman, of West Yellowstone, Montana, drove a team of Malamutes using a whistle and never a voice command. The team was gathered with a long whistle with a rising inflection. The dogs started with a series of short, sharp whistles. A right turn was signalled with one long blast and a jerk on the gangline, a left turn with two distinct blasts and two jerks on the gangline. Increased speed or rallying were accomplished with short sharp blasts repeated with enthusiasm.

Your training has begun with the lead dog. Then one or two dogs have been added to your beginning team. From this point on you will find that most of your effort and direction will be in training new dogs to add to your existing team. We have pictured here the tandem hook-up or double-line of two abreast with a single lead dog. This method of harnessing is most satisfactory as you will have a shorter over-all length of the team and it will thus be easier to handle in wooded or mountain areas, or amidst the crowds, parages, and traffic of our modern life.

Equipment for training is basically a harness and various types of lines and collars. The most versatile harness is the Siwash type as it may be used for training and working. There are many other types for racing but they do not give the control needed for newly trained dogs. The Siwash harness which you see pictured in this book may easily be made of webbing and sewn by hand or riveted. Approximately sixteen feet of webbing material is adequate for one dog.

"There they go!" Notice rear gait and tree bar of harness attached to tug line making the gear comfortable.

261

Remember to fit an individual harness for each dog. Make all strain and pressure rest upon the shoulders, neck, and chest of the dog. Never permit pressure upon the throat or back. Allow the utmost freedom to both the forelegs and hindquarters. The use of the ring in the rear of the harness prevents tangles and the pulling sideways of the harness in action.

In training your new additions to the team, do not expect too much at first. Place your new dogs next to and behind an experienced dog if possible. Maintain a slow pace with new dogs in the team and stop immediately if a new dog is dragged or thrown off his feet. A dog once frightened is very difficult to train. Do not punish the new dog in harness, as he does not know what is expected. Beginners rarely pull their share of the load, so be content if they run freely along.

The question of: "How young may we start?" will vary from breed to breed and according to size within the breed. Generally puppies are started at the age of six to eight months. Do not expect him to pull. In fact, many drivers do not hook puppies in with a tug line, but just with the neck line. If possible, avoid placing puppies in the wheel position, just in front of the sled, as a wheel dog must be strong and solid. Simple maneuvers are best when puppies and new dogs are in the team. Puppies will limit your length of training time to a few hours until they are at least ten months old.

While the dogs are important, the driver will create the happy team. By making the sled work fun and not allowing bad habits to develop, one trainer will be more successful than another. Most tangles and hurt dogs occur when a driver permits the sled to run up on the team, as the main gangline then becomes slack and even the best lead dog cannot maintain a straight team line. A good driver will move dogs around in a team, as some prefer or work better in one spot than another. The successful trainer does not punish a dog in the team, but only when the dog is out of it. Perhaps the one thing that distinguishes the good driver from the inept is that he drives his team from the rear without someone leading them.

If your sled team training progresses beyong the pastime stage you may be working by yourself in isolated areas, and a few words of caution are needed.

Harnessing and unharnessing are times when great problems may occur unless you have a consistent system which the dogs understand. A good method is to fasten the main gangline to the sled and stretch it out upon the ground. Anchor your gee line to a post or stake in the ground. The gee line runs from the tug line ring to the driver, usually under the sled, and trails loosely. With the sled thus secured a runaway team is prevented. Now the leader is hitched with the command "Stay," or "Hold It." This keeps the tug line taut and prevents the remaining dogs from becoming tangled. With all dogs harnessed, place the steadier dogs in the team first and command, "Down" to each as they are hitched in place. Do not hitch up a team too long before you intend to start, as the dogs' natural eagerness to go will be lost.

In unharnessing a team, the sled must be again anchored from the rear by fastening the gee line to a post or tree. It is interesting to note that Leonhard Seppala carried a metal rod which he drove through a hole in his brake lever, deep into the snow to hold his team on every halt. Many drivers merely turn the sled on its side. Unharnessing usually begins with the swing and point dogs, as the wheel dogs cannot be very easily entangled with others as they are fastened to the sled, and thus cannot go very far sideways or backwards. This is an excellent time to check pads of the feet and bodies for chaffing from the harness.

Working Your Dog in Harness

The following letter from Mrs. Pat Enslen tells it all to the owners of Samoyeds:

Fourteen years ago, I purchased two lovely male puppies, an Alaskan Malamute and a Samoyed, Winter Frost of Whitecliff.

At that time I leaned toward participating with the Malamute group because they were eager to get the most out of their dogs by working and training them, rather than just showing. With this in mind, we formed a club and started our project "Working Our Dogs in Harness." None of us knew how except one member, who had made his own equipment. We measured our guys, at a meeting, for a joint venture in making freighting type harnesses.

Finding a tire alongside the road, I couldn't wait to hook Smoky and Frosty up to see how they would do their pulling act. Smoky, a Malamute, gave the dying third act scene, flattening himself on the ground, screaming and hollering so loud that the neighbors called the police and Humane Society. The cruelty charges against me were dropped as I promised never to harness the Malamute again.

The only one left to turn to was . . . Frosty, ha! When Frosty was 3½ years old, he really did not like the weight pulling, but he was getting so much attention, he did fairly well. The sled dog people put on a Weight Pulling Contest and Frosty won, pulling over 650 lbs. I was more elated over this win than the 3-pt. major he received the week before. Our club wanted to do more on training and purchased plans on How To Build a Training Cart. A work shop teacher in San Jose made 14 for us.

Now I had my harnesses and a new cart and a wheel dog. All I needed was a Lead Dog. Gung-ho, I presented the plan to work our Sams to a local club meeting and received only one response. The dog of this new participant was a little female named Pickles (Blance Reyna of Snow Ridge). I put her in harness and away we went on a 2-mile trail and she brought me back. *This was the beginning of sledding!* How she loved it. We added Mr. Duke of Whitecliff, a cousing to Frosty, and for two years were running in the Three Dog Class at Lake Tahoe. Oh, this was far from an overnight success. Many hours of training in all kinds of weather were involved.

Not only did the dogs love doing this, but they acquired tremendous conditioning. Mr. Duke was jumping higher and achieved his C.D.X., and then his U.D. and Tracking degree. Winter Frost lost 30 lbs. and at 71 lbs. received his championship in the fall of '73 at the age of six.

The following April, Frosty sired General Custer and Sister Shana. At 9

263

Not a single dog with all four feet on the ground. Walt Schirber and Warlord Kennels' team in 1981 Saratoga, N.Y., race. At lead: Nikki and Omak; Tasha, point; Butch and Buck, wheel.

Pat Enslen with her 5-dog team at Soda Springs, 1976. At lead: General Custer (left) and Pickles; at swing: Shana and Molly (hidden); and at wheel, Ch. Winter Frost of Whitecliff.

264

months they made their debut in my now five-dog team. This really sparked up the team. With a name like Custer, he wanted to be leader of the Troops. He learned his Gee and Haw commands and was learning how to pass other teams, when Papa Frosty died in my arms at 9 years of age. The bottom fell out of the team, but somehow God performs miracles. A repeat breeding of Custer brought me Linus at an early age. The first day in harness he took over his father's place running wheel on the team. That year I bred Shana to Ch. Yeti of Whitecliff and produced two good running males—Sasha and Sierra Sleigh. The next year I was running ALL FAMILY.

I have to give full credit to Pickles, now a grand old lady of 12. Without her, this would never have come about. How fortunate I was to experience having two natural lead dogs to keep sledding alive. Pickles still likes to practice on the Salt Flats but cold snow is out. Custer loves a blizzard.

Looking back over 10 years that I have received pleasure in working my Samoyeds in harness, I must say that every one that has been on the team is a credit to the breed. They have proven themselves on the trail, in Obedience, Tracking and in the Show Ring. Hopefully their bloodlines and willingness to work will be carried on in those coming up. How better can I express my enthusiasm than to say that I am the proud owner, handler, dirver and trainer of Ch. General Custer and his troops!

> Mushing along,
> *Pat Enslen*

P.S. The easiest thing to remember of the past ten years is pushing that damn cart through the mud!

Working Samoyeds

Walt and Judy Schirber of Warlord Kennels are ardent supporters of the Organization of the Working Samoyeds (O.W.S. to the sledding Samoyed enthusiasts in our country and around the world). Three years ago, they moved to the Western edge of the Adirondack mountains and rebuilt a 200-year-old farm house and barn into perhaps the most ideal and efficient Samoyed kennel in the United States. Now they can train, condition, race and raise their Samoyeds in a natural environment, much as Msgr. Keegan did 50 years ago. The vanishing heritage of our breed is being revived by them.

The Schirbers report:

Our kennel is suited to the particular needs of the northern breed dog and our north country climate. The Samoyed dog has a thick outer coat and an even denser undercoat. This renders the dog almost impervious to weather conditions which might kill some other breeds. Our dogs, 9 adults and 3 youngsters, seldom seek their inside kennel runs. We have looked out during a blinding snow storm and found them happily curled up, tails over their noses, OUTSIDE. For three months of the year our weather does not go above freezing, and the range is from 10 to 15 above zero to 40 below during the coldest months. Snowfall averages 290 inches per year. The Samoyed was bred for this climate.

Keeping a northern breed dog indoors in a heated situation during the winter does a great disservice to the breed and is a major cause of skin problems. We use a wood barn environment for indoor kennels instead of the concrete building used by most kennels. In our winter climate, moisture and condensation occurs and with a concrete building the temperature would drop even lower. One could heat the building but this would be an unhealthful and unnatural environment.

We weigh each dog weekly to carefully monitor any gains or losses and have for years kept weight charts as well as health records for each dog. Even an extra two pounds can slow down a racing dog. We never leave food in a kennel run after feeding time. What the dog does not eat within the allotted feeding time is taken away. We never have had anything but eager eaters.

With the cold weather the water pails freeze. In order to get the dogs to drink and thus prevent dehydration we water them three times a day. However, we water thusly: we soak two cups of dry food in 1/3 gallon of warm water, and give this morning, noon, and after the evening meal. This mixture of "doggy soup" is given two hours before a sled race and after a race.

Our dogs are let out of their kennel runs three times a day to play with each other and receive our attention. This is the time for brushing and inspection. There are raised sleeping benches in the runs which the dogs seem to prefer, as they do their raised box kennels in the inside runs.

Training adult dogs begins as soon as the weather permits in the fall. We use wheeled rigs. We have a light one made from bicycle parts for three dogs and a heavy Hall rig for teams. We begin with short runs and always vary the training trails.

Let the dogs set their own pace in early training. All young adult dogs are trained first with the "on foot" method before using the rigs. If a problem develops with a dog, it is back to the "on foot" method until the problem is worked out. We begin with half mile runs and gradually work up to twice the distance the team will be running in the coming race season.

Dogs are tried in different positions on the team to locate the dog's best running position. Some dogs run best in the same position year after year. Much training is needed to get the dogs to reach a level of acting in unison; all going at the same speed, all responding at once to the commands. Walt does not tolerate dogs not getting along or fighting while in the team. We have males that normally try to dominate each other in the kennel but they will tolerate each other and run well together because they KNOW fighting is NOT permitted within a racing team.

The unique thing about this breed is the slow development. The males develop and grow and continue to be puppies until they are three years old. We have one male coming into his own at six years!

The Samoyed has been "our breed for almost 15 years and our involvement with our dogs is total. My fascination with these beautiful dogs continues and both Walt and I are learning constantly from them. Our prime interest is racing, although we do show. We aim to breed only the best in conformation, racing performance, temperament and mental attitude, a desire to work and run as essential. A good friend of ours said, 'Form follows function in the Husky.' We believe him to be absolutely correct. We are dedicated above all to preserving the working qualities of our breed. The Samoyed's beauty is exceeded only by the dog's great stamina and mental fortitude.

266

Packing

Dog packing is as old as sledge team driving. Many of the natives of the north use their dogs to carry belongings over terrain which is too rough for sledding. There is practically no place a pack dog cannot go with a load.

Loads by the natives generally average one-half of the dog's weight. For week-end excursions to the mountains the hiking clubs of the Samoyed owners limit the weight to one-third of the dog's weight.

Training consists of learning to follow behind the hiker. A dog that has been taught to "Heel" is at a definite disadvantage upon a narrow trail. The command here is "Back," and the dog is taken out on a lead and tapped gently upon the nose until he remains in back. "Down," "Stay," and "Come," are of course very necessary for the protection of the small packs which the dogs carry.

The pack consists of two pouches, one on each side of the dog, held on by a breast strap and a belly strap. A dog is a loose skinned animal, and thus cannot be packed on the same principle as a horse. The pack must be balanced and stabilized upon his back. For serious and heavy work a breeching strap is advisable to keep the pack from slipping forward.

When the pack is first used it is usual to load it with bulky and light loads such as straw, to accustom the dog to the art of missing trees and rocks with the projecting pack.

Hunting with Samoyeds

Everyone does not wish to work their dogs in harness and mush through the snow, and something should be said for other activities. There have been only two experiences known to us personally of using the Samoyed for hunting—once for ducks and the other for deer when it was legal to use dogs on a leash.

The dog that was used for retrieving ducks was purchased by the woman in the family because she wanted a dog at home when her husband went hunting with his Labrador Retriever. These people lived near Fresno, California, a great area for water fowl. The Samoyed was taken along first because there was no dog-sitter at home. He romped and played until a duck was brought down. In he plunged with the Labrador to get the duck, and the bird was carried downstream by the current. Jack, the Samoyed, didn't get the duck. On the second downed bird, this two-year-old Samoyed took one look at the duck floating downstream, ran ahead down river, jumped in and retrieved the duck. Quite a time was had by all to get that first duck away from him, but by mid-morning Jack was bringing them in like a retriever. When Blackie, the Labrador, passed on, our duck hunting friend used a Samoyed to retrieve for the next seven years.

Ch. Alpine Glo Nuvak Chin-Mana ("Chin'A"), weight-pulling bitch par excellence, owned and trained by Carole Harrigan-Rost, Nuvak Samoyeds, Pennsylvania. Entered in the 50-80 lb. class, she is pictured pulling 1138 pounds at the ALPO International competition at Lake Saranac, N.Y., Winter 1980-81. *Photo, Jon Nedele.*

Ch. Alpine Glo Nuvak Chin-Mana pulls her weight in more ways. At left, mothering a litter. At right, in championship show form. Bred by Dr. and Mrs. Michael Cook and owned by Carole Harrigan-Rost.

268

Weight Pulling

An unusual Samoyed bitch has appeared on the Weight Pulling contests scene. Ch. Alpine Glo Nuvak 'Chin-Mana owned by Carole Harrigan-Rost of Irwin, Pa. "Chin'a" pulled 1138 lbs. at Saranac Lake, New York, an all-time record for a Samoyed bitch. This by a bitch who weighs less than 50 lbs.! Chin'a won the Organization for Working Samoyeds Club Award for Weight-Pull for 1981, and also the Trailbreaker's Sled Dog Club Weight-Pull Dog of the Year 1981 Award. Trailbreakers is an Ohio-based club, with over 100 members in five different states. Chin'a is the first Samoyed to have received an award from this club.

Chin'a was bred to work as well as look good. She is what mushers call a natural leader. Carole reports that many mushers express chagrin over the fact that she is a Samoyed. The Malamute people want her bigger—the Husky/cross people want her taller.

Chin'a and her owner began with Fishback's *"Training Lead Dogs My Way"*; then borrowed a few other dogs and began training in the Fall of 1979. In the winter of 1980 Chin'a ran lead on a three dog team some of the time, but her really outstanding mark was made in the Weight-Pull area. Chin'a was undefeated in the Under 50 lb. class in 1980, and placed 1st out of nine dogs in the 50-80 lb. class against other breeds at one race. In 1980-81 season, she pulled 292 lbs. in 11.2 seconds, 792 lbs. in 17.1 seconds, 422 lbs. in 4 seconds and 842 lbs. in 17.9 seconds in three separate weight divisions at Chardon, Ohio; Espyville, Pa. and Newbury, Ohio.

Carole believes that the bitch's attitude is a great part of her ability. The steady training does it, too. They run during the early fall and in early winter. Chin'a runs with the team weekends, averaging about 4-5 miles a run. During the week, they run as singles at the local high school track to emphasize building muscle tone and endurance rather than just high level weight pulling. Carole uses a child's plastic sled that can be used on a dry track or on snow. It is designed so that you can add items for weight such as an old tire or two. By jogging alongside the sled and dog, the trainer becomes conditioned for the racing season.

Carole believes that there is nothing like experience as a teacher; she and Chin'a put on weight pulling demonstrations and participate in "fun" pulls at matches and training seminars.

Probably the hardest part in pulling is to have the dog understand the technique in "breaking the weight." Sled dogs, who have always had the sled follow easily behind, are often confused by the resistance. Starting with easier weights, and building up, will aid in keeping the dogs attitude "up." Always make certain that the dog finishes a pull. Even if they can't do it on their own, walk them through it to show them that it can be done. Remember that Sammies are quite intelligent and usually pace themselves. Do not ask the dog to do something he is not physically or mentally ready to do.

Following the racing and pulling season Chin'a was bred and had eight healthy puppies and a very easy whelping. Chin'a is 20½″ tall, and weighs in at 40-50 lbs. An excellent mover, which fits with her soundness and well-balanced physique, she was owner-handled to her championship.

Carole advises newcomers to use the proper equipment, as her dog quickly learned the difference between a racing harness and a weight pulling harness. Both harnesses came from Mel Fishback-Riley. Weight pull is a good area for many one or two dog Sammy owners. You do not need an entire team or a lot of equipment. Just be sure that your dog is in good health and proper condition, and you can have many pleasurable winter weekends together.

THE ORGANIZATION FOR THE WORKING SAMOYED

by Judy Schirber

The Organization for the Working Samoyed (OWS) was the brainchild of Mel Fishback, longtime friend of the working dog. A small group of Samoyed owners had been requesting advice on training and equipment for sled work and racing. Samoyed owners knew that these dogs are unique among Northern Dogs and required special handling and training methods for their special breed personality. Mel suggested a pooling of knowledge and the publishing of a Bulletin on the subject.

Thus the OWS was born. A member donated the insignia and club patches, and racing rules and point schedules were set up to initiate a ranking and training evaluation.

From this small beginning, OWS has grown to 90 members worldwide. Not all are able to participate physically, but all believe heart and soul in the working abilities of the Samoyed. In its nine years, OWS has raised the esteem with which the Samoyed is held by the canine world. No longer do Samoyed people look back on the past and wonder if the breed could produce a great herder, great leader, or great weight puller in our modern times.

Larry and Ginny Corcoran of Colorado have succeeded in all fields with their dogs. They train Samoyeds for weight-pulling, Obedience, sled team work, herding, and Tracking. Their dog Sukhona's Arrogance ("Ornery") has earned C.D.X. Another bitch, "Sunny" is working on a T.D. Robin of Sukhona, C.D., T.D. is approaching T.D.X. Their dogs show the amazing versatility of the working Samoyed, and what's possible if owners have the necessary patience and are willing to put in the hours of training.

Carole Harrigan-Rost is an OWS member. We have already told the story of Carole and her record-setting weight pulling bitch, Chin'a, who is also an AKC champion.

Bob and Katie LeCour of Wyoming have a dog, Vufka (who also is a conformation champion) that runs as a sprint dog, freighting race dog and works as an outstanding weight puller. Vufka, in 1975, pulled 1,015 at Jackson Hole, Wyoming and shared the honor of being Colorado Weight-pull Champion. The versatility of this Samoyed underscores the OWS desire to promote and develop the natural abilities of the breed.

Lori and Terry Plampin of Colorado own Puffy Cloud of Golden, C.D.X. and another Samoyed, Toby, with a C.D. Both dogs are working at herding. Puffy is being trained in tracking while being shown in conformation. Puffy, who is under 65 lbs., is a weight puller who has a lifetime, 4 year average of 600 lbs. per pull. He is also only one of three dogs of any breed to win the Colorado Weightpull Championship for three years in a row. For this contest the weight must be pulled both ways, with only a ten minute rest between pulls.

Merle and Carolyn Mays of Colorado have had as many as 24 Samoyeds in their kennel and participate in sled work, racing and weight pulling. Merle states: "I always choose a weight puller by attitude, a willingness to please and initiative." Koppy, a dog owned by them, competed in the over-65 division for over 10 years. A consistent winner, in 1971, blind and 11 years old, he pulled 1,125 lbs. at Grand Lake, Colorado. The Organization for the Working Samoyed is bound together with the one purpose to retain the structure, nature, attitude and physical abilities of the Samoyed. Two members, Bruce and Cara Berryman, initiated the first sled dog demonstration in many years at the SCA Specialty, in Atlanta, Ga. Larry Corcoran and Geoff Abbott have requested a Sled Dog Class be allowed with the SCA Specialties. It is the desire to demonstrate to all owners and judges the abilities of our breed, the structure required, and to demonstrate that he is a versatile working breed and grand companion.

Judy and Walt Schirber's Warlord Kennels, N.Y., in summer, 1981.

271

Mrs. Carol Chittum, author of the accompanying article, is shown spinning on a wheel from Norway, with her Ch. Belaya Sergeant Pepper watching. Carol gave a demonstration of drop spindel spinning on the Romper Room television program, and she teaches classes in all art forms of work with fleece.

18

Spinning Samoyed Fur

Contemporary Considerations

by Carol Chittum

T HERE is nothing lovelier or more unique than an article of clothing made from the fur of our beautiful Samoyeds. This article aims to give you some practical suggestions about this fascinating by-product of your involvement in our breed.

It is not our thought here to provide an actual course in spinning. A glance at the yellow pages of most cities will yield the names of weaving and spinning supply stores where one may take classes. Such stores can also be goldmines of books on the subject, or a place to discover the names of qualified teachers. If you want to make good progress, and become skillful, I urge you to take a class. It is possible to learn from a book, and using Samoyed fur to start with (I did), but it was so painstaking that I finally listened to my good friend and experienced spinner, Gertrude Adams, and took a workshop. The difference was remarkable. Now there are so many more resources available that there is no need to experience such frustration. You may also obtain the names and locations of local guilds of spinners from the Handweavers Guild of America, whose address is 65 LaSalle Road, West Hartford, Conn. 06107. Such guilds frequently offer workshops or demonstrations of the various aspects of spinning and using handspun fibers.

Collecting the Fur

Not every part of the undercoat is as lovely and usable as another, so I will discuss this elementary step in achieving the end product you wish, whether a garment or other article.

Since it is much more pleasant to spin clean fur, and since spun yarn is easier to wash than loose fur, let's start with a clean dog. As soon as you see that first telltale loose tuft in the lower stifle area, bathe your dog. Then, frequent attention with the slicker brush will yield clean, spinnable fur, with no other preparation required.

The most desirable fur for garments comes from the sides and shoulders. Therefore, I always brush those areas first, and put that fur in a separate brown paper bag, labeled and dated. Sort your fur as you groom, as it is very tedious and consuming to do it later. Keep each quality of fur stored separately, for ease in planning your projects. Back, ruff and pant fur often yield too much guard coat to be pleasant (unless you are fond of hair shirts!), but this coarser mixture may be spun into a textured and usable yarn. Leg fur below the elbow and stifle, and tail fur are not worth saving as spinning material, but can be useful as pillow or quilt stuffing. It also goes without saying that matted or damaged coat should be discarded.

Designing Your Yarn

In order for any yarn to be sound (i.e. to hold together), the individual fibers must wrap 1½ times around the diameter of the finished yarn. This is necessary to avoid weakness, especially important in garments where friction is a factor, as in elbows of sweaters or fingers of mittens. Thus, due to the short length of the Samoyed fiber (not usually more than 1½"), it is necessary to spin it into a moderately fine yarn if you want it to wear well and not shed excessively. A bulkier yarn should be achieved by plying two or more singles together rather than spinning a heavy single.

Interesting and beautiful yarns can also be created by a blending of Sam fur with other fibers. A blend with wool yields a soft but much stronger yarn. Blending is done in the carding process, and fibers should be nearly the same length. (Longer fibers such as wool will need to be cut.) I have successfully blended Samoyed fur with wool, alpaca, llama, mohair, cashmere and angora. I suggest using 40% or less of the other fiber so as not to overpower the downy quality of the Samoyed. The lovely heathery tones produced by the admixture of any of these other animal fibers can be surprisingly pleasant.

Sam fur can, of course, be dyed. I suggest using those dyes specifically formulated for protein fibers. Due to the molecular structure of the fur, it is difficult to achieve bright, high-intensity colors. Most dyes seem to yield more pastel shades. It is interesting to dye a wool-Sam blend, as the wool takes up the color more intensely and the resulting yarn will be a heather tone.

It is essential to remember the Samoyed's sub-polar origins when designing yarn for a garment. Keep in mind that the fur is *very* warm in spite of its feather lightness. Many spinners spend hours making sweaters that

274

The sweater starts with the combings. Mrs. Agnes Mason, whose White Way Samoyeds contributed so much to the development of the breed, combing the loose hair from Ch. Herdsman's Chattigan, sire of our Ch. Starchak, C.D.

A Samoyed sweater made from the hair of the two Samoyeds in the picture. The sweater was made by Frances Roe for Chloe Witcher, and the two Sams were owned by the Witchers many years ago. They were Ch. Tzarina of the Palace and Ch. Sergi Sashi.

Ruth Tausend of Wisconsin using an Ashford spinning wheel to spin a pile of "fur" from Frostam's Breath of Spring who keeps her company. The painting on the wall is of Tsiulikagta's Taku Koryak and is by artist John Wixey. Note carding tools on the floor.

could only be warn in mid-January in Minnesota because they are not aware of this fact. This is another excellent reason for using a finer two-ply in a more open or lacy pattern, unless you live in a very cold climate. Consider making shawls, scarves or hats from your fur, as they can be useful and appreciated nearly anywhere.

Miscellany

—Be sure to keep fur from your different dogs labeled and separate, as there are many shades of white, ecru, cream and even pale beige Sam undercoats. This is important if you want your project to be all one color.

—Store in brown paper bags. Plastic does not breath, and fur stored for a long time tends to get an "old wet dog" odor about it.

—Spin the fur, regardless of diameter, with a fair amount of twist, and your yarn will shed less. If you want a softer finish, you can achieve this by lightly tapping the finished garment with a slicker brush. This will raise a napped finish similar to brushed mohair.

—Refrain from offering to spin your friends' and relatives' dogs' fur unless you know in what condition the dog is kept, and unless you can give them the sorting instructions beforehand. It is very time-consuming and frustrating to sort years of combings into usable lots.

—Always wash your spun yarn after spinning, then again after completing the project. Samoyed fur gets a grayish, dingy look from the handling, both from the spinning and the subsequent processes. Your finished project should be the same sparkly white as a freshly-bathed Samoyed. Treat your Samoyed yarn and articles as you would any fine woolen. Avoid very hot water, detergents and agitating in washing.

Learn, experiment, innovate and create with this beautiful fiber! There is no satisfaction quite like the one you will derive from seeing your Sam's fur become transformed into a unique, usable article. It makes all the other time and work expended in your dog's care seem so much more worthwhile.

Facing page:
Ruth Tausend spins "Fiber Fabricators" from the world of dogs. The exhibit shows 32 samples of skeins of dog hair with breed pictures above the samples. Ruth is willing to answer questions about spinning and dyeing hair, and can be reached by phone at (Wisconsin) 414-453-3303.

One year's shedding of one dog usually provides one pound of yarn. One ounce of single ply yarn can be spun in one hour or less. A cap requires about 3 ounces of 2-ply yarn; a scarf requires 5 ounces; a stole 16 ounces; and a sweater, 24-30 ounces. Spinning one ounce (2 ply) costs about $3.50, plus postage and insurance.

"It never shows dog hair," says Mrs. Vincent Duffy, pictured with her Samoyeds, Dondianes Siberian Ranook and Dondianes Czaruke, on the 8 × 10 foot rug she made of their hair. "After saving 10 pounds of the wooly combings from the undercoat of my dogs, I sent it to Martha Humphriss to be spun into 4-ply yarn. I had an awning company sew three strips of white canvas together. Since the rug is made for my octagonal dining room, I cut the edge to the shape of the room. This I bound with white tape.

When the yarn came I started tufting. Every ½ inch, I sewed through the canvas, and tied three 3-inch strands with each knot. At the finish, I brushed liquid rubber on the back, and placed the rug on a mat. It cleans well with detergent or dog cleaner, and seldom needs the vacuum."

Truly an angel for Samoyeds. Frances Roe, here pictured tracking with Foge's Snow Job, C.D., T.D., is an Obedience trainer and a spinner and knitter of dog hair. Together with the Cragens and Wilna Coulter, Frances founded the San Francisco Samoyed Rescue, through which over 200 Samoyeds have found new homes since 1973. 99% of them have been spayed or neutered by the Rescue, which is supported by an annual all-breed charity match. There are no paid employees, and all proceeds go directly to aid Samoyeds.

A PICTORIAL PEDIGREE.

At top, the grandparents. Left, parents of the litter's dam: Ch. Herdsman's Faith with Ch. Petrof Lebanof from Agnes Mason's White Way Kennels. At right, parents of the sire: Snowy Dawn, owned by Elizabeth Wyman, and Ch. Starchak, C.D., owned by the Wards. In the center row, the dam, Ch. Suzanne of White Way, owned by Ed and Gertrude Adams, and the sire, Ch. Rainier, bred by Betsy Wyman and owned by the Wards. Below, the Suraine puppies at about 6 weeks of age.

Can. Ch. Brydawn's Winter Chinook, an all-breed Best in Show winner at 8 months of age. Whelped 9/8/80, by Am. & Can. Ch. Polar Mist's Dr. Pepper ex Can. Ch. Rocco's Brandy of Rurik. Breeders: Mr. and Mrs. Brian Rebus. Owners: Mr. and Mrs. Alan M.M. Toomey, Alberta, Canada. Handler: Carol Graham. Chinook's early winning included 11 Best Puppy in Show and 3 Group Firsts.

Can. Ch. Silky Tassel, pictured at 17 months going BOW at Samoyed Club of Canada 1979 Specialty. Owner, Patricia Row, Ontario. Mrs. Row has combined the English bloodlines of Eng. & Am. Ch. Delmonte This Is It and the U.S. lines of Kubla Khan and Ch. Joli White Knight.

Can. Ch. Orenopac's Mogul, Best Puppy in Show at Northern Alberta Canine Assn., 1984. In companion show the previous day, won the Group under F. Cartwright (U.S.A.). Wh. 9/28/83, Mogul is an Ice Breaker grandson, by Ch. Orenopac's Chaena ex Orenopac's Every Boy's Dream. Breeder, T. Murphy. Owner, J.T. Hay.

19

The Samoyed in Canada

THE FIRST official registration of the Samoyed in Canada was in 1925.

The Canadian Standard, while maintaining the English suggested height ranges for dogs and bitches, adds several variations. The "general appearance" section is more descriptive and comprehensive. The desired head is described in greater detail, and there are separate sections on temperament and on gait.

Under disqualifications, the Canadian Standard goes further than the American or English. Specifically, they add as disqualifications: Blue eyes, dewclaws on the hindlegs, and any color other than pure white, cream, biscuit, or white and biscuit. The American Standard has some of these, but the English none.

The Canadian standard continues to include a point schedule—this has been dropped from the English and American standards. Both the Canadians and Americans heavily penalize bad disposition toward mankind and unprovoked aggressiveness toward other dogs.

Official Canadian standard for the Samoyed:

General Appearance: The Samoyed, being essentially a working dog, should present a picture of beauty, alertness and strength, with agility, dignity, and grace. As his work lies in the cold climate, his coat should be heavy and weather resistant, and of good quality rather than quantity. The male carries more of a "ruff" than the female. He should not be long in the back as a weak back would make him practically useless for his legitimate work, but at the same time a close-coupled body would also place him at a great disadvantage as a draught dog. Breeders should aim for the happy medium, a body not long but muscular, allowing liberty, with a deep chest and well-sprung ribs, strong arched neck, straight front and especially strong loins. Males should be masculine in appearance and deportment without unwarranted aggressiveness; bitches feminine without weakness of structure or apparent softness of temperament. Bitches may be slightly longer in back than males. They should both give the appearance of being capable of great endurance but be free from coarseness. Because of the depth of chest required, the legs should be moderately long. A very short-legged dog is to be depreciated. Hindquarters should be particularly well developed, stifles well bent and any suggestion of unsound stifles or cowhocks severely penalized. General appearance should include movement and general conformation indicating balance and good substance.

Temperament: Alert and intelligent and should show animation. Friendly, but conservative.

Size: Dogs, 20-22 in. (51-56 cm) at the shoulder; bitches, 18-20 in. (45-51 cm); weight in proportion to size.

Coat and Colour: The body should be well covered with a thick, close, soft and short undercoat, with harsh hair growing through it, forming the outer coat, which should stand straight away from the body and be quite free from curl. The legs should have good feathering. Colour pure white, cream, biscuit, or white and biscuit.

Head: Powerful and wedge-shaped with a broad, flat *skull, muzzle* of medium length, a tapering foreface, not too sharply defined. The stop should not be too abrupt—nevertheless well defined. *Nose* and eye rims black for preference, but may be brown. Lips black, flews should not drop predominantly at corners of the mouth. Strong jaws with level teeth. *Eyes* dark, set well apart and deep with alert intelligent expression. *Ears* should not be too long but rounded at the tips, set well apart and well covered inside with hair. Hair short and smooth before the ears.

Forequarters: Forelegs straight and muscular. Good bone.

Body: Back medium in length, broad and very muscular. Bitches may be slightly longer in back than males. Chest broad and deep. Ribs well sprung, giving plenty of heart and lung room.

Hindquarters: Very muscular, stifles well let down. Feet long, flattish and slightly spread out. Soles well padded with hair.

Tail: Long and profuse, carried over the back when alert, sometimes dropped when at rest. A judge should see the tail over the back once when judging.

Gait: A Samoyed should gait with a good, well-balanced movement. He should move with an easy, agile stride that is well timed. The gait should be free with a good reach in the forequarters and a sound, driving power in the hindquarters.

Faults: Unprovoked aggressiveness. Over and under allowed height. In or out at the elbow. Cowhocks or straight stifles. Double hook in the tail. Choppy or stilted gait.

Disqualifications: *Blue eyes. Dewclaws on the hind legs. Any colour other than pure white, cream, biscuit, or white and biscuit.*

Scale of Points:

Gait	15
General appearance	10
Coat	10
Head	10
Back	10
Chest and ribs	10
Hindquarters	10
Forelegs	10
Feet	10
Tail	5
TOTAL	100

Can., Am. & Bda. Ch. Samovar's True Grit ("Trooper"), top winning Samoyed in Canada for 1978. BIS at Ottawa, 1979. Wh. 12/18/75, by Ch. Willinda's Drifting Snow ex Samovar's Snowmiss Tosca. Breeder-owner-handler: Myriam Mantle, Quebec.

Two of Canada's oldest Samoyed kennels have united efforts in recent years with aim of producing better movement and good fronts, and still retaining the essential qualities important to the breed. Basic stock includes a strong White Way influence blended with other lines.

Nepachee Kennels, owned by Bill and Betty McHugh, imported Am. & Can. Ch. Bai of Lucky Dee and Blache Encore of Kamisin. More recently descendants of these dogs have had two litters at Nepachee sired by Am. Ch. Ice Way's Ice Breaker.

Glokon Kennels, owned by Mr. and Mrs. A. G. Aitchison, imported Silveracres Sir Glokon, Silveracres Jane of Glokon (linebred to Ch. Nachalnik of Drayalene), Bowlsam's Echo and her daughter (inbred to Ch. Startinda's Robochi), Bowlsam's Flamett of Glokon. Ch. Silver Storm of Kombu, a Canadian-bred dog, has also added to the breedings.

K-Way's Tabor Reveille (linebred to Ch. Ivan Belaya of Taymylyr, C.D.) has just come to Canada, and is co-owned by Nepachee and Glokon to complete their breeding plans.

A daughter of Flame and Storm is with the Von Taymir Sea Kennels in Germany, and has had her first litter—a large healthy one—there. Both kennels are doing outstanding conformation winning, and are engaged in sledding and obedience. Bai finished his Canadian championship undefeated, as did Storm.

Samovar Kennels in Mille Isle, Quebec, began in 1967 and has had great success. Myriam Mantle's first bitch became Can., Am. & Bda. Ch. Karatina, Can. CDX and Am. & Bda. CD. This bitch when bred to Jac-Lin's Debsign Legend produced Samovar's Snowmiss Tosca, who produced eight champions: Can., Am. & Bda. Ch. Samovar's True Grit, Can. & Am. Ch. Samovar's Trademark, Can. & Bda. Ch. Samovar's Sweet Gypsy Rose, Can. & Bda. Ch. Samovar's Sacha Snowcharm, Can. Ch. Samovar's Something Special, Can. Ch. Samovar's Snowangel O'Alexann and Can. Ch. Samovar's Kaddak Hy-Jinks. These splendid champions in three litters places her in the select few of the top producers of our breed.

True Grit ("Trooper"), whelped 12-18-75, won many Best Puppy in Group awards and became a Bermudian champion at 8 months of age. He finished to his Canadian championship the following week with a Best Puppy in Show. He acquired his American championship in 1978 with two majors on one weekend (two Group placements). Trooper was Canada's top winning Samoyed in 1978, and in 1979 was Best in Show at the Ottawa Kennel Club over 780 dogs.

Jack and Sandra Post, Jasam Samoyeds, in St. Albert, Alberta, Canada is the home of Am. & Can. Ch. Pinehill's Bjelkier Rurik and Am. & Can. Ch. Elsamjo's Sasha of Rurik, C.D. The Posts are active in the Edmonton Kennel Club, as well as with Sams and Chow Chows.

Shebaska Samoyeds, owned by Frank and Helga Gruber of Cheltenham, Ontario, Canada, began in 1969. Their kennel name of Shebaska was awarded to them by the Canadian Kennel Club in 1978. Registered kennel names in Canada are not merely taken and applied for with your first dog; you must earn them over a period of time with success and exemplary conduct.

In their very first litter, the Grubers had two champions. Since then 15 of their homebreds have made their championships. In 1980, their Am. & Can. Ch. Shebaska's Diamond Dazzler, Can. C.D., was shown in the United States by Annie Jureziz. At the Canadian National Specialty in 1980, their now Ch. Shebaska's Titu Laka At Samsu, was Best of Winners. Titu is a 5th generation breeding and is owned by Rosie H. Varjassy, Samsu Reg. An outstanding bitch, the now Can. & Am. Ch. Gonalda's Kosca Tamara, finished with four majors in the United States.

Shebaska Kennels must be especially proud of their obedience record. Their first C.D., Glow's Grand Finale of Khingan ("Shauna"), was highest scoring dog at the SCA Specialty in Wisconsin in 1972, also highest scoring dog in Trial the next day at the all-breed show. In 1974, with Ch. Shebaska's Chumikan Express, the Grubers again won Highest Scoring Dog in Trial at the SCA Specialty Show at Seattle, Washington with a score of 196½. In 1976, with Shebaska Sulaykha Pakova, C.D., they won Highest Scoring Dog in Trial at the Erie County KC (Pa.) show with a score of 197. Pakova was awarded the Samoyed Club of America Top Winning Obedience Award for 1976, and earned the Dog World Award for Canine Distinction with 3 consecutive scores of 195.5, 197.5 and 198. This bitch also has won four successive Highest Score in Trial awards at all-breed shows.

The Grubers breeding program is largely based upon line breeding to the English Snowland line through Snowland Sarnac, Snowland Rooski and Snowland Janice of Frostyways, all champions. For pedigree interest, they trace in five generations to Buck of The Glacier, who was a full brother to Am. Ch. Siberian Nansen of Farningham of Snowland. Glacier's dam, Eng. Ch. Sandra of the Glacier, was a daughter of Eng. Ch. Snow Chief of the Arctic. So you see, their bloodlines are not too different from some

Can. & Am. Ch. Shebaska's Diamond Dazzler, C.D. (left) and his sister, Can. Ch. Shebaska's Vashti Bathsheba, C.D. Breeder-owners: Frank and Helga Gruber, Ontario.

dominant ones in the United States. Their first stud was Ch. Khingan's Chu the Magnificent. Chu sired 6 Canadian champions and 5 of these have their Obedience titles, which is certainly a record. Chu has set the type for the kennel. He is 23″, well-balanced, beautiful-headed, with white and silver stand-off coat and a lovely disposition. Through Eng. Champion Derek the Piskeylated he goes to Nathan of Snowland, who is a full brother to Garin of Snowland, one of England's most dominant studs.

Shebaska has always kept a tight linebreeding program to Snowland. In 1974, they bred out to Am. & Can. Ch. Oakwood Farm's Kari J'Go Diko and kept the now Ch. Shebaska's Diamond Dazzler, CD, and his sister Ch. Shebaska's Vashti Bathsheba, CD. Another sister is Shebaska's Candida, CDX, owned by Rory Norman of Toronto.

In 1974, they were fortunately able to buy a linebred Snowland bitch, Ch. Chetereh's Kazanna Teki ("K-C"), whom they had seen win at two Canadian National Specialties. As the Grubers say, "By the time we had learned to appreciate her structure and movement, and knew that these do not come around very often." "K.C." has produced some lovely bitches including: Ch. Shebaska's Tiffany, and granddaughters, Ch. Shebaska's Blue Diamond and Shebaska's Mountain Willow, owned by Dr. and Mrs. T. C. Mountain, Mountaiga Reg.

Can. Ch. Shebaska's Malyenki, Am. & Can. CD & TT ("Kipna"), bred by the Grubers, is owned by Dr. Judith L. Wasserfall. In 1983, Kipna was the top Canadian obedience Sam, having the highest number of points ever accumulated by a Sammy. She achieved her Canadian CDX with an average score of 197, winning a Dog World award. She was also one of the top winning American Obedience Samoyeds tested for herding instinct and passed with flying colors.

285

Eng. Ch. Grenadier of Crensa ("Scotty"), holder of the all-time record for CC's won by a Samoyed—44. (Author Robert Ward awarded him Best in Show at the Northern Samoyed Society Championship Show, 1977.) "Scotty," owned by J.H. James, won his first CC at 15 months.

Judge Robert Ward selects Novskaya Khan Lefay as Best Puppy in Show at Northern Samoyed Society Championship Show, 1977, at Whitworth, England. Owner-handler, Capt. Townsend. Dolly Ward presents sterling perpetual trophy plaque. (Bred by Betty Moody who later moved to New York.)

20

The Samoyed
in Other Countries

England

Diane Chenault, of Orlando, Florida, visited Edinburgh, Scotland in August, 1981, and narrates her impression of the English and Scottish dogs and dog shows:

"I stayed with my friends in Edinburgh—Alan and Anne Brownlee and their daughter Serena, who shows their dogs. They have acquired two bitches from Mrs. Eileen Danvers (Fairvilla Kennels) as well as much advice and guidance from her.

"The night before the show was set aside for grooming as they already had their baths. The only grooming was combing and brushing, for no whiskers, no feet are ever trimmed over here. Grooming tables and crates are not commonly used here, in fact equipment like ours is not available.

"At the show-ground I saw another difference: no motor homes, and very few vans. It was my first benched show. There was an entry of 50 Samoyeds for Mr. James to judge. He is the owner of the famous Ch. Grenadier of Crensa, the all-time Challenge Certificate holder for Samoyeds in England.

"The dogs were beautiful, much more beautiful than I had expected from the pictures I had seen of English dogs. The bitches were breathtaking. I had always preferred the males until I saw the English and Scottish bitches. (I've been going to show for five years, including the Samoyed Club of America Specialty when it was in Atlanta.) The difference in coat was the outstanding difference. Apparently they do not bring them out unless they are dripping in coat. Most of the coats are longer than ours, and just a lot more of it.

Ch. Fairvilla Katrina, Best of Opposite Sex at the 1977 Northern Samoyed Championship Show judged by author Robert Ward. Owner: E.T. Pont.

Kim of Crownie, an outstanding English stud circa 1950. By Scaf ex Eng. Ch. Aura of Silver Frost. Kim, owned by Mr. Hopkin, was sire of 5 champions, and is the linebred grandsire of Eng. Ch. Grenadier of Crensa and Cavalier of Crensa.

Samont Sameric (at 10 months). By Eng. Ch. Fairvilla Emperor ex Samont Missy Missy. Owner: E.T. Pont, England.

288

"Another thing you notice right off is the absence of professional handlers. The presentation of the dogs is very casual. In fact, no one uses bait, yet many of the dogs would stand motionless for some time, alertly looking at their owners. I only saw one girl stack her dog. I don't know why they have so many classes for dogs to enter, but they do, and every one seems to enter more than one class with the same dog. The judge never changed the order of the dogs he had already judged. When new dogs would come in, he would judge them and then place them among the dogs already judged. From a spectator's and picture taker's viewpoint this was good, because the dogs were in the ring a long time and it gave you a chance to study them.

"I saw two dogs that day in Scotland that made quite an impression on me. One is Fairvilla Snowivan of Nenetsky. He is the most beautiful Sam I have ever seen. He was three years old, and stood about 22 inches tall. The Fairvilla dogs are known for their gorgeous heads and coat. He was far and away the best showman of the day. The judge didn't like him as well as I, for he was Reserve Challenge that day. Mr. James put a bitch Best of Breed. A dog needs 3 Challenge Certificates to become a champion and Ivan has only two at this time. Remember all the champions are in the Open Class so a dog must beat champions usually to win the C.C.

"The other dog I liked is Ch. Grenadier of Crensa, called "Scotty." The best word for description is breathtaking. He was so special, it brought tears to my eyes just to see how great a dog he really is. I had asked the Brownlees if Mr. James, the judge, would bring Scotty for me to see. After the judging Mrs. James brought him to the judging area. She had him on a long lead and he came bounding into the crowd. He was 11 years old, but could have been any age. He was like a spirited puppy with great dignity. He was larger than many of the other dogs I saw that day, heavier boned and more masculine looking. He was just outstanding!

"As I was watching Scotty, I was reminded of a Samoyed I saw several times on the Florida Circuit—Ch. North Starr's King Ransom. I do not know how many people have seen both dogs, but to me they were very much alike. I thought Ransom was outstanding with the same spirit and dignity. They are also the same age with similar show careers.

"Here I began talking of how wonderful the bitches were, and have ended up really liking two special males the best. But my next dog will be a bitch from England. I think my boys would like that the best."

Mr. and Mrs. J. H. James, Top Acre, Selston, Notts, England sent us this letter of their impressions of dogs they have seen in England:

"When I first saw Fairvilla Istvan of Airebis who later became an English, American, and Canadian champion as a young puppy in 1967, I thought him to be quite outstanding. We eventually mated him to a young bitch of ours, Venus of Crensa. Venus produced seven puppies, all males.

289

Ch. Naduska Grit of Kiskas (at 2½ years). By Ch. Grenadier of Crensa ex Kiskas Silverstar. Owners: Gerald and Kathy Mitchell (Kiskas).

Karaholme Samoyeds, "Chocolate and Sara." Owners, Tom and Joyce Stamp.

Fairvilla Dancing King (wh. 1975, by Ch. Golway Mr. Chan ex Ch. Fairvilla Michelle). Breeder: Eileen Danvers. Owner: P. Blewitt. Pictured winning Reserve Group at Rose of Tralee Int. all-breed championship show, 1980, under judge Robert Ward.

One of these was Cavalier of Crensa, owned by Mrs. Brenda Thompson. He had an outstanding career as a puppy but unfortunately was not campaigned extensively. Mrs. Danvers also had a puppy from this litter which she sent to Sweden; he became a Swedish Champion and did valuable stud work in Scandinavia.

"We repeated the mating to get a bitch, and would you believe it—this time Venus had six puppies, all male! They were all sold, although I kept a very handsome puppy back until last. The purchaser did not show up so I decided to keep him. This was, of course, Grenadier of Crensa, or "Scotty" as he is called.

"He was quite a shy puppy and it was a long time before he settled. He finally enjoyed showing. He gained his Junior Warrant whilst still a puppy. He won his first Challenge Certificate at 19 months, and was a champion at 22 months. This was a very unusual feat for those days. He was a Working Group Winner twice and Reserve three times. He has been Best in Show at the Northern Samoyed Society twice in succession.

"Scotty has won 43 C.C.'s and 33 Bests of Breed. This is a Samoyed breed record.

"Ch. Grenadier of Crensa is a sire of champions in England, South Africa and the USA, and at 12½ years, has just sired a litter to one of our bitches. He is a wonderful companion in the home.

"I don't suppose we will ever have another dog as good, but he is the standard we have set for ourselves.

"We look forward to another twenty years of showing and breeding for the quality we have had in the past."

Mrs. Eileen Danvers of Leicester, England, under the prefix Fairvilla, has been active most successfully in the breed for over twenty years, since 1959. Her breeding and bloodlines have contributed to the success of Novaskaya (Moodys) and the Ponts through Ch. Fairvilla Katrina, and of Kiskas (Mitchells), Karaholme (Stamps) and Crensa (James) through Eng., Can. & Am. Ch. Fairvilla Istvan of Airebis. It should be noted that Ch. Fairvilla Katrina was Best of Breed at the Cruft's Dog show in London three times. Mr. and Mrs. Geoff Grounds of Whitewisp, have combined the old English Kobe lines also with Fairvilla.

The Kiskas Kennel was founded in the early 1960s by Gerald and Kath Mitchell of Chesterfield, England. The foundation stock was descended from Ch. Snowland Rooski, linebred from the Snowland Kennels. Their first male (from John Hopkin) was Orion of Crownie, who was linebred to Kim of Crownie. Orion was the first Kiskas male to become a champion. The bitch, Owlie of Crownie, was then acquired. She excelled in style and soundness and correct type of coat. Owlie won two C.C.'s and 17 Reserve C.C.'s.

Linebreeding has always been the plan of this kennel whose motto is, "Tis not the gale but the set of the sail that steers the ship to progress." Thus careful thought has produced get who have all displayed the qualities of soundness, head quality, eye shape and color and coat texture for which this kennel is noted. Every Samoyed in the kennel has won either a C.C. or Reserve C.C.

Christmas '76 saw the birth of perhaps the most famous dog from this kennel, with a most illustrious early show career—three C.C.'s before the age of 11 months. Ch. Naduska Grit of Kiskas had to win another C.C. after the age of 12 months to meet the English Kennel Club's requirement for a Championship, because of his age. He now has 10 C.C.'s. He is noted for excellent substance, soundness and lovely true Samoyed head and eye. Another star is the young Ch. Trushka Trinket of Kiskas, who has been bred to "Grit" to carry on the linebreeding to the Snowland blood of Ch. Orion, and hopefully carry on the typical heads, eyes, style and lovely Samoyed temperament.

As judges, Gerald and Kath Mitchell have awarded Challenge Certificates since 1975 in England and at Championship shows in Holland, America and Spain. They have written "A Guide to Samoyed Care and the Illustrated Standard for England." Gerald is Chairman of the British Samoyed Club and Kath the Secretary of the Northern Samoyed Society. Gerald is also Breed Liaison Representative to the Kennel Club and a Kennel Club Member.

One of Ch. Orion's daughters, Lisa of Crownie, owned by T. & J. Stamp, produced a litter by Cavalier of Crensa (full litter brother to Ch. Grenadier of Crensa). The Mitchells purchased a male puppy from this litter which they were enticed to sell to the authors in 1972. He became Ch. Kiskas Karaholme Cherokee, who was the Samoyed Club of America Top Stud Dog in 1980. It is interesting to note that Cherokee was born in 1970 and Grit in 1976. They have almost identical breeding, their sires are litter brothers and their dams half-sisters by Orion.

Mr. and Mrs. Tom Stamp (the Karaholmes) have been in the breed for 25 years. They got their first Sammy, Beauty, in 1968 and acquired Lisa of Crownie to fill that empty feeling. Lisa was bred by John Hopkin of "Red Carnation" fame. Lisa won well in the show ring and had a CC and a Res. C.C. Lisa's litter, by Cavalier of Crensa, was whelped August 29, 1970. Their daughter, Rosalyn, chose a bitch puppy and named her Ballerina. Rosalyn and Rina had success in the show ring and won Best Puppys, BOB and RCC and a 1st at Cruft's on Rosalyn's thirteenth birthday. In 1975, Rina was mated to Samont Mistvan and they kept Karaholme Bronya and Karaholme Carpenter. Karaholme Sultan went to Eddie and Margaret Dalton. All have won well, Brony has 2 C.C. and 2 Res. C.C. When written up in the critiques, all are described as excellent movers and being of the essential type, good heads and excellent temperament.

In 1977, Bronya was bred to Ch. Grenadier of Crensa, a full brother to Cavalier. They kept Karaholme Chocholate who was named by their son Robin. Chocolate has won the Junior Warrant and 1 Res. C.C. They nicknamed her Squeals on Wheels, because she always wants attention. Her sister, Karaholme Karamac, is owned by Liz and Ian Mackie in Scotland.

Karaholme Sara won the Dog of The Year Award at the Scunthorpe Canine Association in December, 1981.

Joyce and Tom Stamp write: "In being owned by Samoyeds, we have met some lovely people who became friends. The world of dogs is also a human world with all that entails. One of my favourite quotations, 'Beauty is Truth, and Truth is Beauty, that is all you know and all you need to know,' epitomizes the Samoyed breed."

Mrs. Muriel Hopkin is their doyen of the Samoyed world. The Stamps' dogs are linebred to her Kim Of Crownie. Mrs. Hopkin's knowledge and hard work was the foundation of their stock. They are a small kennel. They aim at breeding good Samoyeds with soundness, type, movement and balance. Tom states, "We are very proud to have bred Ch. Kiskas Karaholme Cherokee in the first litter with Lisa."

The Samoyed in Holland
by Martin Hozeman, Stranja Severa Kennels

The very first Samoyed imported into Holland was Farningham Ikon of Samoya. He was imported in 1924 by Miss Nelly Dickhoff and was bred by Mrs. Kilburn-Scott. Ikon, as he was called, attracted much attention, so Miss Dickhoff imported more and formed a kennel partnership with Miss Bea Kuipers under the kennel name "Of Samoya."

More people became interested in the breed and 30 Samoyeds were imported between 1924 and 1934. Twenty-five of these were of British origin, 3 were bred in Norway and 2 came from Germany.

As other kennels came into existence, the *Nederlandse Samojeden Club* was formed in 1934. One year later the name was changed to *Nederlandse Poolhonden Club*. This was done at the insistence of the *Raad van Beheer* (Court of Management), as Poolhonden is Dutch for polar dogs and thus the owners and fanciers of other Nordic Breeds could become members of the one club.

In 1939 there were over 100 Samoyeds registered in Holland and then the war came. In 1940 there were two litters at the "Of Samoya" Kennels, owned now only by Miss Kuipers. Three years later, even during the war when food was so scarce, Mrs. Van Ogten had a litter at her home in 1943. Miss Kuipers and Mrs. Van Ogten combined their dog activities in Mrs. Van Ogten's house in a bomb shelter under the house. The dogs had their own special shelter. Nevertheless, at the end of the war only a few Samoyeds were left. Miss Kuipers was bombed out twice and Mrs. Van Ogten's house was destroyed by artillery fire.

293

In the immediate postwar period there was no interest in dog breeding because of the desolate position of the country and the lack of food for everyone. Even when the country had been reestablished by hard work and the Marshall-Aid, there was no interest in dogs, not even the lovely Samoyeds of Holland. When Queen Wilhelmina abdicated in 1955, her daughter, Queen Juliana, presented her with the Samoyed bitch "Ibur Stella." Interest stirred. Stella was imported from Norway. Her granddam, Snowland Elena, was bred by the well-known Mrs. Ada Westcott and exported to Norway. Snowland Elena was sired by Martingate Snowland Taz. The Queen-Mother (then titled Princess Wilhelmina) had Stella bred twice and her puppies went all over Holland. At this time the Club was renamed again to *De Nederlanse Samojeden Club* and began its glorious recovery. In 1957, Rippleby Davy was imported from England; in 1960, Tamaya of Kobe from England and Anka von Eismeer, bought from Germany even though she was of original Crownie bloodlines. The Hozemans imported their first Samoyed, Arkhan of Crystalline, in 1965. He was bred by Mrs. Hozeman's sister in England. Within four years "Sammy" became a Dutch, International, Belgian and Luxemburg champion.

Miss Kuiper, who had begun 30 years before, again renewed her interest and with vicar Dr. Hohan Kabel revived the oldest existing Samoyed kennel in Europe.

Dr. Kabel imported four Samoyeds from England: two dogs and one bitch from Rose Lewis' Snowcryst Kennels, and another bitch from Ted Ironside's Leasam Kennels. The Hozemans imported a dozen Sams, all from the Sworddale and Fairvilla Kennels of England. They kept three for themselves. The last import is a Crensa, bred by John and Betty James. Garin is by the famous Grenadier of Crensa, the holder of 43 Challenge Certificates. Other imports came from Norway, Sweden and Finland. In the middle of the 1970s, the Club attained a high point of 800 members. Now, due to economic problems, they have about 750. This is a remarkable number when we realize the Samoyed Club of America has only a few hundred more. The Dutch Samoyed Club is the largest on the West-European continent. Only the Finnish Club is a bigger one.

There are about 2,000 Samoyeds in Holland, most in small kennels. The name Samojeed is pronounced "Sa-mo-yaid" and the plural form as "Sa-mo-yai-dun."

To become a Dutch National Champion, a dog or bitch must win four C.A.C.'s in Holland under at least three different judges. The C.A.C. can only be given if the dog is at least 15 months old and qualified Excellent by the judge. The rules for becoming a National Champion differ from country to country; the rules for becoming an International Champion are set by the F.C.I. Here the dog needs four C.A.C.I.B.'s, won in at least three countries. At least one must be won in his own country. There must be at least 12 months between the first and fourth award; thus no dog can become an International Champion under the age of 27 months.

There are no special Samoyed clubs in Germany, Belgium and Switzerland. The Sams there, together with all of the Nordic breeds, are combined into one Club, but they all show in each other's shows across the borders. The Scandinavian countries cannot participate in this interchange of shows because they have quarantine regulations. The Dutch contacts with the English clubs are quite good, even though they too cannot show because of quarantine, but many of the Dutch Samoyed owners are also members of the English clubs and vice versa.

France

Mrs. Connie Humphrys, Norilsk Kennels, Reg'd., provided us with more recent information of Samoyeds in distant lands.

She shipped Danook of Norilsk to Paris to a Dr. Michel de Muzan in 1974. Danook became a French Champion and later was awarded the C.A.C.I.B. (International Title) by the F.C.I. He was used for the Breed Standard in France.

Danook has many progeny in Europe and some are winning. Ch. Nansen of Norilsk, a brother to Ivonoff and Mysam Sonya from Norilsk was being shown in Switzerland.

Another one, Norilsk Okwari, was sent to Israel to live on a kibbutz, the Gesher Haziv, where there was a female. They produced the first litter of Samoyeds in Israel. Norilsk Okwari was by Ch. Nansen ex Ch. Norilsk Lady Terra.

Belaya's Uffda of Kauzja was the first American-bred Samoyed exported to France, from Carol Chittum's Belaya Kennels. More recently Belaya I'm A Pepper Too, winner of Best in Sweepstakes at the SCA National in 1982, was exported by her former owner, Teena Deatherage, Crizta Kennels and has arrived safely and is happy with her new owner, Mme. Periot, Trevous, France.

Sweden

Bergit Hillerby and Lasse Carlberg of Stockholm, Sweden, are ardent supporters and breeders of the Samoyed in the Scandinavian countries.

With the kennel name of *Explorer's Samojedhunder,* they have added to their stock with imports from the United States. Int. Nord Ch. Kauzjas Cochise of Snowcliff is a Nordic and Finland winner. He is the only Samoyed to own both titles, and the first Samoyed to win an All-Breed Veterans Class. He has sired 18 champions and 12 of them have won Certificates of C.A.C.I.B. Bergit also imported a bitch from Jo Anne

Birgit Hillerby with Swedish and Norwegian Ch. Kauzjas Cochise of Snowcliff, export to Sweden from the U.S. Cochise is sire of 18 champions, 12 of which have earned C.A.C.I.B. certificates.

Swedish, Finnish and Norwegian Ch. Jenathan Jashuaja, bitch, twice Best in Show in extensive winning in the Nordic states. Breeder-owner: Mrs. Jnma Kivimurtu, Savonlinna, Finland.

Norwegian Ch. Maiken's Katja-Nova, dam of BIS winner, Ch. Mjaerumhogda's Toya.

Ch. Mjaerumhodga's Toya, bitch, Best in Show at Vasteras, Sweden 1977, over 3,000 dogs. Judge (at left), author Dolly Ward. Center, ring steward and translator, Mikael Nordenstedt. Owners: Greta Else Mjaerum and Elvind Mjaerum. Toya, by Swedish and Norwegian Ch. Kauzjas Cochise of Snowcliff ex Norw. Ch. Maiken's Katja-Nova, was also Best in the Specialty Show at Stockholm, judged by Robert Ward.

Marineau named Shatazah of Antares, sired by Ch. Midnight Sun Kimba ex Larissa of Taymylyr. Shatazah is a champion but lacks one certificate for the C.A.C.I.B. She has two daughters by Geronimo that are exceptional.

Lady JoAnn is both a Nordic and Finnish winner and has Group Placements. She was Best of Breed at their Samoyed Specialty in 1979. Bergit has bred her dogs to Samoyeds of Grete-Sofie Og Eivind Mjaerum in Norway and produced Mjaerumhogda's Toya, a splendid champion bitch, to whom your author awarded Best of Breed at a Samoyed Specialty in Stockholm, Sweden, in 1977. The ultimate award to her breeding was the selection of the bitch, Ch. Lady JoAnn, for the breed representation picture in the Swedish Kennelklub magazine, and a double centerfold at that!

Parvovirus struck Sweden in the fall of 1979 and all dog shows were cancelled until May 1980. All dogs are now required to be innoculated for parvo. The Swedish dog owners participate in a health and life insurance plan for their animals. Several years ago it cost 200 Crowns per year (about $42.) and covered accidents, illness and greatly reduced prices for shots and X-rays and $250. life insurance. All of the established breeders sold their puppies with such a policy included. Bergit and Lasse have exported their puppies to Finland, Norway, Denmark and France. One bitch, Explorer's Skeeter of Sweden, has been exported to Texas in the USA.

297

Samoyed entries at Swedish shows range from 20 to 50. Your author judged a specialty of approximately eighty (counting stud and brood classes) and they are a most impressive event. In each breed, each dog in the class is assessed, critiqued and rated 1, 2, or 3 or 4. This critique is written openly and read orally to the exhibitor. All of the 1's remain in the ring and are placed 1st, 2nd, 3rd, 4th. From all of the class winners the winner is selected. The Champion class is also assessed and critiqued in writing and the winner competes for Best of Breed and the C.A.C.I.B. Certificate. All of the written Critiques are published in the Kennel Club magazine each month. Therefore, really poor specimens do not return for competition, lacking encouragement.

Denmark

Kennel Kaissa, owned by Kirsten and Folmer Jorgensen of Aalborg, Denmark, has a most unusual group of fine Samoyeds with a true international background.

Kirsten's bitch, Kaissa Petrowa is English; Explorer's Universal Soldier is from Sweden; Yakir, a male is from Kenya, South Africa; and Int. & Danish Ch. BDSG Sir Jonah of Banff is from the USA. Most amazing is that the last three (all males) have a common ancestry of similar English and American lineage. The Swedish dog is from Birgit Hillerby of Stockholm; Jonah is from Mardee Ward. Jonah, a double grandson of Ch. Ice Way's Ice Breaker, has won many Group Firsts and a Best in Show.

For the pedigree buffs, Yakir has Ch. Nachalnik of Drayalene as a grandfather; Int. Nord Ch. Kauzjas Cochise of Whitecliff and Swedish Ch. Explorer's Lady Jane are the parents of Universal Soldier (Victor); and Ch. Kiska's Karaholme Cherokee is behind Jonah.

The Jorgensens train their dogs in harness and sled work, as well as in show and obedience.

Australia

Mr. and Mrs. Robert Willis, owners of the Taz Kennels and judges of the Samoyed in Australia, have provided us with this report:

The breed in Australia is now catered for by specialist clubs in Western Australia, South Australia, Victoria, New South Wales, and Queensland. All the dogs are descended from about 100 imports from the United Kingdom and New Zealand. The majority of these have come into the country in the last twenty years. To prevent the importation of rabies, the quarantine laws only permit dogs to come into the country through the

Samoyeds in Denmark. Explorer's Universal Soldier ("Victor"), and the bitches, Kaissa and Anuska, from the Kennel Kaissa, owned by Kirsten and Folmer Jorgensen, Aalborg, Denmark.

Danish Ch. Sir Jonah of Banff, exported by Mardee Ward to Kirsten and Folmer Jorgensen, Kaissa Kennels in Denmark. Jonah, an Ice Breaker grandson, met Yakir from East Africa (a combination of Pinehill and Silveracres) and Kaissa (who carries the English lines of Whitewisp plus the Swedish Explorer lines of Antares and Kauza). With a family of six, the youngest in kindergarten in 1983, what a haven for Samoyeds!

Author Dolly Ward judged the Samoyed Club of Queensland's 11th Specialty in July, 1981. Best in Show and winner of the bitch CC was Aust. Ch. Samlaki Vada Gabriella (Aust. Ch. Zarbelle Dartanyan ex Aust. Ch. Alpayo Miksu Varinka). Owner, Mrs. C. Warwick. At right, Graham Bray, club president.

At left, Reserve BIS and winner of the dog CC at the 1981 Queensland Specialty was the Reynolds' Aust. Ch. Saranvar Taras Altai (by Fairvilla Tsarovitch, imp. UK ex Aust. Ch. Lesamek Silver Tamyra). At right Bloric Vaymac Velvet, Reserve Challenge bitch and Best Minor Puppy, owned by Olive Singer. Aiding judge Dolly Ward is ring steward Bev Hartland.

300

United Kingdom, where they must spend a year (six months in quarantine kennels and a further six months in residence) before coming to Australia, where they must spend another three months in a quarantine kennel before joining their owner. There are no restrictions between Australia and New Zealand, other than compulsory worming plus veterinary inspections at both ports. Dogs have often been taken from one country to the other for showing and mating.

There were undoubtedly Samoyeds in Australia earlier than the 1930s, for Antarctic Buck was known in 1909, but the earliest fully documented and accepted for the pedigree book was Ch. Yukon Queen, whelped February 2, 1929, and imported from Miss Leonard in England by L. Maike. She was by Snow Elf ex Snowvit. Yukon Queen was the dam of the first Australian born champion, Ch. Blackeyed Susan. However, in the Royal Agricultural Society of New South Wales annual of 1927 the show results include in All Other Varieties Not Specified, under 45 lb.—1st in Open Dog, Prince Zero, whelped November, 1925, by Zero ex Snowqueen (Samoyede), owned by Mrs. S. Hart.

Interestingly, Mr. and Mrs. Willis report that the largest show entries are at the breed club shows, not the Royal shows. This is because the breed club shows have a full seven class entry, and are held on weekends. The Royal Agricultural Shows are held during the week and are in conjunction with all types of exhibits. They only have four classes for dogs—puppy, junior, intermediate and open—and are open only for Champions and dogs under three years of age. Thus entries at the Royal Shows average approximately 60 to 80 Samoyeds, while the club championship shows average 100 to 110 Samoyeds.

To acquire an Australian championship, a dog needs to earn 100 points. Points are obtained as follows:

> Five points are awarded for each Challenge Certificate, plus 1 point for each dog/bitch defeated. (For example, if there were 5 dogs and 7 bitches in attendance, the Dog Challenge would be worth 10 points, and the Bitch Challenge 12 points.)
>
> A Best in Group is worth 5 points plus 1 point for each dog and bitch beaten in the Group, up to a maximum 25 points each show.
>
> Best in Show earns no points unless the Group win was less than 25 points, in which case the dog's count is supplemented up to 25 points (taking into account the dogs beaten in other Groups).

Dogs are bred and judged by the English standard, and this standard cannot be changed or altered except by permission or instruction of the English Kennel Club.

Aust. Ch. Kalina Major Module, Best Exhibit at Perth Royal, 1977. Breeder-owners: Mr. and Mrs. J. Sydenham-Clarke, Victoria, Australia.

Aust. Ch. Silvasam Snow Rocket, placed Best Veteran at the 1981 Samoyed Club of Queensland Specialty by judge Dolly Ward. Snow Rocket, whelped 9/17/74, is by Aust. & N.Z. Ch. Kalina Imperial Eureka ex Aust. Ch. Mulawa Karinne. Owner-handler, Mr. Bloomfield. In 1975, Robert Ward judged the Cranbourne KC show in Melbourne and put Snow Rocket Best Minor Puppy. Dolly put him on to Best Puppy in Group and Graham Head (Australian judge) awarded him Best Minor Puppy in Show.

New Zealand

The history of the breed in New Zealand can best be traced through the imports starting with the introduction of dogs from the Antarctic expeditions at the turn of the century. Captain Scott was known to have presented five Samoyeds to the Wellington Zoo, and these were later added to by imports from England and Denmark. The zoo bred their last litter in 1941 and the Samoyeds were then sold to the public, hence an influx of breeding stock to establish the breed further. Other dogs were believed to be smuggled into this country by any means possible.

The first Samoyeds registered with the N.Z. Kennel Club were in 1903. The N.Z. Kennel Club adopted the standard of the breed from The Kennel Club (England) and it is still observed to the present day. The first Samoyed to gain a Championship title was Mrs. W. Richard's Ch. Doctor. The first Samoyed bitch to gain the title was Mr. Brain's Ch. White Princess of the Yukon.

In the 1930s there were several imports from England and Australia. The first dog of real note was Eng. Ch. Rex of the Arctic, imported from England by Mr. & Mrs. Woodhouse of Dunedin. Rex was the first Samoyed to be awarded Best in Show in New Zealand. Mrs. Y. Sydenham Clark's Kalina Kennels in Australia and Neilmar Fraiser in Christchurch played an important part in the lineage of today's dogs in New Zealand. Imports such as Aust. & NZ Ch. Kalina Kuts, Kalina Madonna, Kaline Sabrina, NZ Ch. Kalina Saschina, NZ Ch. Kalina Smirnoff, Aust. & NZ Ch. Kalina Stardust, NZ Ch. Kalina Wanderer, NZ Ch. Kalina Zanetta, NZ Ch. Kalina Zeigred, NZ Ch. Kalina Silver Knight and NZ Ch. Kalina Major Module are perhaps some of the better known imports. These Kalina dogs were bred from such English parentage as Aust. Ch. Starya of Kobe, Aust. Ch. Icemist Beauty of Kobe, Eng. & Aust. Ch. Darryl of Tamitsa, Aust. Ch. Eureka of Kobe and Fairvilla Tsarovitch. These dogs virtually form the basis of today's breeding stock. Two other English imports to arrive in Australia were also to have an influence on present day Samoyeds: Eng. & Aust. Ch. Imperial Rebel of Kobe and Eng. & Aust. Ch. Silver Dart of Sworddale.

New Zealanders have also imported Samoyeds from England. Some of these include White Hunter of Kobe, Aust. Ch. Tatina of Kobe (Imp via Aust.), Wings Gem of the Arctic, NZ Ch. Rex of the Arctic, Viking of the Arctic, Silver Light of the Arctic, NZ Ch. Glamour of the Arctic, Beauty of the Arctic and NZ Ch. Rippleby Borodino. Later imports of note were Whitewisp Snow Elf, Prince Hal of Kobe, NZ Ch. Fairvilla Elvrina, Carwood Snow Nanette, Lealsam Shigalov, Aust. & NZ Ch. Novaskaya Silva Zaravitch (via Aust.), NZ Ch. Novaskaya Silva Sunspark of Kimchatka, and Novaskaya Sleigh Chief.

The top winning Samoyed in New Zealand history is NZ Ch. Ruski of Tsilma, born February 3, 1965, bred and owned by Mr. & Mrs. T.

Rushbridge of Christchurch, N.Z. At all-breed shows, he was awarded 11 Bests in Show, 5 Reserve Bests in Show and 19 Bests of Group.

Samoyeds are of a high standard in this country, and there is no doubt that the importation of Australian and English breeding stock on a regular basis has contributed to the caliber and success of present day specimens.

Note that due to the rabies quarantine in the United Kingdom, animals are in quarantine for one year (at $6. per day) before being released to the new owners. The cost of transportation is usually more than the cost of the dog.

Trevor and Eleanor Maitland of Paeroa, New Zealand, who contributed the history of the Samoyed in New Zealand above are actively involved in breeding and exhibiting their Samoyeds. Their first dog did not become a show winner, but he did succeed as a stud. He sired three champions: Toska of Kimchatka, Toga of Kimchatka and Marcia of Kimchatka. When they tried inbreeding, they had what was for them disastrous results . . . they did not get the length of neck and leg that they felt they needed. They bought a dog from Australia from Vic and Aileen Perry who had the style and height they wanted. He was Snosheen Sadi Sahib and he became a New Zealand champion and sired their next Ch. Kimchatka Silver Prince.

Again thinking of English dogs, they wrote to several kennels and decided upon Novaskaya for the type they wanted. In the meantime they acquired a bitch from Christchurch, NZ who was a granddaughter of Fairvilla Tsarovitch. She, Ch. Foxworth Melitopal, grew up to have the substance and leg length they always wanted in a bitch.

Their English import, Novaskaya Silva Sunspark of Kimchatka was an instant success story and proved the turning point in their breeding and showing career. She became a champion and won several Group awards. Their next import was Novaskaya Tsarina Lafay who was sent in whelp to Whitewisp Arrogance. From this litter, a male was sent to Hawaii to Amy Sakata, and Brenda Blewitt bought Kimchatka Alpine Alexi.

Of her own breeding, Mrs. Maitland is especially proud of her bitch Silva Sunspark's litter with Ch. Sikandi Silver Joker, which produced Kimchatka Sun Heritage ("Henry"), who made breed history by winning Best in Show all-breeds at the tender age of 8 mos, 3 days. He is New Zealand's top winning puppy of all time.

Brenda and Tony Blewitt (Vashka Samoyeds) of Auckland, New Zealand, write: "Our first Samoyed took over our hearts and home as an eight-week-old pup and was immediately classified as a family pet, with perhaps the odd outing to ribbon parades. Nothing serious like championship shows with all their strange terminology and mountains of equipment was for us. Four years later, what do we have? Many thousands of miles on

304

Ch. Kimchatka Alexei ("Kermit"), owned by Brenda (pictured handling) and Tony Blewitt, winning Best in Show under the American judge, Mrs. Maynard Drury, at Auckland Non-Sporting Dog Association show, October 1983. Kermit was bred in England and whelped (2/10/80) in quarantine in New Zealand. In 1982 he scored all-breed Bests in Show at Napier Kennel Assn. under judge Jean Gillies (NZ), at Otago and Manawatu KA under Kevin Brown (Aust.) and under Samoyed specialist judge Valerie Auckram (NZ).

Norm Fraiser of Christchurch, New Zealand, pictured in 1975. Wife Nielmar was away judging in Sydney.

the speedo, a wealth of experience, many new friends and a champion dog. Yes, we are hooked. So much so that we were involved in bringing out to New Zealand from England a bitch, Novaskaya Tsarina Lafay, in whelp to Whitewisp Arrogance in the hope that she would produce bitches. She only produced one bitch so we have a dog we hope to make up to a champion.

"The reason we have gone to the U.K. for our breeding stock, is that New Zealand follows the English standard and most, but not all, of our dogs are bred from or can be traced back to English stock. We are firm believers of linebreeding as opposed to outcrossing. Being so far removed from other countries has its disadvantages and advantages. It permits us to observe what has happened to the breed in other countries and hopefully enables us avoid their mistakes, as we see them.

"Unfortunately, when you look at a lot of Sammies it is very difficult to visualize them in the role and environment from which they originated. So many breeders have developed a pretty animal which may or may not look good in the show ring, but more importantly would not stand up to the rigors of a northern winter. There is no substance in the animal once you go beyond coat. Prettiness in the show ring has been a main criteria to the detriment of the breed."

A personal note. The authors judged in New Zealand in August, 1981. Dolly judged Samoyeds and the Non-Sporting Group at the Hauraki Plains Canine Assn. Championship all-breed show at Paeroa. The Dog C.C. went to Eischiedvik Pearlonna, bred by Fran M. Wilson and owned by J. E. Watts of Wellington. Pearlonna, who Dolly feels resembled their daughter's Ch. Hoof 'N Paw's White Knight, was from the Junior Class and went on to win Best Junior and Best Non-Sporting. The bitch C.C. went to Schmiroff Pola Panda, bred and owned by A. and P. Naylor. She excelled in both gait and type, and had good quality of coat.

We fully enjoyed our week in Auckland as house guests of Brenda and Tony Blewitt, ably assisted by Ch. Vodka, and the newly arrived English import "Kikki" and Kimchatka Alexi. All three knew our guest room bed and we welcomed them as they welcomed us.

Guatemala

Randy and Irving Young have a small boarding, training and breeding kennel in the town of Chimaltenango, which has an elevation of 6,000 feet and a year-around temperature of 65°. The Youngs are professional handlers of the International Latin-American circuits.

They have a young Samoyed male, Ch. Glacier Maker of Polar Mist, acquired from Lynette Hansen. Glacier has finished his Guatemala, Costa Rica and Puerto Rico championships and the C.A.C.I.B. title. They are

Aust. Ch. Mulawa Kael Annastarsy, Best Veteran Bitch and First in Open Bitch at Queensland Specialty. By Eng. & Aust. Ch. Imperial Rebel of Kobe (UK import) ex Elgianto Cherkassy. Breeder-owner: Olive Singer.

New Zealand Ch. Kimchatka Achilles ("King"), whelped 10/2/80 in New Zealand. By Whitewisp Arrogance ex Novaskaya Tsarina Lafay (English import). Owners: Trevor and Eleanor Maitland.

Novaskaya Georgia Mist ("Kiki"), bred by Betty Moody (then in England, now in New York). Imported and owned by Brenda and Tony Blewitt, Wiri, NZ.

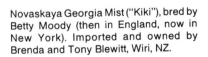

planning upon additional titles of: Mexican (1 point away), South American (2 points away) and International and Champion of the Americas. This would give him more titles than any other Samoyed we know of to date. They are also looking to show him in the United States and possibly Canada to complete the title list. Glacier is a Ch. Ice Way Ice Breaker son.

Brazil

The Samoyed breed has been revived in Brazil by Werner Degenhardt of Sao Paulo, Brazil.

Samoyeds have been in Brazil before. In 1957 Mrs. Tucker, Encino Kennels, exported one. Assis Chateaubrian, a very prominent Brazilian journalist who introduced television to the country, was an owner and great booster of the breed from 1940 until his death in 1968; however, none were ever registered with the Kennel Club until 1975.

Mr. and Mrs. Werner Degenhardt brought a bitch from Denmark named Jenisej's Laci. She became a Great Brazil and Int. Champion and the foundation bitch of their Bjelkiers Kennel. Their next dog was Nanook Salton from Canada and he is a Great Brazil and International Champion. Nanook and Laci have had two litters registered with the Brazilian Kennel Club. The get have done very well at the shows and most of them have Group placings. Great Brazil and International Ch. Jenisej's Kirova of Bjelkiers is the first Samoyed bitch to receive the title South American Champion, won at Montevideo, Uruguay in 1979 during the II. Sicasud Show. Am. and Braz. Ch. Silverseas Ivan of Arandale also won this award. Ivan was imported to Brazil to help maintain the quality of the Samoyeds. Another import is the now Am. and Great Brazilian Ch. Pooka's Centurion of the Pines, by Ch. Silveracres Chief Polar Bear ex Ch. Pooka's Surprise O'Frosty Morn, C.D. Centurion has been in Brazil since 1980 and is doing very well.

In 1984 the Degenhardts took their bitch, Jenisej's Rebecca of Bjelkiers to the Am. & Mex. Ch. The Hoof 'n Paw White Knight in California. From this breeding, they raised a litter of two. The male, Rebecca's Orion of Bjelkiers, stayed with them. The bitch, Rebecca's Olinda of Bjelkiers, was sold to Marie-Louise and Borge Lakjer in Espergaerde, Denmark.

Another export from Bjelkiers went to Italy—the Samoyed Blue, sired by Sabarkas Kurgan of Silvertip out of Jenisej's Zahrina of Bjelkiers, went to Mrs. Renata Fossati, Corno Bianca Kennels in Durfo, near Milan.

Several Brazilian dog magazines have published articles on the Samoyed breed and interest is being shown by new owners.

The Brazilians have adopted the American breed standard. Werner Degenhardt reports the difference in Best in Show in Brazil. "From the six Group winners a Best in Show is chosen; then the dog that was Second in

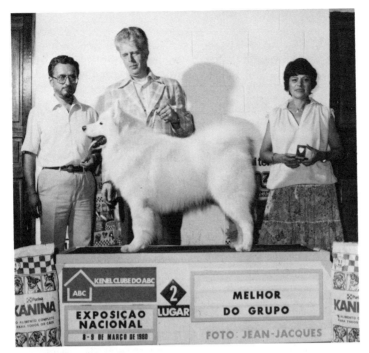

Samoyeds in Brazil. Above, Ch. Jenisey's Turgay of Belkiers (18 months) in 1978 win under Argentina judge, Mrs. Celina di Pacci. Owner-handler, Werner Degenhardt of Sao Paulo. Turgay is by Braz. & Int. Ch. Nanook Salton ex Braz. & Int. Ch. Jenisey's Laci. Laci, imported to Brazil from Denmark, is the foundation bitch of Mr. and Mrs. Degenhardt's Bjelkiers Kennels, and is pictured below with her six weeks old litter by Ch. Silverseas Ivan of Arandale.

that Group comes in as a Reserve replacement; now a 2nd Best in Show is chosen; again the second to that dog returns as a replacement to compete for 3rd Best in Show and this continues until 4th place Best in Show is selected.''

Brazil is a member of the *Federacion Cynologique Internationale* (FCI) and CACIBs (Certificate for Aptitude for Championship of International Beauty) are awarded only at International shows under FCI rules. To become a champion in Brazil, a dog must win 5 and a bitch must win 4 CACIBs by different judges. The judge may award one certificate for each 25 dogs in the ring. He awards one for the dog and the bitch. For final championship they must win Best of Breed at least once.

To become a Great Brazilian Champion a dog must win 60 points and a bitch 40 points. Not more than 5 points are awarded to a sex at a show. At least three Bests of Breed must be won under three different judges.

The Orient

While unregistered Samoyeds from China were shown in California and Texas in the 1920s, none were ever registered, and none appear in present bloodlines. Good examples of the breed did find their way to the Orient in 1934. Miss Hazel I. Shadell, a stenographer missionary, purchased a puppy from Mrs. Ivy Kilburn-Morris, then in Shanghai. Mrs. Kilburn-Morris had lived in Japan in 1932 with her two dogs, Farningham Polar Bru and Farningham Tosca, and five litters were placed in that country also. Miss Shadell's puppy, Snow Wrangle, travelled far and came to Mrs. John H. Thomas of Mt. Vernon, Ohio, and Mt. Rainier, Maryland. Here this Samoyed bloodline completed its trip around the world. A litter by Ch. Siberian Nansen of Farningham of Snowland out of Snow Wrangle was pictured in the Washington *Post*. Many people came to see these dogs, described as rare in 1940. Most startling was the fact that a puppy, Snegurochka, went to the Russian Ambassador, Mr. Constantine A. Oumansky, who had sent his undersecretaries to purchase the puppy for his daughter.

In 1984, Crizta Kennels exported two puppies to Japan. One was a 6-months-old male, Billy Casper (by Ch. Ice Way's Flash Cube ex Crizta's Charismic Chinook), and the other an 8-months-old bitch, Crizta's Power Winder (by Ch. Ice Way's Flash Cube ex Hoof 'n Paw NDN Rain Dance). Their new owner is Mitsuyoshi Matsudaira of Saitama (near Tokyo).

Mrs. Ivy Kilburn-Morris with Samoyed "Polar Bru," swimming in the waters of Hong Kong in 1940.

Keta Ku Tse Ne of Asgard, which in Japanese means Arctic Fox. Bred by Ruth Mary Heckervoth. Owned and named by Terry Sonnier, California.

Ch. Davina's Frosty Bear, finished to championship in Alaska in 1981. Bred by Bobbie Smith, Frosty Bear is a son of Ch. Ice Way's Honey Bear. Owner: Phyllis Gerow, Sunnyhill Samoyeds, Alaska.

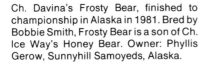

APPENDIX

Samoyed Club of America Specialty Winners

NOTE: *First line of listing identifies date, show at which held, number of entries and judge. Name of owner is in parentheses following the dog's name.*

1. Sept. 14, 1929—Tuxedo KC—40—Louis Smirnow
BOB—Ch. Tiger Boy of Norka (Mr. and Mrs. H. Reid)
2. Sept. 13, 1930—Tuxedo KC—12—Mrs. F. Romer
BOB—Ch. Storm Cloud (Mrs. E. Hudson)
3. May 29, 1937—Morris & Essex KC—19—Louis Smirnow
BOB—Krasan (Msgr. R. F. Keegan)
4. May 28, 1938—Morris & Essex KC—43—Msgr. Keegan
BOB—Ch. Norka's Moguiski (A. V. W. Foster)
5. May 27, 1939—Morris & Essex KC—31—Enno Meyer
BOB—Ch. Prince Kofski (B. M. Ruick)
6. May 25, 1940—Morris & Essex KC—20—Ruth Stillman
BOB—Ch. Prince Igor II (Msgr. Keegan)
7. May 31, 1941—Morris & Essex KC—29—C. H. Chamberlain
BOB—Ch. Alastasia's Rukavitza (A. L. McBain)
8. March 28, 1943—International KC of Chicago
Cancelled because of war regulations.
9. Oct. 19, 1946—International KC of Chicago—46—A. Rosenberg
BOB—Ch. Frolnick of Sammar (J. J. Marshall)—on to GR1
10. June 8, 1947—Pasadena KC—47—Dr. Richard Walt
BOB—Ch. Staryvna of Snowland (Mr. and Mrs. R. H. Ward)
11. Apr. 25, 1948—Los Angeles KC—35—Dr. Wm. H. Ivens
BOB—Ch. Gay of White Way (Agnes and Aljean Mason)
12. June 25, 1950—Harbor Cities KC—110—Chris Knudsen
BOB—Ch. Verla's Prince Comet (Shirley Hill)—on to GR4
13. Aug. 3, 1952—San Mateo KC—78—J. W. Cross
BOB—Ch. Verla's Prince Comet (Shirley Hill)
14. Sept. 11, 1953—Westchester KC—40—Ruth Stillman
BOB—Ch. Zor of Altai (A. V. Ruth)
15. Apr. 13, 1954—International KC of Chicago—51—E. D. McQuown
BOB—Ch. King of Wal-Lynn (E. M. Smith)
16. Sept. 11, 1955—Westchester KC—16—C. H. Chamberlain
BOB—Ch. Tazson's Snow Flicka (A. E. Ulfeng)
17. Nov. 26, 1955—Los Angeles KC—83—Alf Loveridge
BOB—Ch. Polaris Pan (G. Klein and M. Mueller)
18. Feb. 25, 1956—Seattle KC—35—A. E. Van Court
BOB—Ch. Bunky Jr. of Lucky Dee (Mr. and Mrs. B. P. Dawes)—GR2
19. Sept. 9, 1956—Mason & Dixon KC—22—Mrs. M. B. Meyer
BOB—Ch. Nordly's Sammy (J. M. Doyle)—GR2
20. May 25, 1957—Monmouth KC—39—Chas. A. Swartz
BOB—Ch. Nordly's Sammy (J. M. Doyle)—GR1, Best Am-bred in Show

21. Feb. 29, 1958—International KC of Chicago—49—W. H. Reeves
    BOB—Ch. Nordly's Sammy (J. M. Doyle)
22. Feb. 22, 1959—Santa Clara KC—71—Major B. Godsol
    BOB—Ch. Nordly's Sammy (J. M. Doyle)
23. Oct. 2, 1960—Maria-Obispo KC—38—O. C. Harriman
    BOB—Ch. Shoshone of Whitecliff (Mrs. J. Blank)
24. Sept. 9, 1962—Westchester KC—32—C. H. Chamberlain
    BOB—Ch. Elkenglo's Dash O'Silver (E. L. Miller)
25. Apr. 6, 1963—International KC of Chicago—34—V. D. Johnson
    BOB—Ch. Winterland's Kim (Heagy)
26. May 31, 1964—Framingham DC—35—Mrs. N. Demidoff
    BOB—Ch. Sarges Silver Frost (R. N. and W. C. Parry)
27. 1st parent Samoyed Club of America separately-held Specialty
    July 24, 1964—Miramar Hotel, Montecito, Calif.—92—A. E. Van Court
    BOB—Ch. Shondra of Draylene (J. M. Dyer)
    BOS—Ch. Noatak of Silver Moon (R. J. Bowles)
28. Apr. 3, 1965—Western Pa. KA—22—Theodore Wurmser
    BOB—Ch. Winter Kloud of Silver Moon (J. A. Helinski)
29. 2nd separately-held SCA Specialty
    Aug. 20, 1965—Bellevue, Wash.—83—Virginia Keckler
    BOB—Ch. Shaloon of Draylene (L. R. Wacenske)
    BOS—Ch. Shondra of Draylene (J. M. Dyer)
30. Sept. 20, 1965—Colorado KC—34—Robert H. Ward
    BOB—Ch. Kenny's Blazer Boy of Caribou, CDX (D. Yocum)
31. Sept. 25, 1965—Ox Ridge KC—28—Alva Rosenberg
    BOB—Ch. Snowpack Silver Melody of Kobe (Ashdown)
32. Oct. 24, 1965—San Fernando KC—60—Forest N. Hall
    BOB—Ch. Danlyn's Silver Coronet (L. L. Torres)
33. Mar. 6, 1966—Natl. Capitol KC—50—Mrs. L. W. Bonney
    BOB—Ch. Park-Cliffe Snowpack Sanorka, CD (McGoldrick)
34. 3rd separately-held SCA Specialty
    Sept. 24, 1966—Inglewood, Calif.—92—N. L. Kay
    BOB—Ch. Sayan of Woodland (J. and E. Kite)
    BOS—Ch. Tsarina of Lassen View (E. J. Burns)
35. May 7, 1967—Trenton KC—28—Mrs. Eve Seeley
    BOB—Ch. Venturer of Kobe (Donald Jordan)
36. 4th separately-held SCA Specialty
    June 30, 1967—Madison, Wisconsin—47—Robert H. Ward
    BOB—Ch. Star Nika Altai of Silver Moon (Lucile Miller)
    BOS—Ch. Bradley's Powder Puff (C. and B. Bradley)
37. 5th separately-held SCA Specialty
    Sept. 23, 1967—Inglewood, Calif.—71—Mrs. Helen Wittrig
    BOB—Ch. Sayan of Woodland (J. and E. Kite)
    BOS—Ch. Tei Juana Cayenne of Virburnum (L. L. Bill)
38. 6th separately-held SCA Specialty
    Sept. 13, 1969—Thousand Oaks, Calif.—94—Mrs. Joyce E. Cain
    BOB—Ch. Sayan of Woodland (J. and E. Kite)
    BOS—Ch Hoti-Ami of Starchak (Mr. and Mrs. R. H. Ward)
39. 7th separately-held SCA Specialty
    Aug. 14, 1970—Renton, Wash.—122—Joseph Faigel
    BOB—Ch. Darius Karlak Cheetal (LaVera Morgan)
    BOS—Ch. Tsonoqua of Snow Ridge (Margo Gervostad)

40. Sept. 11, 1971—Somerset Hills KC—135—J. M. Cresap
    BOB—Ch. Elrond Czar of Rivendell, C.D. (E. and M. Gaffney)
    BOS—Ch. Babe's Gypsy Magic of Gro-Wil (H. E. and S. L. Dewey)
41. Oct. 7, 1972—Janesville, Wisc.—Nelson Radcliff
    BOB—Ch. Midnight Sun Kimba (K. Horton and Art Mondale)
    BOS—Ch. Silveracres Charm (H. and D. McLaughlin)
42. Sept. 15, 1973—San Leandro, Calif.—Phil Marsh
    BOB—Ch. Kipperic Kandu of Suruka Orr, C.D. (D. and D. Hodges)
    BOS—Ch. Reddison of Vellee (E. and J. Coloma & L. and D. Kusler)
43. Aug. 16, 1974—Seattle, Wash.—Howard Dullnig
    BOB—Ch. Stormy of Mistyway (McCarthy and Baird)
    BOS—Ch. Ice Way's Ice Cube (M. and B. Smith)
44. Oct., 1975—W. Friendship, Md.—Ramona VanCourt
    BOB—Ch. Frosty Morn's Big Blizzard (Donald Zeeb)
    BOS—Ch. Weathervane's First Million (M. Million)
45. June 3-4, 1976—Denver, Co.—Robert Hamilton
    BOB—Ch. Oakwood Farm's Kari J'Go Diko (Lueck)
    BOS—Ch. Rickshaw's Mandarin Lady (E. and G. Wong)
46. Aug. 18, 1977—Lake Orion, Mich.—Melbourne Downing
    BOB—Ch. Kristik's English Autumn (Lynda Zaraza)
    BOS—Ch. Lady Kara Kristilla Del Sol (A. and A. Peil)
47. Oct. 5-6, 1978—Portland, Ore.—Derek Rayne
    BOB—Ch. Nordic's Wynter Sunniglo (Anderson/Matthews/Hodges)
    BOS—Ch. Starctic Aukeo (R. and D. Ward)
48. Oct., 1979—Marrieta, Ga.—J. D. Jones
    BOB—Ch. Sulu's Mark of Distinction (Hoehn)
    BOS—Ch. Suzuki's Final Edition (Kirms)
49. Aug., 1980—San Diego, Calif.—V. Lynne
    BOB—Ch. Shawndi of Mid-Night Sun (Hoeffecker)
    BOS—Ch. Northwind's Running Bear (J. and H. Feinberg)
50. Oct. 6-7, 1981—Madison, Wisc.—Mrs. Peter C. Guntermann
    BOB—Ch. Ice Way's Ice Crush (Ann Bark)
    BOS—Ch. Dajmozek's Miss Ruff Stuff (J. and D. Orr)
51. Aug. 25, 1982—Everett, Wash.—Peter Thomson
    BOB—Ch. Northwind's Maraiva Bearfoot (Lytle)
    BOS—Ch. El Sol's Kovsh Kim O' Whitecliff (Coulter and Molineaux)
52. Oct. 11, 1983—W. Friendship, Md.—Mrs. James E. Clark
    BOB—Ch. Quicksilver's Razz Ma Tazz (Middleton/Curtis)
    BOS—Ch. Moonlighter's Ima Spark O' Bark (R. and K. Lense)
53. Sept. 7, 1984—Littleton, Co.—Judith A. Goodin
    BOB—Ch. Quicksilver's Razz Ma Tazz (Middleton/Curtis)
    BOS—Ch. T-Snow Star's Name of the Game (M. and D. Ragsdale)

Winners of the
Samoyed Club of America Annual Awards

TOP WINNING DOG

1969—Ch. Sam O'Khan's Chingis Khan (Sheets)
1970—Ch. Sam O'Khan's Chingis Khan (Sheets)
1971—Am./Can. Ch. Maur-Mik's Kim (Aldred)
1972—Ch. Lulhaven's Snowmist Ensign (Hyatt/White)
1973—Ch. Czar's Dorak of Whitecliff (Walker)
1974—Am./Can. Ch. North Starr King's Ransom (Hritzo)
1975—Am./Can. Ch. North Starr King's Ransom (Hritzo)
1976—Am./Can. Ch. North Starr King's Ransom (Hritzo)
1977—Am./Can. Ch. North Starr King's Ransom (Hritzo)
1978—Am./Can. Ch. North Starr's Heir Apparent (Dunham/Dr. Hritzo/
    Kathy Hritzo)
1979—Ch. Di Murdock of Seelah (Evans)
1980—Ch. Di Murdock of Seelah (Evans)
1981—Ch. Northwind's Running Bear (Feinberg)
1982—Ch. Murdock's Marauder of Seelah (Evans)
1983—Ch. Quicksilver's Razz Ma Tazz (Middleton/Curtis)

TOP WINNING BITCH

1969—Ch. Honey Babe of Gro-Wil (Walls)
1970—Ch. Orion's Mishka of Marcomar (Eggiman)
1971—Ch. Honey Babe of Gro-Wil (Walls/J. Baer)
1972—Babe's Gypsy Magic of Gro-Wil (Dewey)
1973—Ch. Kipperic Kandu of Suruka Orr (Hodges)
1974—Ch. Kipperic Kandu of Suruka Orr (Hodges)
1975—Ch. Bubbles LaRue of Oakwood (Price)
1976—Ch. Bubbles LaRue of Oakwood (Price)
1977—Ch. Que Sera's Karaimee (Wiley/Hoehn)
1978—Ch. Nanank's Bathzarah (MacArthur)
1979—Ch. Blue Sky's Pound Cake (Hooyman)
1980—Ch. Snowblaze Sugar Cookie (DeVoe)
1981—Ch. Tasha of Sacha's Knight (Mardee & Dolly Ward)
1982—Ch. Tasha of Sacha's Knight (Mardee & Dolly Ward)
1983—Ch. Me Too of Bubbling Oaks (Price)

TOP STUD DOG

1969—Am./Can. Ch. Saroma's Polar Prince (Beal)
1970—Ch. Nachalnik of Drayalene (McLaughlin)
1971—Ch. Nachalnik of Drayalene (McLaughlin)
1972—Am./Can. Ch. Saroma's Polar Prince (Beal)

1973—Ch. Kondako's Dancing Bear (Richardson)
1974—Ch. Nachalnik of Drayalene (McLaughlin)
1975—Ch. Kondako's Dancing Bear (Richardson)
1976—Ch. Sulu's Karbon Kopi O' Baerstone (Hoehn)
1977—Ch. Sulu's Karbon Kopi O' Baerstone (Hoehn)
1978—Ch. Sulu's Karbon Kopi O' Baerstone (Hoehn)
1979—Am./Can. Ch Oakwood Farm's Kari J' Go Diko (Lueck)
1980—Ch. Kiskas Karaholme Cherokee (Ward)
1981—Ch. Kondako's Sun Dancer (Richardson)
1982—Ch. Di Murdock of Seelah (Evans)
1983—Ch. Ice Way's Ice Breaker (Smith)

TOP BROOD BITCH

1969—Ch. Tempest of Misty Way (McCarthy)
1970—Can./Am. Ch. Sam O'Khan's Tsari of Khan (Fitzpatrick)
1971—Ch. Honey Babe of Gro-Wil (Baer)
1972—Ch. Honey Babe of Gro-Wil (Baer)
1973—Silver Sonnet of Gro-Wil (Baer)
1974—Ch. Silver Trinkets of Misty Way (McCarthy)
1975—Ch. Silver Trinkets of Misty Way (McCarthy)
1976—Ch. Kim's Ladybug (Lycan)
1977—Tsartar's Somewhere My Lara (Wiley)
1978—Ch. Weathervane's Katie-Did (Scovin)
1979—Ch. Snow Fire's Bo Peep, C.D. (Evans)
1980—Ch. Snow Fire's Bo Peep, C.D. (Evans)
1981—Ch. Snow Fire's Bo Peep, C.D. (Evans)
1982—Ch. Dor Kei's Pepeta (Knoblock/Evans)
1983—Ch. Dor Kei's Pepeta (Knoblock/Evans)

TOP OBEDIENCE WINNER

1969—Ch. Snowline's Joli Shashan, C.D.X. (Mayfield)
1970—Ell-Tee's Square Do Tasha, U.D. (Gormley)
1971—Silver Charm of Starfire, C.D. (John & Addie Decker)
1972—Snowman of White Hall, C.D.X. (Keith & Carla Smith)
1973—Snowman of White Hall, C.D.X. (Smith)
1974—Ch. Tsarevich of Kobray, U.D. (Ruby)
1975—White Glamour of Starfire, U.D. (Decker)
1976—Sebaska Sulaykha Pakova (Gruber, Canada)
1977—Am./Can. Ch. Dajmozek, Am. U.D.T./Can. C.D.X., T.D. (Orr)
1978—Winterway's Owenover Mistaya (Lee)
1979—Barron's White Lightnin', C.D.X. (Barbara Horne/Dan Cole)
1980—Barron's White Lightnin', U.D. (Horne/Cole)
1981—Stasia's Tad of Winterway, C.D. (Lee)
1982—Darshan's Honey Bear, C.D. (Schiddell)
1983—O.T. Ch. Barron's White Lightnin' (Barbara & Dan Cole)

The bond between man and dog sometimes exhibits itself in unusual forms. If Charlene Taran had not used her head (keeping it above water and not panicking), this story might have had a different ending. Charlene and her Samoyed, "Dolly," were walking near City Park Lake in Fort Collins, Colorado. Dolly slipped her leash, mischievously took after a flock of Canadian geese, and fell through the ice. Charlene was horrified and went to her pet's rescue, but herself fell into the 37-degree ice and water. Dolly (45 lbs.) pulled herself out and the Poudre firemen rescued Charlene after 15 minutes of freezing. (Ironically, Dolly's dam is Lynthea's Miss Conduct, by Ch. Ice Way's Ice Breaker.)   *Photo by William W. Posell, Chief Photographer, The Coloradan.*

The Samoyed—A Dog to Admire

by Vincent G. Perry

(Mr. Perry was one of America's top all-rounders for many decades. His passing, in February 1985, was a great loss for the fancy.)

It was such a long time ago, yet I remember well my first glimpse of a Samoyed on this continent. It was at Westminster, of course, and my reaction to that magnificent white dog was instantaneous. "Gee, what a truly beautiful dog," I found myself exclaiming, and in the many years that have passed since then, that has been my reaction each time of the many times I have judged this now well-established breed. He is still a beauty, but he is more than that, much more. He is a well-boned dog without being clumsy, rugged in structure, built with the strength of a hard working dog, never dainty, always handsome and the correct moving dog moves with the accuracy and determination of a true worker. On top of that he has those grinning lips, and the laughing eyes.

Oh, yes; I have seen those just pretty dogs that have won in some areas, occasionally, but their reign was short-lived. I have also seen a period when leggy, narrow dogs of the breed seemed to find favor with judges, but no more. Today, across the land the good dogs of this breed are the sturdy ones, always favored by the sincere students and breeders of this breed which is still growing in popularity and is well-represented at most shows in America.

Always an admirer, in the ring and from a distance, it was not until this writer purchased two Sammies for my number one granddaughter that I became acquainted with the Samoyed intelligence and devotion. Samoya was the first one. She was a doll, and a thinker. At eight weeks old, she became the constant companion of my grandson-in-law. On the day he raked the leaves from the front lawn, she left his side only to run and pick up the leaves his rake had missed and carry them to the big basket he used for carrying the leaves to the compost heap.

Shiloh was the second Samoyed, this time a male. Two little daughters had increased the family to four, and before he was a year old, Shiloh was established as the fifth member. They didn't own him, he had become part of them. He was playmate and devoted guardian. As he neared maturity he had established a routine. Each night before going to his own bed in the kitchen he visited each bedroom to make sure everyone was safely tucked in. Once satisfied that all was well, he would give a sigh of relief, then seek his own rest. What a watchdog! What a companion! What a truly great dog. No wonder we all loved Shiloh!

BIBLIOGRAPHY

ALL OWNERS of pure-bred dogs will benefit themselves and their dogs by enriching their knowledge of breeds and of canine care, training, breeding, psychology and other important aspects of dog management. The following list of books covers further reading recommended by judges, veterinarians, breeders, trainers and other authorities. Books may be obtained at the finer book stores and pet shops, or through Howell Book House Inc., publishers, New York.

BREED BOOKS

AFGHAN HOUND, Complete	Miller & Gilbert
AIREDALE, New Complete	Edwards
AKITA, Complete	Linderman & Funk
ALASKAN MALAMUTE, Complete	Riddle & Seeley
BASSET HOUND, Complete	Braun
BLOODHOUND, Complete	Brey & Reed
BOXER, Complete	Denlinger
BRITTANY SPANIEL, Complete	Riddle
BULLDOG, New Complete	Hanes
BULL TERRIER, New Complete	Eberhard
CAIRN TERRIER, Complete	Marvin
CHESAPEAKE BAY RETRIEVER, Complete	Cherry
CHIHUAHUA, Complete	Noted Authorities
COCKER SPANIEL, New	Kraeuchi
COLLIE, New	Official Publication of the Collie Club of America
DACHSHUND, The New	Meistrell
DALMATIAN, The	Treen
DOBERMAN PINSCHER, New	Walker
ENGLISH SETTER, New Complete	Tuck, Howell & Graef
ENGLISH SPRINGER SPANIEL, New	Goodall & Gasow
FOX TERRIER, New	Nedell
GERMAN SHEPHERD DOG, New Complete	Bennett
GERMAN SHORTHAIRED POINTER, New	Maxwell
GOLDEN RETRIEVER, New Complete	Fischer
GORDON SETTER, Complete	Look
GREAT DANE, New Complete	Noted Authorities
GREAT DANE, The—Dogdom's Apollo	Draper
GREAT PYRENEES, Complete	Strang & Giffin
IRISH SETTER, New Complete	Eldredge & Vanacore
IRISH WOLFHOUND, Complete	Starbuck
JACK RUSSELL TERRIER, Complete	Plummer
KEESHOND, New Complete	Cash
LABRADOR RETRIEVER, Complete	Warwick
LHASA APSO, Complete	Herbel
MASTIFF, History and Management of the	Baxter & Hoffman
MINIATURE SCHNAUZER, Complete	Eskrigge
NEWFOUNDLAND, New Complete	Chern
NORWEGIAN ELKHOUND, New Complete	Wallo
OLD ENGLISH SHEEPDOG, Complete	Mandeville
PEKINGESE, Quigley Book of	Quigley
PEMBROKE WELSH CORGI, Complete	Sargent & Harper
POODLE, New	Irick
POODLE CLIPPING AND GROOMING BOOK, Complete	Kalstone
ROTTWEILER, Complete	Freeman
SAMOYED, New Complete	Ward
SCOTTISH TERRIER, New Complete	Marvin
SHETLAND SHEEPDOG, The New	Riddle
SHIH TZU, Joy of Owning	Seranne
SHIH TZU, The (English)	Dadds
SIBERIAN HUSKY, Complete	Demidoff
TERRIERS, The Book of All	Marvin
WEIMARANER, Guide to the	Burgoin
WEST HIGHLAND WHITE TERRIER, Complete	Marvin
WHIPPET, Complete	Pegram
YORKSHIRE TERRIER, Complete	Gordon & Bennett

BREEDING

ART OF BREEDING BETTER DOGS, New	Onstott
BREEDING YOUR OWN SHOW DOG	Seranne
HOW TO BREED DOGS	Whitney
HOW PUPPIES ARE BORN	Prine
INHERITANCE OF COAT COLOR IN DOGS	Little

CARE AND TRAINING

COUNSELING DOG OWNERS, Evans Guide for	Evans
DOG OBEDIENCE, Complete Book of	Saunders
NOVICE, OPEN AND UTILITY COURSES	Saunders
DOG CARE AND TRAINING FOR BOYS AND GIRLS	Saunders
DOG NUTRITION, Collins Guide to	Collins
DOG TRAINING FOR KIDS	Benjamin
DOG TRAINING, Koehler Method of	Koehler
DOG TRAINING Made Easy	Tucker
GO FIND! Training Your Dog to Track	Davis
GUARD DOG TRAINING, Koehler Method of	Koehler
MOTHER KNOWS BEST—The Natural Way to Train Your Dog	Benjamin
OPEN OBEDIENCE FOR RING, HOME AND FIELD, Koehler Method of	Koehler
STONE GUIDE TO DOG GROOMING FOR ALL BREEDS	Stone
SUCCESSFUL DOG TRAINING, The Pearsall Guide to	Pearsall
TEACHING DOG OBEDIENCE CLASSES—Manual for Instructors	Volhard & Fisher
TOY DOGS, Kalstone Guide to Grooming All	Kalstone
TRAINING THE RETRIEVER	Kersley
TRAINING TRACKING DOGS, Koehler Method of	Koehler
TRAINING YOUR DOG—Step by Step Manual	Volhard & Fisher
TRAINING YOUR DOG TO WIN OBEDIENCE TITLES	Morsell
TRAIN YOUR OWN GUN DOG, How to	Goodall
UTILITY DOG TRAINING, Koehler Method of	Koehler
VETERINARY HANDBOOK, Dog Owner's Home	Carlson & Giffin

GENERAL

AMERICAN KENNEL CLUB 1884-1984—A Source Book	American Kennel Club
CANINE TERMINOLOGY	Spira
COMPLETE DOG BOOK, The	Official Publication of American Kennel Club
DOG IN ACTION, The	Lyon
DOG BEHAVIOR, New Knowledge of	Pfaffenberger
DOG JUDGE'S HANDBOOK	Tietjen
DOG PEOPLE ARE CRAZY	Riddle
DOG PSYCHOLOGY	Whitney
DOGSTEPS, The New	Elliott
DOG TRICKS	Haggerty & Benjamin
EYES THAT LEAD—Story of Guide Dogs for the Blind	Tucker
FRIEND TO FRIEND—Dogs That Help Mankind	Schwartz
FROM RICHES TO BITCHES	Shattuck
HAPPY DOG/HAPPY OWNER	Siegal
IN STITCHES OVER BITCHES	Shattuck
JUNIOR SHOWMANSHIP HANDBOOK	Brown & Mason
OUR PUPPY'S BABY BOOK (blue or pink)	
SUCCESSFUL DOG SHOWING, Forsyth Guide to	Forsyth
TRIM, GROOM & SHOW YOUR DOG, How to	Saunders
WHY DOES YOUR DOG DO THAT?	Bergman
WILD DOGS in Life and Legend	Riddle
WORLD OF SLED DOGS, From Siberia to Sport Racing	Coppinger